THE WORK OF JESUS
IN
CHRISTIAN THOUGHT

BY

ALEXANDER McCREA, M.A.

THE EPWORTH PRESS
(EDGAR C. BARTON)
25–35 CITY ROAD, LONDON, E.C.1

THE WORK OF JESUS
IN
CHRISTIAN THOUGHT

To

THE MEMORY OF

MY

FATHER AND MOTHER

CONTENTS

	PREFACE	9
1.	INTRODUCTORY	13
2.	SIN	28
3.	THE MEN WHO CRUCIFIED CHRIST	47
4.	THE CROSS AND THE RESURRECTION	64
5.	ST. PAUL'S INTERPRETATION OF THE DEATH OF CHRIST	80
6.	THE DEATH OF CHRIST IN THE SYNOPTIC GOSPELS	101
7.	THE DEATH OF CHRIST IN THE TEACHING OF ST. PETER	124
8.	THE DEATH OF CHRIST IN THE EPISTLE TO THE HEBREWS	134
9.	THE DEATH OF CHRIST IN THE JOHANNINE WRITINGS	147
10.	THE DEATH OF CHRIST IN THE PATRISTIC WRITERS	166
11.	THE DEATH OF CHRIST IN THE PATRISTIC WRITERS (continued)	182
12.	AUGUSTINE AND ANSELM	200
13.	THE MORAL INFLUENCE SCHOOL	214
14.	MORE RECENT TRENDS IN INTERPRETATION	240
15.	SUMMARY AND CONCLUSION	261
	EPILOGUE: PERSONAL AFFIRMATIONS	285
	INDEX	287

CONTENTS

PREFACE 9

1. INTRODUCTORY 13

2. SIN 68

3. THE MEN WHO KILLED OUR CHRIST . . . 87

4. THE CROSS AND THE RESURRECTION . . . 94

5. ST. PAUL'S INTERPRETATION OF THE DEATH
   OF CHRIST 86

6. THE DEATH OF CHRIST IN THE SYNOPTIC
   GOSPELS 101

7. THE DEATH OF CHRIST IN THE TEACHING OF
   ST. PETER 128

8. THE DEATH OF CHRIST IN THE EPISTLE TO
   THE HEBREWS 131

9. THE DEATH OF CHRIST IN THE JOHANNINE
   WRITINGS 147

10. THE DEATH OF CHRIST IN THE BAPTISM
    166

11. THE DEATH OF CHRIST IN THE ATONEMENT
    184

12. SACRIFICE AND DREAM 200

13. THE MORAL INFLUENCE THEORY . . . 244

14. THE RIGHT ELEMENT TRUTH IN INTERPRETATION 250

15. SUMMARY AND CONCLUSION 269

APPENDIX: PERSONAL AFFIRMATION . . . 281

INDEX 283

PREFACE

It may save time, possibly wasted in mis-directed criticism, if the writer explains why he felt constrained to commit the following pages to print. It fell to his lot, from time to time, to address groups of University and art students on certain questions of Christian doctrine. He was impressed by three facts: the genuine interest revealed in any doctrine that seemed to be related to life and character. Secondly, a general chaotic state of mind in some, in which fragments of out-worn and often unethical theology were mingled with vital truths. Thirdly, a difficulty in distinguishing between what is timeless and vital and certain antique and misleading forms in which it had been presented. This was particularly true in regard to the work of Christ in His Passion and Death. There seemed an obvious need of a survey of the main historical interpretations of Christ's death.

Nothing, it seems to the writer, is a better preparation for constructive work on this subject, even by the ordinary layman, than an understanding of what has been done already in Christian history. Obviously to include the name of every writer on the Atonement, even if the present writer were familiar with them all, would be to turn these pages into a colourless catalogue of names, and defeat the end in view. Instead of this, he has sought to group

9

writers generally under the three main systems of thought to which they severally belong, and to leave a broad outline rather than crowded detail.

If students who are not reading for the Christian ministry, as well as others who are, can be persuaded to enter on a patient study of our Lord's work, they will probably reach two conclusions; first, that the mode of interpretation was conditioned by the age and environment in which the thinker lived and, as the environment changed, a restatement of the truths of Christian experience became necessary; secondly, that every theory propounded, however out-moded and even grotesque it may now appear, has still clinging to it the aroma of some vital truth. By patient comparison of past labours, we see in theology, as we see in the Holy Scriptures, a blending of the divine and human. No theory of interpretation is sacrosanct and the work of the past should point to something nobler beyond itself.

The omission of some important themes from our subject will be obvious. Little is said about Atonement in the Old Testament; little or nothing about the transformation of the idea of Messiah to embrace the thought of the suffering Servant, and too little is said about our Lord's consciousness of His mission as the suffering Servant and Son of Man. In a larger work something would be required on the implications of the Atonement in the sphere of social conditions and, above all, the burning question of the Cross and pacificism. But some limit had to be set and it seemed best to keep to the salient aspects within Christian history.

The writer is under a greater debt than he can express to the Rev. Professor Harold Roberts, of Wesley College, Headingley, Leeds, for his great kindness in reading the typescript and making valuable suggestions, many of which have been incorporated. This makes Dr. Roberts in no way responsible for the defects that are sure to be found. Also he is greatly indebted to the Rev. Professor Howard, of Handsworth College, Birmingham, for reading, and making helpful emendations embodied in Chapter 6.

He wishes also to express his thanks to the Rev. Alan R. Booth, B.A., LL.B., for reading the proofs; and to Mr. A. H. McCrea for preparing the index.

Finally, he would remind readers that this is a book for beginners and not for the professional theologian. If it helps such, even a little, to see that the death of Christ is the wisdom and power of God, a revelation of love and a ground of forgiveness, this will suffice.

A. McC.

EDGEHILL COLLEGE,
BELFAST.
1939.

Chapter 1

INTRODUCTORY

Few who are in any wise familiar with the New Testament and with modern preaching will deny that a marked contrast exists between the emphasis given to our Lord's death in the Scriptures and that given in the modern pulpit. One may search the tables of contents of many recent volumes of sermons in vain for any allusion to atonement or forgiveness. Among students this aspect of Christ's work is often received with ill-disguised impatience.

The reasons given for this attitude are varied: The element of mystery in an age of science, the baffling paradox of wrath and mercy, the persistent repetition in fundamentalist schools, so-called, of obsolete interpretations, the repellent similes and imagery of a bygone age, the confusion between fact and its interpretation, the influence of the age, environment, education and the personal factor on the theory of the particular writer, the swing of the pendulum to-day from interest in individual salvation to enthusiasm for the redemption of society and the solution of international problems, and, finally, the alleged misinterpretation of the character of God through an approach to the work of Christ from Old Testament conceptions—in other words, that that which has been called Christian soteriology has too often been Jewish.

The general impression left on the minds of some young students may be illustrated by two quotations. One student writes: 'The view of Christ's death which I was taught, that one person's death is accepted instead of another and that there must be blood in an atonement, is to me black magic.' Another writes: 'Such words as "transactions in the Godhead", "satisfaction to God", and even "atonement" sound unreal, and mean to me just nothing.'

It is obvious that any theology that confuses the issue and blocks the road to Christ has failed of its function. It is only at our intellectual and moral peril that we continue to repeat shibboleths which fail to illuminate our minds and express reality; first and foremost, we must come to the inquiry with unfettered minds.

Before we examine these minor questions in any detail, we shall consider some of the broader issues that divert interest from the Christian doctrine of redemption. These will include a reconsideration of God, Sin, Human Nature, and the Influence of the Age Spirit.

1. *Concerning God.* The entire Biblical doctrine of reconciliation rests on the belief that God not only *is*, but is personal. However much more personality may mean in Him, in inclusiveness and originality, He is at least, and in the same sense as we are, personal. In the Old Testament this view is carried to an extreme degree of anthropomorphism. In the New Testament He is represented as a father,

distressed over the fall and alienation of His children and seeking at infinite cost to restore them to Himself. Similarly, this has been the generally accepted view of God in St. Augustine, Anselm, Calvin, and Wesley—to name no more. Sometimes the creative, sometimes the sovereign, sometimes the judicial aspect has been stressed, but all are agreed that God is a personal Being who regards men as His own.

But modern thought is not prepared to accept this view with such unanimity. The newer views may not have permeated the minds of the masses (that process may be expected), but they have certainly reached the student classes. One writer,[1] himself no apostle of doctrinal orthodoxy, says: 'Philosophers stretch the meanings of words until they retain scarcely anything of their original sense. By calling God some vague abstraction which they have created for themselves, they pose as deists, as believers before the world, they may even pride themselves on having attained a higher and purer idea of God although their God is nothing but an unsubstantial shadow and no longer a mighty personality of religious doctrine.' By writers like Bergson He is conceived as an impersonal vital urge, by writers like Schopenhauer as immanent will, or 'cosmic libido', by members of the Freudian school itself He is an imaginary but comforting defence mechanism projected by timid souls, who have no longer any earthly parent to protect them from the buffets of life, and who find consolation in a fantasy that they call God. This generation is not irreligious in the sense that it has no interest in

[1] Freud. See Brightman, *Belief in God*, p. 57.

15

another world. Spiritualism, necromancy, theosophy, and 'Christian science', so-called, show that many who have rejected the Christian faith of the New Testament are deeply interested in a spiritual world of some sort, but the prevailing trend is towards a neo-mysticism that is on the verge of pantheism. Men want to commune with the infinite or unseen, but they definitely object to worshipping a personal God. A deceased German thinker, Fritz Mauthner, whose writings seem to have had considerable influence on the continent of Europe and in America wrote: 'By religion I mean mysticism, and mysticism is communion with art and poetry. It is a feeling of longing and of union, a longing for unity, no more.' Disciples of Reventlow and Hauer say that the religion of Germany must find its object in the soul of the nation and at the same time be the expression of the national life—a view that seems to be a reversion to animistic beliefs among certain African tribes, such as the Ashantis. Another German writer, Herr Ziehen, says that God is essentially law, law as ordered uniformity in the universe and he crowns his belief with the name of 'nomotheism'. He says: 'God is law not a person; He is above personality. He or it, as one must say, consists of logical laws (laws of thought), causal laws (laws of physical nature), epigenetic laws (the laws of consciousness and value).' This points in the direction of God as 'the great mathematician'. Now, the plain man finds it hard to conceive of any laws, particularly those of 'consciousness and value', apart from a personality. Yet this must be done. Law, we are told, is higher than personality and subsumes personality within itself. Our homage must be paid to impersonal, all-pervading law, but we are not permitted to rise (these writers would say descend) from law to a personalized God and Father. As Dr. Rendel Harris said: 'We are not permitted to believe in a personal God because we have found out the way He does things.'

It need not be pointed out that so long as God is a name for anything impersonal—will, force, law— so long will all questions of disobedience, guilt, and reconciliation fall to the ground. The garment of Christian theology is without seam, woven throughout, and each great doctrine is interwoven with the others. If students are shaky about the idea of God as personal and moral they may well come to regard the doctrine of atonement as 'black magic'.[1]

2. *Concerning Sin.* If Freud's criticism of loose thinking and careless expression of ideas concerning God was well founded, much more does it hold concerning sin. A century ago sin was thought of inevitably in relation to God. It was rebellion against a sovereign personal will; it was a culpable violation of His moral kingdom, it was an affront to His majesty and a challenge to His crown rights as Creator and Governor. Repentance was a restored recognition of His will and a turning away from all that conflicted with it. Faith was a perception of His graciousness and an appropriation of His mercy, made available through Christ in His

[1] It lies outside the scope of these pages to discuss the being and nature of God, but we commend to beginners Canon Quick's *Doctrines of the Creed* (Nisbet & Co.) and the Bishop of Gloucester's *Christian Theology* (Oxford University Press).

death. It was a consideration of the relations between a man and his God.

Since then two currents of thought have flowed like streams of corrosives over this view of sin and forgiveness, viz. the Hegelian doctrine of God, or the Absolute Spirit, and the application of the theory of evolution to morals and religion. It is not easy to state either doctrine clearly and briefly, but so pervasive has been the influence of each that an attempt must be made.

(a) Hegel conceived of the eternal absolute spirit as seeking self-conscious realization, a coming to awareness of itself. This is achieved by a three-fold principle or movement. Spirit moves forward against matter, seeking to overcome and use it. In the clash spirit has an awareness of resistance that makes it at the same moment aware of itself. Through the action of spirit on matter, matter is also modified and both spirit and matter are taken up into a new synthetic existence that results in self-conscious Being. Though this three-fold movement runs throughout the universe appearing in history, religion, and every other phenomenal manifestation of reality, yet it is most clearly seen in man and in the Man, Christ Jesus, who was the perfect synthesis of spirit and matter. In man, as we too well know, the synthetic harmony is incomplete, 'the flesh warreth against the spirit and the spirit against the flesh and these are contrary the one to the other'. Until the final harmony is realized man is incomplete. Now, this is where the crux of Hegelian philosophy emerges. Sin is not resistance to a personal God, sin is incompleteness, lack of self-realization, a defect in the carbon that refuses to allow the current to set up incandescence, a failure in the fusion of flesh and spirit into one self-conscious whole. What we call sins are only ineffective experiments in self-realization, efforts of spirit to find harmony in our material bodies.

'According to this view,' as Dr. Lidgett says, 'sin is right as a stage, but wrong as a result—a factor in the process of becoming good which is cancelled when the state of being good is attained.' At once we realize we are breathing here the stuffy air of pantheism and theosophy. In both climates morality and personal responsibility cannot thrive; and if we, each, are but fragments of absolute spirit realizing itself in us and in nature, all questions of sin and reconciliation must be recast and the old words must be made to mean new things. The influence of Hegel's philosophy on British theology presented a challenge thirty years ago and though it is generally repudiated by theologians to-day its backwash can still be felt among students who read Hegel for the first time and think they find in him a deliverer from all anti-scientific dualism in man and the universe. It has been suggested that 'spiritualism' is a fresh manifestation of this pantheistic conception but 'spiritualism' seems rather to be a reversion to animism with its belief in the survival of personality and its apparatus for seeking to call up departed spirits.

(*b*) The application of the theory of evolution to morals and religion. For the Christian, morality is of binding obligation because it comes out of the character of God. This does not mean that a thing is necessarily right because a deity wills it; it means that since God has revealed Himself in Christ Jesus as perfect that which we see and recognize as perfect in Him must be our law. 'Ye shall be holy, for I am holy.' 'He that loveth not, knoweth not God, for God is love.' Turning to evolutionary ethics, we find that once the concept of physical development in varying species, by slow increments captured the mind and particularly the imagination, it was inevitable that the theory would be applied to morals. Herbert Spencer gave the attempt classic expression in his *Data of Ethics*, and a succession of writers followed to show that morality with its sanctions and taboos can be accounted for in the same way as we can trace the development of the Derby winner from his humble four-toed ancestor in a primeval swamp. Sin is anything but a violation of a divine will or of communion with God. It finds its basis in no transcendental authority whatever. It arises only when man is anti-social, when by independence and self-assertion he weakens the social bond. Beyond the well-being of the tribe or race there is no moral law. That this is the earliest form in which the idea of sin comes to primitive man is a possibility, but that it is the only content in the word sin to-day is open to challenge. It is enough to note that the idea reached practical expression in the Positivism of Auguste Comte and Frederic Harrison last century and now raises its head afresh in the totalitarian doctrine of the State in Germany. The saint is the man who prostrates himself on the altar of State supremacy; the sinner is the man who dares to ask if behind and beyond the State there may be a kingdom of God. The Jew who wrote 'against Thee, Thee only, have I sinned', is to be banished the realm. We may sin against State law, or efficiency or civic prosperity or even our neighbours' well-being, but beyond that there is no God or law. Nietzsche does not mince matters in *Thus Spake Zarathustra*: 'Once did people say God when they looked out upon distant seas. . . . Now, however, I have taught you to say Superman. . . . If there were Gods I could not endure not being one. Therefore there are none.' Whether we consent to the logic or not, we are left in no doubt about the new orientation given to such words as 'God' and 'sin'.

3. *Humanism*. Here we come to a trend of thought, noble in many of its aspects, that diverts interest in a deeply pervasive way from the cross. It may be described as an attitude to life that relies solely on man's resources, especially his intellectual powers and creative faculties. It has an ancient lineage and goes back from the present through the fifteenth-century renaissance and the Augustan era to the Greek domination in Palestine in the second century B.C. The prophet Zechariah and the writer of Daniel are keenly aware of the difference between its viewpoint and that of the Hebrew prophets. (*a*) Humanism is grounded in an optimism about human nature. Man is intellectually, if not morally, self-sufficient. Some humanists leave God and the Christian religion peacefully in the background. They admit that there are individuals of the tenderfoot type who need and get help out of faith in Christ; no gentleman would

deride or offend such, but for the full-blooded young pagan humanism is the message. Man can be his own saviour. A sound education, self-confidence, freedom from all moral inhibitions, a fine disdain for moral lapses which are only ways of learning, and a demand for a full-blooded, thrilling life—lived fully; a life that includes what the ages have taught of art, science, and adventure—this is the life for to-day. This noble humanism, as represented in England by the Huxleys and in America by the late Irving Babbitt and Walter Lippmann, is concerned with service, not salvation. With what man can do for others, not with what God can do for him. It appeals to youth infinitely more than statements on sin, the Cross and forgiveness. It sounds like the gospel for youth. It draws men into Rotary, Toc H, newsboys' clubs and camps, and all manner of humanitarian societies and activities. It desires, above all, to do something and to give something. It is keeping the world from timid despair by its dash and daring. It was the spirit that helped the Allies to win the Great War, and no doubt humanism will respond to another call in the youths who now only know of the Great War by hearsay. If we can be kept out of war, this spirit is ready to face social and international reconstruction. Though all humanists are not unselfish and some youths are not eager to die for any ideals whatsoever, yet it is only just to say that on its nobler side there is here a spirit of self-sacrifice that easily goes round to the way of the Cross. It was the presence of this spirit in young soldiers, otherwise out of touch with the Christian faith, that made them so responsive to the message of the Cross, and the Lord's Table during the Great War.

In all this, then, so far, there is nothing at which we should cavil. No one exalted the worth of the individual more highly than our Lord. It was He who set the Good Samaritan above priests and who taught that in the final analysis men shall be judged, not by creeds or denominations, but by kindness and love to the hungry, thirsty, naked, and imprisoned. It was He, too, who urged men to stir up their intelligence, asking, 'Why even of your selves judge ye not what is right?' Yet if Humanism has in it a potency that diverts man from the Kingdom of God, that lightly regards moral failure, that diverts interest from fellowship with God, and that fosters interest in this life only, then every right-thinking man must probe farther into its principles and explore its defects. Furthermore, it must be said that Humanism does not cast a wide enough net. It suits the privileged, and those who can command the blessings of culture. It has a message for those who are unbroken and free from the withering curse of evil habits. But Humanism has no gospel for the poor. It does not bind up the broken-hearted; it is powerless in presence of broken lives and broken homes and warring nations. It even feeds the arrogance and self-assertion and truculence of men that strut and boast in the capitals of Europe at this hour.

(b) But there is a more militant variety, known as 'scientific humanism', which denies and assails the supernatural order. Mr. Julian Huxley, in his *What Dare I Think?*, p. 174, defines it thus: 'Scientific humanism is a protest against supernaturalism. The human spirit, now in its individual, now in its corporate, aspects is the source of all values and the highest reality we know.' Man has no haven into which he may retire when the storms are heavy except that of his own thought. If Socrates urged men to know themselves and the kingdom of their souls, he still believed in 'gods' or transcendent powers that could come and share their aid in man's extremity; but the gods are all gone. 'The human spirit is the highest reality we know.' To the same effect, a writer in the *Rationalist Press Association Annual*, 1933, says: 'A rationalist denies the efficacy of Heavenly aid in the solution of earthly problems. . . . Rationalism asserts that supernaturalism can find no place in a civilized world-theory. For the practice of mankind has shown that there is no human activity that achieves its purpose by "Divine" intervention. . . . The history of human progress is the history of the emancipation of man from supernaturalism.' One further quotation, taken from Mr. Julian Huxley,[1] must suffice to indicate the resentment with which the scientific humanist regards all thought of God or a transcendental order: 'The universe is not divisible into regions or compartments labelled natural and supernatural, material and spiritual, scientific and non-scientific, and so forth. . . . There are not two regions of reality, one of which is accessible to scientific method and the other inaccessible. Rather there is a single reality but scientific and other ways of approaching it. . . . Man is a part of nature, but

[1] *What I Believe*, p. 9.

not something contrasted with nature. His thoughts and bodily movements follow the same laws that describe the motions of the stars and the atoms.' We are not concerned at this stage to do more than indicate the influence of scientific humanism on certain Christian doctrines, yet we would like to have had an expansion of the words 'and other ways of approaching' reality by Mr. Huxley and something more on the essential oneness of the laws that govern thought and the motions of the atom.

4. *Concerning Secularism.* Yet another reason why there is a decay of interest in questions of redemption is secularism. This is an out-growth of Humanism and has taken different forms. The secularism of Charles Bradlaugh and J. G. Holyoake was a protest against the bourgeois complacency of the nineteenth-century capitalist, who looked on material prosperity as proof of the divine favour, but often forgot the well-being and rights of those who made his wealth. It often happened that such men occupied high places in Church courts, and wealth and religion became in the secularist's eyes as synonyms for hypocrisy.

In the younger universities, secularism took another form. Education had been considered incomplete in the older universities unless it embraced a philosophy that found place for religion. Gradually the word 'science' has taken the place of philosophy, and, worse still, science has come to mean physical science. As Professor Webb has said:[1] 'Sometimes what is harmless enough as a well-understood abbreviation may have mischievous

[1] *Religion and the Thought of To-day*, p. 15 (Oxford University Press).

consequences if it be assumed to carry with it the implication that whatever is not "scientific" in this special sense is not therefore "science" in the wider sense—not knowledge of reality at all.' This tendency is manifest in many—perhaps we may say in most—universities to-day, and it is reinforced by the belief that not dogma only, but also religion tends to keep the intellect in chains. The same tendency is seen in the persistent effort to make secondary education entirely secular. The ordinary student leaves his *alma mater* after three to six years' study with the impression stamped on his mind that all the important values of life are to be found in the natural and not in the supra-natural order.

Already the nemesis of this myopic view of life is upon us. Man has trusted in natural science, he has got the 'machine age' in which to attain to his full stature, and, after half a century, with what result? That god wherein he trusted threatens to destroy him. 'This growth of technics', says Nicolas A. Berdyaev,[1] 'and this mass-democratization of culture involve the basic problem of the present crisis, particularly acute for the Christian conscience, the problem of personality versus society. Personality, striving for emancipation, seems to be more and more oppressed by society, more and more socialized, collectivized. This is what comes of the mechanization and democratization of life, once hailed as "emancipatory".' It is not our task to follow the outworking of industrial secularism in countries like Russia. It assumes that man can live by bread alone. It ignores or denies all those intuitions

[1] *The Crisis of Christianity:* Christendom, No. 2, p. 235.

of an unseen order that persist in flitting across the human mind. It asserts that the Kingdom of Heaven is an ecclesiastical trap to catch the unwary. God is not, and sin and forgiveness are consequent fantasies.

These are among some of the reasons why the word of the Cross to many is foolishness. It belongs to a world quite remote from human thought and experience and is based on assumptions which multitudes think incapable of verification.

Chapter 2

SIN

SINCE sin is the ground and cause of alienation from God, it is impossible to study the atonement without considering in further detail that which occasions it. This raises the question, What is sin? For the present it is enough to say that sin is anything in our lives, to which we consent, that conflicts with the divine purpose and alienates us from God. Meanwhile it will be seen that we postulate a personal God and a moral order based on His character. Where God is regarded as impersonal force, or law, or the soul of the universe, within but not above nature, sin, as we understand the word, cannot arise. It is only by literary licence we speak of sinning against nature or even, in its collective sense, against society.

Sin is the act of one moral agent against another and is the product of personal freedom. The fact of its presence rests ultimately on the reality of human personality itself.[1] It implies that not only is there a personal God, but a moral order. This Kingdom of God is the expression of His nature, its perfection is His glory, and man by his constitution is capable of receiving and sharing the fellowship of this

[1] H. Wheeler Robinson, *The Christian Doctrine of Man*, p. 301 (T. & T. Clark).

28

Kingdom. 'It is your Father's good pleasure to give you the kingdom.'[1]

Conscience is the clearest witness we possess to the reality of a moral kingdom. It is one mark of the divine image in man. St. Paul is not satisfied to use *nous* (reason) as the instrument of moral judgement, but prefers *suneidēsis* (self-knowledge) to express this inner awareness of a moral order. By it man can judge his actions and achievements in the light of his ideal or moral standard, and can approve or condemn himself. Obviously the moral value of conscience is determined by the norm that the individual accepts—tradition, or public opinion, or a code of laws or the perfect life of Christ. We are not to think of conscience as an unerring faculty of equal value in all men everywhere; but rather, as the aesthetic faculty can be trained to appreciate beauty or to catch the wonder of a Beethoven sonata, so conscience as an innate endowment can be trained to appreciate the highest moral standard given and to give its verdict in favour of what is noblest.

At first the child and primitive man respond to arbitrary commands or taboos whose moral reasons may not be evident, but later the response is to moral principles alone. But Bishop Butler carries the nature and function of conscience much farther. He represents it as a delegated principle in man acting in its own right, yet on behalf of God, and with unlimited moral authority.

'There is', he says,[2] 'a superior principle of reflection or conscience in every man, which distinguishes

---

[1] Luke xii. 32.   [2] *Sermons on Human Nature*, pp. 403, 406.

between the internal principles of his heart, as well as his external actions; which, without being consulted, without being advised with, magisterially exerts itself and approves or condemns the doer accordingly. It is by this faculty, natural to man, that he is a moral agent, that he is a law to himself; but this faculty, I say, is not to be considered merely as a principle in his heart, which is to have some influence as well as others, but considered as a faculty in kind and in nature supreme over all others, and which bears its own authority of being so. This is a constituent part of the idea, that is, of the faculty itself, and to preside and govern, from the very economy and constitution of man, belongs to it. Had it strength as it has right; had it power as it has manifest authority it would absolutely govern the world.'

Whether Butler makes good his argument that conscience is *sui generis*, different, e.g. from the practical reason of, say, Kant, and God's vicegerent in man may be open to dispute, yet Butler's entire argument sustains the view that man is the subject of a moral kingdom, that that kingdom for the Christian is embodied in the life of Christ and that conscience is the mentor that institutes comparison between our ideal and our achievement and approves or condemns accordingly. It is not one among many principles that may have some influence but one that judges and if necessary condemns. This sense of obligation is as much a fact of experience as our ordinary appetites.

Nor does the argument of those who hold by an evolutionary origin of ethics invalidate this view.

Both Darwin and Herbert Spencer admit, that, be the historical conditions what they may, conscience functions within a normative science, i.e. in a world in which an obligation to live in a particular way operates. The norm may have been laid down by ancestral usage or be originally due to some self-protective custom of the tribe, yet here we find a clearly marked difference between the laws of a normative science and the laws of a positive science. Darwin's own words in the *Descent of Man* are 'the imperious word *ought* seems merely to imply the consciousness of the existence of a rule of conduct, however it may have originated'.[1] Why, we ask, add the word 'merely'? The awareness in man of an ideal to which he should conform is something entirely significant.

Spencer sought to decry the significance of the moral ideal. 'Supernatural ethics', he wrote, 'is defunct. Moral injunctions have lost the authority given by their supposed sacred origin and the secularization of morals is becoming imperative.'[2] This view belonged to the thorough-going deterministic evolution of forty years ago, and has been through the fires of criticism often since. The main and most devastating criticism has been made by pointing out the difference between the language appropriate in one universe of discourse, but not in another. No legerdemain can turn the law of what *ought to be* into the law of what *is*. It is this fact in man that is at once his glory and his humiliation. Only one capable of receiving the Kingdom of God can in the Christian sense commit sin. Whitman

---

[1] *The Descent of Man*, p. 98 (John Murray).   [2] *Data of Ethics*, p. iv.

does not do man honour when he chides him by pointing out in contrast the equanimity of the cattle in the field.

They do not sweat and whine about their condition,
They do not lie awake in the dark and weep for their sins,
They do not make me sick discussing their duty to God:
Not one is dissatisfied not one is demented
With the mania of owning things,
Not one kneels to another, nor to his kind that lived thousands
    of years ago:
Not one is respectable or unhappy over the whole earth.

To all of which we can consent, only remembering that the cattle are not moral subjects, are destitute of ideals, are incapable of failure, are incapable of regret and are incapable of receiving any higher kingdom. However aesthetically repellent the sight may be to a humanist, a penitent convulsed in sorrow over his failure and stretching out his hands to God for moral victory is a more inspiring picture than the contented cattle dreamily satisfied in their ample pasture.

As Professor Mackenzie wrote in comments on Whitman's words: 'The grass, as Mr. Ruskin somewhere remarks, is green every year; it is only the wheat that, on account of its higher nature, is liable to a blight. . . . Animals are not capable of the higher forms of sin.' It is only man who is high enough to fall. The humanist does man no honour by eliminating life's moral struggle at the expense of the 'divine spark that disturbs our clod'.[1]

So far the position is this: man is capable of

[1] *Manual of Ethics*, pp. 414, 415 (Univ. Tut. P.).

recognizing a nobler existence than that which he now lives. He feels himself challenged by it. He also realizes 'there are many adversaries' and that the life of the flesh is, at the outset, more appealing than the life of the spirit. He may even resist the Kingdom of God and rise in rebellion against the divine purpose. In such conditions we see sin in its Biblical form and we see also the need of reconciliation. Before we come to this, one other point needs consideration.

Exponents of the new psychology have represented human nature and religious aspiration in such a way that the picture we have just painted tends to lose all sense of reality. Thus, in his *Psychology of the Unconscious* Dr. Jung of Zurich, writing as a psychologist, seeks to eliminate the supernatural or 'power not our own' to, whom prayer might be addressed by finding it already in human hearts as an ancestral inheritance. 'Mankind', he says, 'wishes to love in God only their ideas, that is to say, the ideas which they project into God. By that they wish to love their unconscious, that is that remnant of ancient humanity and the centuries old past in all people—namely, the common property left behind from all development which is given to all men, like the sunshine and the air. Thus they turn back to the mother of humanity, that is to say, to the spirit of the race and regain in this way something of that connection of that mysterious and irresistible power which is imported by the feeling of belonging to the herd.'[1]

Here at best the not-self is but an immanent spirit

[1] p. III (Ed. 1921, Kegan Paul).

that dwells in the race; call it libido, *élan vital*, or what not, it is in no sense personalized; secondly, the sense of failure is due in the individual to mal-adjustments in the psychical mechanism, and salvation is accomplished by helping the subject to understand himself. If the subject is alarmed by reality he can by introversion escape within himself, and if he desires to escape from an inner complex to reality he can do it by transference.

Jung as a scientist naturally tries to find a reason within mental phenomena for every psychological problem that confronts him and so far he is true to his profession, but he overlooks two facts: (1) that merely to explain the idea of God by using a psychological phrase such as 'spirit of the race' or 'the feeling of belonging to the herd' is only calling a familiar object by a somewhat unfamiliar name; (2) to explain, however explicitly, the mechanism of the unconscious and human psychoses and to expect healing and harmony to follow from this alone is no wiser than to expect that, given the chemical elements of protoplasm in their due proportions and conditions, life must follow. We know that personality depends on other personalities for its existence and development, and when limited personalities have done all they can for the support and satisfaction of the psychotic subject then nothing remains but that right relations be set up between that soul and (not a 'spirit of the race' but) a personal God.

Indeed, in more recent writings Jung and Freud have come to recognize more clearly than they did where the boundaries of psychology end and where the frontiers of metaphysics and the postulates of theology begin. Behind all the pathological conditions of any soul lies God, and when the fullest understanding of human personality is attained (and for that we may well be very thankful) the individual stands face to face with Him. We conclude this brief observation in words that seem to express the fact: 'Psychology can teach us nothing about the essential nature of sin or original sin. It has thrown much light on the psychical machinery of sin . . . but from the standpoint of pure theology the idea of sin still remains unaffected. Our acceptance or rejection of the Christian view of sin must be determined on other grounds than those of psychology.'[1]

Since sin is so obviously an obnoxious and intractable element in man and society, we must consider the age-long questions, how did it begin? and has the problem any solution? The earliest considerable exposition of the question is that offered by Zoroaster in the Gathas. He, like Gotama, felt oppressed chiefly by the repulsiveness of sensuous evil. He says of himself that he received a commission from God (Ormuzd) to purify religion and purge it from the grossly sensuous elements of *daeva* worship and to uplift religion to a higher purer plane (Yasna 44). So stern was the conflict between the appetites of the flesh and the noble ideals of the mind that, rather than sacrifice facts to a theory, he sacrificed intellectual and moral unity to the facts.

[1] Bicknell, *The Christian Idea of Sin and Original Sin*, p. 78 (Longmans, Green & Co.).

At the beginning of things, he says there existed the two spirits who represented good and evil. The existence of evil is therefore in the world from the beginning. Both spirits possess creative power; in Ormuzd this power is manifested positively and constructively. Ormuzd is light and life and creates all that is pure and good in the ethical world of law order and truth. His eternal rival (Ahriman) is the source of darkness, filth, death, and every form of evil. As Zoroaster develops his ideas he tends to personalize and to give a pre-eminence to Ormuzd over his rival.

From the point of view of later theology, the important aspect of his theory is that he associates ethical and all evil with the action of Ahriman on and through matter. The epic battle is between the spirit and the flesh and between the creations of these deities in these two realms. The human tragedy is that man belongs to both kingdoms. As spirit he is bound to obey the call of Ormuzd. As incarnate spirit he is under the law of Ahriman; consequently he is the victim of endless inner strife. As spirit, too, he is free and can choose to respond to darkness or to light. 'Since thou, O Mazda, didst at the first create our being and our conscience in accordance with thy mind and didst create our understanding and our life together with the body, and works and words in which man, according to his own will, can frame his confession, the liar and the truth-speaker alike lay hold of the word, the knowing and the ignorant. Each after his own heart and understanding' (Yasna 31, 11). Man is not only involved in evil by his incarnation but further involved by his own voluntary response to the flesh.

Not a little of this conception of evil has found its way into Christian thought through Manichaeism and particularly from Mani (*b.* A.D. 215) through St. Augustine into Christian theology. A recent Gifford Lecturer[1] has pointed out that, in his conception of woman, St. Augustine never, even in his post-conversion days, got quite clear of the debasing conception of the flesh that came not from the New Testament, but from Manichaean philosophy. 'Who has not felt astonishment and repugnance when reading the passage in St. Augustine's *Confessions* in which he narrates his heartless dismissal of the faithful woman who for years had been his wife in all but name and had borne him a dearly loved son. He dwells on his own distress but has never a word for hers.' It has been argued that St. Paul, especially in Romans vii, has expressed the same view when he attributes sin to 'the flesh' or 'the body of the flesh' and the nobler aspirations to his spiritual self.[2] Something like a dualistic origin of sin is suggested, but it is only apparent. St. Paul, as a Jew, could not consent to any theory that would bring man ultimately under a dual authority.

'For dualism postulates an original and integral contradiction within human nature itself, and thus provides a key to that enigma of moral conflict which is the very hall-mark of humanity. It assumes an ultimate and irremovable divergence between

---

[1] Bishop Henson, *Christian Morality*, p. 165 (Oxford: The Clarendon Press).

[2] Romans vii. 18, 22.

the physical and moral constituents of human nature, presenting the one as the normal and natural adversary of the other, to be suppressed and destroyed, never to be disciplined and brought into natural harmony. Jewish religion required, not the suppression but the consecration of the material factor. "The earth is the Lord's and the fulness thereof" was the assumption of its ethical doctrine.'[1]

St. Paul's teaching recognizes the necessary restraint that the spirit must exert over the flesh and that men may on occasion require to buffet their bodies to keep them in subjection, but he is also the Apostle who declares that men's bodies are the temple of the Holy Spirit, and who encourages his converts to cleanse themselves from all defilement of flesh *and spirit*.[2] As for our Lord; the fact of the incarnation is the New Testament answer to the Manichaean theory of the origin of evil; and with sure insight and conviction the Church of the second century repudiated Valentinus and the docetic gnostics, who denied that the Son of God was come in the flesh, just as the Catholic Church more ruthlessly dealt with similar heresy in the fourteenth-century Cathari and to a lesser degree in the Waldensians in the next century. Our Lord's emphasis, to the scandal of His rabbinical contemporaries, on the sins of the spirit such as pride, uncharitableness, and hardness of heart rather than on sins of the flesh showed His mind with regard to the origin of moral evil.

The attempt is made in the Old Testament to show the historic origin of sin and this seems to be

---

[1] *Christian Morality*, p. 191.   [2] 2 Corinthians vii. 1.

accepted by St. Paul in the Epistle to the Romans. Probably the best way to a clear understanding of the account of 'the fall' in Genesis iii is to re-read the narrative without importing, consciously or unconsciously, what less-inspired writers have added. Milton cannot be acquitted of having added to the words of Scripture in this matter. Dr. Driver comments: 'It is sometimes supposed that the first man was a being of developed intellectual capacity, perfect in the entire range of his faculties, a being so gifted that the greatest and ablest of those who have lived subsequently have been described as the "rags" or "ruins" of Adam. This view of the high intellectual capacities of our first parents has been familiarized to many by the great poem of Milton, who represents Adam and Eve as holding discourse together in words of singular elevation, refinement, and grace. But there is nothing in the representation of Genesis to justify it, and it is opposed to everything we know of the methods of God's providence.'[1] The Hebrew writer has in Genesis iii. 1-15 given, unconsciously no doubt, a piece of psychological analysis that shines in its own light, that holds good of the human heart to-day, that is recorded in naïve imagery, but that nowhere indicates man's intellectual or moral development, save in general terms. We are dealing, not with Adam, but with human experience as we know it. James Denney wrote over forty years ago words that hold good now: 'The question, what is man? has been treated as if it were convertible with the question, what was

---

[1] 'Genesis', *Westminster Comm.*, *in loc.*

Adam? but it is plain that we do not stand in the same relation to these two questions. Man is before us, or rather, in us; we have the amplest opportunity for investigating his nature and constitution, and we have the whole range of Scripture to guide and correct our interpretation of these accessible facts. But Adam is not within our reach at all; and it is simply exposing ourselves, without any necessity whatever, to refutation by the progress of physical science, when we advance statements about the primitive condition of man which have not only a religious, but a physical and historical content.'[1] If we detach the religious significance of the account in Genesis iii from the form in which it is presented, we find an experience that is verified in the life of each individual at some stage in his growth. At whatever stage in development man attains to awareness of a Power not himself, realizes a sense of obligation and of a need that he comes to believe can be met by that power, and expresses that belief in a definite response, it may be by prayer, sacrifice, or silent adoration, there man has attained to the possibilities of religion.[2] If the Object be a personal Being whose will is revealed, and man has the disposition to disobey that will, we have the conditions of sin. The ethical content of the word 'sin' depends on the character of the God whose will has become law. Sin is man's opposition to the will of God. From the Christian view-point, it is the clash of two personalities; a divine, full of wisdom and compassion, and a human that seeks

---

[1] *Studies in Theology*, p. 78.

[2] cf. Galloway, *The Philosophy of Religion*, p. 83 (T. & T. Clark).

to attain an imaginary freedom by self-will and rebellion.

Philosophical theories that represent sin as an illusion, such as we get in the Vedanta philosophy of India, or as a necessary reaction to temptation, the apparently evil consequence of which is transcended in a fuller life, and seen as such from a higher altitude, as in Hegel, cannot be considered here at greater length. All we can say is that such theories tend to sacrifice moral values and distinctions to the intellectual satisfaction of an all-embracing theory. This can never satisfy the man who believes that justice, mercy, and holiness are more than names. In the words of Dean Inge, 'The notion of a finite God is one that the moralist can never afford to forget nor the metaphysician to remember'.

We conclude by considering something of the teaching of Jesus on sin. To begin with, He seldom discussed any great question in the abstract. This method was alien from Hebrew thought in general and in particular from the quality of His own mind. This was strongly imaginative and pictorial. Every abstract question he approached in a concrete setting and every problem He handled in relation to conduct. A good example is His reply to the question: 'What shall I do to inherit eternal life?' This involves loving God and one's neighbour, and the out-working of this love of one's neighbour is the story of the Good Samaritan.[1]

So it was with regard to sin: Jesus displayed a salutary impatience with any doctrinaire theory

[1] cf. Luke x. 25 ff.

offered to account for it. He rejected out of hand
the notion that sin lay behind all suffering and that
suffering was the visible sign of divine wrath towards
it. Those upon whom the Tower of Siloam[1] fell
were not greater sinners than the others in Jerusalem
who escaped, but such a tragedy is a clear call to
repent. John retains the same tradition in his
account of the man born blind.[2] 'Who did sin, this
man or his parents, that he should be born blind?'
'Neither did this man sin nor his parents but that
the works of God should be made manifest in him.'
The only problem about sin that need greatly
concern us is how we may overcome and be rid
of it.

Again, Jesus regards sin in a purely personal and,
therefore, religious way. Those who sat in Moses'
seat discussed all questions of sin in relation to the
Law. While it is true that at its best, and rightly
understood, the Law was a vivid transcript of the
mind of God, yet for the ordinary Jew it embraced
all sorts of taboos, ritual injunctions, and regulations
of a very subordinate kind. Christ's great task was
to separate the wheat from the chaff, love to God
and man from the washing of hands, cups, pots, and
brazen vessels. It required great moral insight and
courage. Sin had lost its meaning because the
tithing of mint had become as momentous as a
pure heart. It is always dangerous to put laws,
however excellent, as the test of character. It too
easily leads to casuistry and hypocrisy. We shall
see later that attempts to interpret the work of
Christ as a fulfilment of, or satisfaction to, eternal

[1] Luke xiii. 4 ff.   [2] John ix. 1–3.

42

laws break down. According to Jesus, sin must not
be regarded simply as a violation of laws, nor would
He have been satisfied with the statement that sin
is the transgression of the law.

If we are concerned with ethics only, then we may
speak of sin in this way, but Jesus went beyond
ethics to Religion; and Religion is that which binds
two persons—a Divine and a human—in a fellowship of life.

He knew God in the depths of His own consciousness so intimately and so fully that all His thought
and conduct were directed not to abstract laws, but
to the Father's will. Sin could only arise in relation
to the Father's purpose. If the thoughts and intents
and purposes of the heart were right, then even if
circumstances denied them realization in daily life,
there was no sin. If the thoughts and intents were
wrong and only failed of expression because fear of
public opinion or law held them in check, then the
man was a sinner. Consequently, the sin that
summed up all the sins was insincerity or hypocrisy.

This brings us more closely to our Lord's conception of sin. It is a corrupt quality of life due to
alienation from God the Father. Instead of accepting His gracious purpose and plan, instead of sharing
fellowship with Him, the sinner is the man who puts
self in the place of God—self-assertion, self-interest,
self-indulgence. This is the factor that alienates.
Consequently Jesus attacks sin in this citadel. 'If
any man would come after me, let him deny himself, and take up his cross daily, and follow me.'[1]
Once self is central and dominant, God and His

[1] Luke ix. 23.

purpose and grace are rejected, the gulf widens, for sin is cumulative, and the need for reconciliation grows. Sin is thus a religious problem and results in hostility to God.

Jesus shows, further, that it begets a general *malaise* in the soul. 'Sin is not primarily a matter of omissions and commissions, but a condition of the soul analogous to disease in the body. This analogy is implied in the saying: "They that are whole have no need of a physician but they that are sick." . . . Just as bodily pain, sickness, high temperature, and the like are not the disease itself, but only the signs or symptoms of it, so the follies and crimes of men are the signs and symptoms of the morbid conditions of men's souls.'[1]

Consequently, while Jesus lays down clear instruction for the disciple who would follow Him, He is under no illusion about the necessity for a complete renewal of the man's moral nature. It is here He stands in clear contrast with John the Baptist and so uniquely transcends Him in His message. John is a reformer and holds that much can be done by the axe and fire. Society can be cleansed, or at least made safe. But Jesus goes deeper: 'Make the tree good and the fruit good. The good man out of the good treasure of his heart bringeth forth that which is good.' As Dr. E. F. Scott has written: 'The purpose of Jesus . . . was not to enforce a rule that must be followed with labour and difficulty, but to impart a spirit which would take the place of law. The Christian character at its finest has always an-

[1] Manson, *The Teaching of Jesus*, p. 308 (Cambridge University Press).

44

swered to this requirement of Jesus, and this has
been the secret of its charm. We can feel that its
virtues are not the result of painful effort, but are
the outflow of an inner spring.'[1]

Because of this fact, Jesus alone meets the problem
of sin. He is of all teachers the most exacting in
His moral demands. He refuses to let us make compromise with sin, even as He resisted unto blood
striving against it. He transcends the Baptist's
demands for a personal and social respectability.
He pierces to the thoughts and motives which are
the true man within, and yet His ruthlessness fills
us with great hope because He undertakes to give
us moral renewal, to lead us from a self-centred
to a God-centred life and to stir the soul into new-
ness of life as it is swept by the breath of His own
spirit. His demands for a new kind of life are
promises of its fulfilment.

Jesus reveals also His personal hostility to sin by
His action even more than by His words. 'The best
men have opposed sin by setting their life against it,
by placing themselves in its path, at whatever cost,
and constituting their personal being a dedicated
obstacle to its progress. This path Christ pre-
eminently chose. It was for Him not enough to
denounce wrong; He went further and took the last
step; He exhibited an utter opposition to sin by
dying at the hand of sinners. By letting sinful men
vent their utmost hate upon Himself, He revealed
and condemned sin as the absolute contrary of love.'[2]

[1] *Ethical Teaching of Jesus*, p. 20 (Macmillan & Co.).

[2] Mackintosh, *The Christian Experience of Forgiveness*, pp. 199–200
(Nisbet & Co.).

Jesus refused to surrender to sin. He refused to use its own weapons. He refused to render evil for evil. He let sin work its will upon Him and in so doing He was its condemnation and destruction.

One other point deserves attention. Jesus stressed the helplessness engendered in man by his sin. He can alienate himself from God or from his neighbour by it, but once this gulf is opened he can never of himself bridge it. That remains entirely within the power of those sinned against. The sinner is as a lost sheep in a wilderness that cannot find its way home. He is dependent on grace or nothing. He owes what he cannot repay. Consequently, Christ's great work over against sin is His own cross. It witnesses to a love that triumphs over sin and extends a hand of mercy.

Chapter 3

THE MEN WHO CRUCIFIED CHRIST

For two reasons, we must consider in this chapter the motives of the men who crucified Jesus. First, because many entertain in a loose and uncritical way the idea that God fore-ordained that His Son must be made to die for sinners and that therefore, instead of holding Pilate, Judas, or the Priests to execration, we should regard them with pity as pawns in the invisible fingers of One whose will they helped to accomplish. Was it not prophesied that the Christ must die? Some one must be the Pilate or the Judas.

Even Abailard sees no other way of interpretation: 'Grace is not given to all men alike and in the same way, for God chooses His elect arbitrarily in accordance with the right He possesses of disposing His creation in whatever manner He may desire. Akin to the power which the potter wields over his clay, God's power over mankind is tyrannical, and so no injury is inflicted upon a man if God refuses him his gift of grace. Bound by no obligations until an actual promise has been made, utilizing for good both the wickedness of Judas and the sanctity of Peter, governing the universe with strict rationality, God commits no wrong in thus restricting His gifts.'[1]

[1] Quoted from Sikes, *Peter Abailard*, pp. 202–3 (Cambridge University Press).

This short and easy method with divine sovereignty belongs to an age when the character of God was not fully moralized. Amos says, 'Shall evil befall a city and the Lord hath not done it?' (iii. 6); and Isaiah says, 'I make peace and create evil, I am the Lord that doeth all these things' (xlv. 7). The devout Jew was determined at all costs to maintain a strict monotheism. Better to make God responsible for evil than to allow the polytheistic and deadly error that there was another beside God who did the evil and challenged the supremacy of Jehovah.

Further, we need scarcely be warned against the anachronism of making Old Testament writers hold a clear view of scientific or secondary causes. All actions were due to God and He was so real to the prophets' consciousness that intermediate causes were overlooked. To-day the secondary or tertiary causes are so prominent that the primary cause is often forgotten. The devout Hebrew also saw, what the Christian can see more clearly, that God is continually overruling the acts of wicked men and bringing good out of their evil. Thus in the records of Barnardo's rescue work in London we have this story: A drunken father drove his small son on the streets of London. The lad was rescued and educated. To-day he holds a position of trust in Canada more honourable and indeed lucrative than if he had remained under a drunken father in Whitechapel. No one can be convinced that God willed or incited the inhuman cruelty of the drunken father. If so, a demon rules the universe. Yet a devout Hebrew would not hesitate to 'short-circuit' the story and say that God caused the lad to be cast out in destitution that He might save him.[1] However strong the language used about the fore-ordination of Judas and others in regard to Christ's death, the Christian conscience revolts against the idea that the God and Father revealed in Jesus Christ overrides the personality of any of His sons and makes it impossible that they should do other than commit crime. Such a view destroys all meaning in personal responsibility and shatters the moral justice of the universe.

We hope to see rather that despite the moral depravity and the ignorance of His sons God takes hold of tragedy and by the resources of His wisdom, love, and power turns it into victory. The New Testament teaches this, if nothing else, that divine love refuses to be outwitted by man's wickedness and victory remains with love. As Dr. Wheeler Robinson says: 'The paradoxes of our religion become the ultimates of our faith.' Secondly, unless we study the motives and passions that led these men to crucify Christ, we shall miss the important fact that we belong to that common humanity that takes the same attitude to Him in every generation. Christ is as central to men to-day as nineteen hundred years ago. He evokes similar responses.

The chief actors in the drama were Pilate, Judas, the priests, and the multitude, and to this study we turn.

Pontius Pilate. Pilate was no enemy of Jesus. The statement in Peter's speech[2] that 'Pilate was determined to release Jesus' is entirely congruous with the

---

[1] cf. the parallel in Genesis xlv. 5–8.   [2] Acts iii. 13.

Synoptic accounts of what took place at the trial. In an ineffective sort of way he struggled three times to commend Jesus to the Jews and to secure His release. It was not enmity, but the fact rather that he was bound in the fetters of his own past that led to the sacrifice of Jesus. Earlier he had sowed the wind and at the crucial hour he could only reap the whirlwind. He was a man of weak temperament and character. Apart from a fragment in Luke xiii. 1, we are dependent on Flavius Josephus[1] for hints about the administration.

Two incidents shed light on the disaster at the Crucifixion. It was a custom in the Roman Empire that when troops arrived in any colony or province the Imperial standards should be placed in the nearest important temple. Owing to the sensitive scruples of the Jews, and because they were on the whole good citizens, Rome excused the Jewish peoples from this demand. On Pilate's arrival as Procurator or provincial governor, he determined to assert his authority, teach the Jews they were no better than other religious sects, and compel them to admit the offensive and desecrating standards into God's holy house. To avoid immediate clash, the standards were placed in the Temple during the night. When the news spread next morning Jerusalem gathered as one man at the steps leading to the Governor's house and demanded their removal. Pilate, thinking to rise to the dignity of a governor, ordered the spearmen to be ready. He warned the Jews of their danger if they did not withdraw, but the Jews merely bared their necks, showing where

[1] cf. *Ant.*, xviii. 3.

the spears would find them first, and stood un-
moved. Pilate saw he could not begin government
by massacre, ordered the standards to be removed
and returned a beaten man.

Later he came into conflict with the Jews when
he ravaged the Temple treasury for money to pay
for the aqueduct, valuable in itself, which he
directed to be built, to supply Jerusalem. The
Jewish revolt so angered him that he directed
soldiers to go through the crowd stabbing men, here
and there, for no other reason than to afford himself
the miserable satisfaction of revenge. Philo says he
was tactless, insolent, corrupt, and stained with a
murderer's blood. At one stage the Sanhedrin
thought of sending a delegation to Tiberius to lay
an impeachment against Pilate.

Every man meets his day of judgement, when he
is tried as by fire. Only God knows what were
Pilate's moral assets at the outset, but even a pagan
Roman governor knew that his Empire stood for
justice, for equity, and even, on occasion, for mercy.
He did not need to be taught that bullying, insult,
revenge, murder were not the part of a man who
represented the great Lex Romana. A moral
cancer consumed all resistance and courage in his
soul. He knew, too, of the threatened impeachment, and when the savage howl went up, 'If thou
let this man go thou art not Caesar's friend', he
knew that to refuse the Jews their prey meant his
own banishment and possible execution. It was a
terrible ordeal, 'Christ or Barabbas?' To a quiet,
strong man with a clean record, 'whose strength
was as the strength of ten because his heart was

pure', it would have been no ordeal. Pilate was the problem. A governor, whose record was clean, had only to raise his finger and the legions of the then greatest Empire on earth would have moved forward, cleared the court, put justice on the throne, and proved loyal to the Son of God. Instead, we read: 'And Pilate, wishing to content the multitude, released unto them Barabbas, and delivered Jesus, when he had scourged Him, to be crucified' (Mark xv. 15). No one can read the story of Pilate without realizing that so far from commanding our pity, we see the outworking of the unchangeable moral law that whatsoever a man soweth that shall he also reap. Given men in high places like Pilate, and it was a moral certainty that Christ would be handed over to be crucified.

Judas. The part played by Judas in the Crucifixion is so unbelievably infamous that all sorts of explanations and apologists for him have been found. De Quincey set the pace (*Works*, vol. viii, pp. 177 ff.). His argument may be summarized thus: Jesus appeared to Judas as something of a doctrinaire and dreamer who trusted too much in the efficacy of self-sacrificing ideals, but who failed as a realist. Judas believed that Jesus had not only sound principles, but power, and that, if a crisis were forced, then Jesus would rise sublimely to the demands of the occasion, reveal His authority and strength, and set up His Kingdom. Judas, the argument runs, determined to precipitate the crisis, force the hand of Jesus, and be the honoured instrument in revealing His glory. Jesus did not respond. When the stage was set, He refused to play the part. Instead, He submitted without any resistance to be crucified. Horror-stricken and filled with remorse, the well-meaning Judas went and hanged himself.

One would like to think the highest of all the sons of men. We are ashamed to think human nature could sink to such a hell, yet can we accept this interpretation? We must examine the facts before we form the theory. Whatever be his motive in betraying Jesus to the priests, Judas was guilty of distrust towards his Master. He assumed that he knew better than Jesus the time and manner of setting up the Kingdom. Faith always waits until God shows that the hour is come. Even a loyal soldier does not let his impetuous zeal carry him into action before the signal is given.

But according to Mark (xiv. 10, 11) all trace of this high-minded idealism vanishes as we read that 'Judas Iscariot . . . went away unto the chief priests that he might deliver Him unto them. And they when they heard it were glad and promised to give him money. And he sought how he might conveniently deliver Him unto them'. Whether writers like Branscomb[1] fail to find evidence of cupidity in Judas or not, it seems certain from the conjunction of these two sentences, 'they promised to give him money' and 'he sought how he might conveniently deliver Him', that Mark regarded the bribe as finding response in Judas. Matthew represents the tradition of thirty years later. 'Judas went unto the chief priests and said, what are you willing to give me and I will deliver Him unto you?' (xxvi.

1 'St. Mark', *Moffatt's Commentary*, p. 247 (Hodder & Stoughton).

14–16). Luke says: 'Satan entered into Judas . . . and he went away and communed with the chief priests and captains, how he might deliver Him unto them' (xxii. 3–4). The Synoptic writers may have been mistaken in their analysis of Judas's character and motives, but, right or wrong, it seems certain they regarded Judas as a disappointed man who felt that money payment for revealing the whereabouts of his Master was not unattractive.

So it becomes a choice between modern apologists for Judas and the obvious belief and tradition in the first century. On the whole, the unpleasant ancient view is more convincing. The moral development of Judas seems to have been this: When Jesus called him to be one of the Twelve, he was like any other young man, a mass of possibilities for good. Else why did Jesus call him? We cannot conceive that He called a man to be an apostle who was only a covetous, ambitious traitor. But in every man there are distinct propensities full of moral danger. To such men come glimpses of a nobler life; unless such glimpses are cherished and stabilized in character, the natural propensities to lust, envy, ambition, covetousness reassert themselves and settle like a dark night upon the soul. The stars are eclipsed and disaster becomes a certainty. Contact with institutional religion is no guarantee that such moral deterioration will not ensue. Many beside Paul must needs pray that after having preached to others they may not become castaways.

Judas was with the new Messiah but failed to

appreciate his new ideals; he was with the party, but not of it. Judean dreams of a Messianic dictatorship took the place of the picture of the suffering servant, until, chagrined and disappointed, Judas came to despise the pacific principles and self-sacrifice of Jesus his Master and moved in his sympathies more and more to the circumference. His soul had gone over in response to the old ideals of the chief priests before he set up negotiations. As in all harvests, the ripening at the close was rapid and disaster followed. Christ's effort at the eleventh hour to hold him back (Mark xiv. 18 and Luke xxii. 21–3) gives no support to the theory that he was in the grasp of an inescapable fate other than that of responsibility for the way in which he had cherished his early and noblest ideals, and of the inevitable consequences of neglect.

Caiaphas. We may take the High Priest as genuinely representative of the ideals and motives of the 'Sons of Annas'. If we follow his reactions to the ministry of Jesus, we shall not go amiss concerning that of the leaders in the Sanhedrin. For reasons peculiar to his aim, the Fourth Evangelist makes the occasion of the collision between Jesus and the chief priests to lie in the raising of Lazarus. The Synoptic writers make it to lie in the cleansing of the Temple just before the arrest and trial. This cleansing John puts at the beginning of Christ's ministry. Since John handles his material derived from Synoptic sources with great freedom, being more concerned to reveal the majesty of the eternal Son than to trace a history of events in chronological order, we accept the Synoptic record (cf. Mark xi. 15–18) as expressing the true order of events. Mark says that on the cleansing of the Temple 'the chief priests and scribes heard it and sought how they might destroy him' (xi. 18).

To account for this hatred, we must consider the position of the High Priest and his party. Caiaphas held his office as High Priest under Tiberius from A.D. 18 to 36. He was a kind of Jewish Caliph. His office was dual; as head of the Jewish community or State, he was President of the Sanhedrin, dealt with all civic questions and presided at the trial of offences up to those requiring the death penalty. But, more important for our purpose, he was head of the body that directed the national religious cultus. He was married to a daughter of the ex-High Priest Annas, and as Annas had succeeded in having four of his sons appointed to the High Priesthood, the cultus had come to be in the hands of a close corporation or limited company. The Temple was designed to be God's house of prayer for all the nations. As a matter of common knowledge, it had become the instrument of an unscrupulous and avaricious party.

The 'Sons of Annas' had estates on which herds were raised for Temple sacrifices. These were a necessity to Jews of the Dispersion who came to the Passover. The market was opened within the Temple precincts. As Gentile money was ritually unclean, brokers were appointed to exchange it for Jewish shekels. An immense revenue was reaped from commission on exchange alone. The rate lay entirely in the hands of the priestly party. Meat inspectors, sellers of wine and of doves, and attendants of the sacrificing priests constituted an industry and made the Temple a busy market place. Little imagination is needed to see the repulsive conditions in which the priests filled their coffers. Animal filth, litter, highly pitched bargaining voices, lowing cattle, bleating sheep, and men on the strain to make money or cut down prices—this was the centre of the religious life of Judaism. Is it any wonder Professor Burkitt sees in Christ's entry into Jerusalem a public recall to religion by the purification of the national worship? The House of Prayer for the nations had become a den of robbers under the aegis of the High Priests. Some were literally robbers who sought sanctuary in the Temple, others were robbers of man's moral and religious privileges. The priests were Sadducees who resented the ethical teaching of the prophets as modernism. They were content with the Pentateuch. They set small store on life beyond the grave and so sought to make the most of this life. They upheld the things Jesus made secondary and they buried under a mass of lucrative institutionalism the knowledge of God and eternal life which Christ came to bestow. Religion was secularized, commercialized, and turned into money. Though writers like Mr. Middleton Murry[1] have tended to discredit the moral character of Jesus for His cleansing of the Temple, yet the soul of Christendom has always felt that desperate diseases need desperate remedies and that spiritual freedom could not have come to Israel until this incubus was attacked in its citadel.

[1] *The Life of Jesus*, pp. 241–2 (Cape).

Jesus condemned the policy of the priests, He discredited their authority in the eyes of the people, He endangered their financial prosperity, and He repudiated their religious half-beliefs. 'It is not surprising that from this point on the priests appear in the story as actually plotting the destruction of this rebel who had led the attack on their prestige and authority if not on their income.'[1]

The Scribes and Pharisees. These two parties were really one. The Scribes were only a specialized group of jurists within the Pharisees and were only distinguished because of their peculiar function. The cause of conflict between the Pharisees and Jews was on a higher level than that of the Chief Priests. It was on the Pharisees side a misguided but largely sincere struggle to retain morality and religion. Yet the difference between the teaching of Christ and of the Pharisees goes to the roots of real religion. It is a question of human effort versus divine revelation, of human merit over against a free gift, of works over against faith in God. Nothing can be more vital since it means salvation by outer reform or by inner renewal. The issue was fought out afresh by St. Paul, especially in the Epistle to the Galatians, by Luther in the sixteenth century, and by John Wesley in the eighteenth century. The issue is repeated in almost every individual who seeks to attain to righteousness before God. Dr. T. W. Manson states the issue with great clarity.[2] 'The opposition between Jesus and the Scribes and Pharisees is thus a fundamental difference of

---

[1] Branscomb, *Mark*, p. 205 (Hodder & Stoughton).
[2] *The Teaching of Jesus*, p. 300 (Cambridge University Press).

principle. It is the opposition of two conceptions of virtue. For Jesus, good living is the spontaneous activity of a transformed character; for the Scribes and Pharisees it is obedience to a discipline imposed from without. The Scribes and Pharisees rightly perceived that these two ideals were incompatible, and that if the ideal of Jesus prevailed, it meant, not a reform of the Law, but the substitution of something else for it. They therefore opposed the new teaching with all their might, just as at a later date they opposed the Pauline restatement of it.'

Jesus asserted ideals and principles of conduct for His new community so lofty that men were staggered when He uttered them and men still declare they are beyond human nature, a counsel of perfection. They go far beyond the exacting 613 tests of the Scribes. 'Except your righteousness shall exceed the righteousness of the Scribes and Pharisees ye shall in no wise enter the Kingdom.' But the wonder of Christianity is just here. Christ declares that human nature can be re-made from within, and that He can communicate a new quality of heart to men that will provide a passion and a motive that will change thought and feeling as well as action. 'Make the tree good and its fruit good.' This regeneration or becoming as little children is a matter of obedience to and faith in Himself, and the reflex influence of His Personality on those who come to Him. He is not afraid to mingle with the disreputables of His day. He says little about the Law or even repentance and faith. He eats with alienated men and women. The Pharisees see in His method only a condoning of sin. The Law is belittled by one who consorts with law-breakers. They murmured saying, 'This man receiveth sinners and eateth with them'. They had not moral discernment to see that the best way to float out rubbish is to bring in a high tide. Christ's standard demands Christ's power and Christ's power is communicable.

But the question that filled Scribes and Pharisees with alarm was this: If men take this way of Christ, what of the Law and all its time-honoured precepts? What of the Temple and the Scribal office and the national history? What of Moses? Has their religious history been a prolonged mistake and is even God to be arraigned at this new bar set up by the prophet of Galilee?

The Scribes and Pharisees seem to have history and precedent on their side. It does seem as if law and social decency are to be brought into contempt. If Christ is believed in by mankind, He will become the end of the Law, and such a disaster must be averted even by the death of this misguided enthusiast. So the Scribes joined the elders and Chief Priests at the High Priest's house[1] to consult together how they might destroy Jesus. The motive of the Scribes, then, was similar to that of the priests in one point. Both parties knew that their prestige and office must perish if the teaching of the Nazarene prevailed, but certainly some credit must be given to the Scribes as showing a real concern for what they believed to be the only way to acceptance with God. A trace of the heresy-hunting spirit that always marks literalists and legalists is also present.

[1] Mark xiv. 53; xv. 1.

This the Fourth Evangelist is at pains to show.[1]

The Multitude. According to Mark xv. 11, the Chief Priests 'stirred up the multitude' and in v. 13 the multitude cried out 'crucify Him'. Also in v. 15 we read, 'Pilate, wishing to content the multitude . . .' The question to be decided is who are this multitude? Two words are used in the Gospels both translated 'multitude'. *Plethos* means a vast aggregation regardless of the moral character of the individuals, but *ochlos*, the word used in all the above examples, means a crowd with riotous tendencies, an irregular mob. It seldom is used to indicate our colloquial 'the public', or mass, thought of only collectively. From this we conclude that the multitude who cried 'crucify Him' had no relation to the multitude who listened with wonder and astonishment to Jesus, or to 'the people of the land' or to that multitude in Jerusalem of whom the Scribes and Pharisees had such a wholesome fear that they plotted to have Jesus arrested in their absence 'lest a tumult should arise', or to those who broke down branches from the trees and strewed them in honour of Jesus and cried, 'Hosanna to the Son of David'.

It is, of course, obvious that the multitude who cried, 'Away with Him' were drawn from the *plethos*, the general populace. But as great moral differences exist between people in the plebeian as in the upper classes. Certain psychological elements are peculiar to human nature in the mass, and the less the cognitive or critical faculty is developed, the more strongly these elements reveal

[1] cf. John vii. 47-9.

themselves. The multitude is dangerously liable to 'mass' suggestion. Primitive instincts such as fear or combativeness flourish in a mass. Emotion corresponding to such instincts is quickly stirred to boiling point. In mass emotion almost any object suffices upon which to find release, and an unscrupulous demagogue has a golden opportunity to work for a party advantage. 'The irrationality of the crowd is notorious, its cognitive powers being limited to the bare recognition of objects or symbols which excite its affects and impulses. The rational powers of the individuals composing it are in abeyance, when once its instincts are excited. The ease with which the crowd is excited and led by a skilful crowd-leader who knows how to play on its instincts, or by a chance individual who can gain its ear and can pass, for the moment, as a leader, or even by any accidental happening which acts as a stimulus to its instincts—these are things too well-known to need illustration.'[1] For these reasons, one is compelled to dissent from Branscomb's view that Mark's statement that 'the High Priests stirred up the crowd' is a lame explanation of Pilate's surrendering Jesus to the multitude and releasing Barabbas.[2] In addition to the exploiting of mob emotion by the priests, there may have been elements of disappointment in the minds of some that made them more susceptible to their leaders' incitements. The multitude were ready to follow Jesus when He appeared as a popular Messiah. He was fashionable as a Healer, a Controversialist, an

[1] Tansley, *The New Psychology*, p. 231 (Allen & Unwin).
[2] See Branscomb, *Mark*, p. 289 (Hodder & Stoughton).

outspoken and fearless Leader, but when He became less of a philanthropist and more of an ethical Teacher calling upon men to surrender all, even life itself, for His sake, then a painful reaction followed in many minds and enthusiasm turned to disgust. This would probably have taken no outward expression but for the party leaders. The demagogue flourishes best when he finds a man with a grievance. The motives of the multitude at the trial were apparently due to artificially stimulated passion, as well as chagrin over a disappointing leader.

Chapter 4

THE CROSS AND THE RESURRECTION

THERE were four counts in the indictment brought against Jesus: First, that He was usurping authority to which He could lay no legitimate claim;[1] secondly, that He was a menace to the security of the Jewish state;[2] thirdly, that He was a corrupter of truth and a blasphemer, representing Himself as initiating a new way to fellowship with God that transcended that of Moses and the Law;[3] and, fourthly, that He was a dangerous demagogue[4] both in politics and religion, 'stirring up the people throughout all Jewry and beginning from Galilee even unto this place'. These were not formulated in this order at the trial, but they seem to have been the grounds of antagonism on which the great accusations were based. At the trial, religious heresy and political agitation were the formal charges and the latter was the factor that weighed most with Pilate. It is evident that even with the help of suborned witnesses, it was no easy task to secure a verdict of 'guilty'. Contradictory evidence cancels itself out, and when it came to anything approaching dispassionate examination of Christ's teaching it had to be unearthed in parable and

[1] cf. Mark xi. 28.   [2] John xi. 48.
[3] Matthew xxvi. 65.   [4] xxiii. 3–5.

epigram. It was a message of great moral principles
and these had an unpleasant way of confronting
those who began to examine them, as both Pilate
and Herod knew to their cost.

But, waiving all this, the verdict of both Church
and State, of ecclesiastics and political leaders, of
highly placed officials and the irresponsible masses
was that Jesus ought to be crucified. Pilate lacked
the moral strength to oppose the demand, the
priests were concerned to be rid of one who imperilled the entire cultus, and the Scribes and
Pharisees resolved that venerable institutions and a
tradition that held ground for centuries should not
be thrust aside or overthrown at the word of a young
teacher whose origins and credentials were hard to
determine.

The Crucifixion was effected. It expressed in a
most appalling manner the estimate in which men
held Jesus. The Cross is the world's verdict and
judgement upon Him. Jesus bore witness to truth
as He knew it. Men denied it and condemned Him
as in error. He had various roads by which to
evade the issue. He could retire to Galilee, or He
could compromise, or He could recant completely.
This He refused to do. Herein lies the moral
necessity of the Cross. By this we understand such
words as 'Behoved it not the Christ to suffer these
things?'[1] If eternal life is to come by the knowledge
of God then Christ's witness must be borne even
in and by death; so the cup that the Father gave
Him to drink He did not evade.

We must tarry a moment to enter as far as

[1] Luke xxiv. 26.

reverence permits into the meaning of this hour.
The Agony in the Garden cannot be explained by
the nails and the thorns, the mockery and derision
alone. To One so sensitive to life and friendship
as Jesus was this was a poignant grief, but more lay
behind the distress than anything men could do.
Jesus stood at this hour quite alone. Of the people
there was none with Him. The sleeping disciples
were receding to the circumference of His thought
and travail, and soon even they would fail to utter
a word in loyalty or defence. 'The hour is come
that ye shall be scattered, every man to his own
and shall leave me alone.' In such a moment the
sensitive man is staggered. The temptation comes
to his heart with withering power: 'Am I alone in
possession of truth?' 'Is the mind of God not more
likely to be known in a group or a multitude than
in a solitary soul?' 'By what authority doest thou
these things?'

In such an ordeal men are tempted to turn for
corroboration to the multitude and to doubt the
deliverance of their own consciousness. Compromise follows and the saving vision fades. At this
hour, as in the wilderness, our Lord had to stake
everything on His own immediate consciousness
of the Father's will. It is the greatest adventure of
faith recorded in human history. Jesus made His
choice. He rested His soul on the immediate
knowledge of God and fellowship with the Father
that had hitherto sustained Him. Men might
say sincerely or in malevolence, 'Thou hast a
devil and art mad', but He was content to go
forward in the light that never dimmed in His

66

own soul. 'I am not alone, because the Father is with me.'

That point brings us to the main idea in this chapter. Christ's own confidence and serenity, what He called 'my peace', left Him in no doubt but that He was treading the way of God and redemption, yet it was personal and subjective, and could hardly suffice for the world. He was crucified, but who or what was to decide the issue between His way and that of the world? How could men determine whether He was a dangerous fanatic or the perfect revelation of God? The world had given its verdict on the Cross, but what of Heaven? It remained silent, and what an ominous silence! If the burial of Jesus is the end of His mission then we may well believe that the universe is the sport of demons, and all confidence in the reality of a moral Kingdom, of spiritual values, of a reign of God is so much blind credulity. In the silent hours after the body is laid in the tomb, all that is noblest in Heaven and earth calls for an assertion of God and a resurrection of some kind. A silent Heaven will spell an indifferent or immoral universe. The moral necessity of the Resurrection can hardly be exaggerated.

Before we come to examine the records about the Resurrection itself it should be noted that uncertainty about the moral validity of the Crucifixion swiftly set in. Questionings sprang up even before the deed was done. The forced trial by a thrice illegal process,[1] a trial that ended in a travesty of law, showed that the Chief Priests were not too

[1] cf. Shaw, *The Trial of Jesus Christ* (Hudson).

happy about their action. Judas was so quickly overtaken by a sense of the enormity of his act that he preferred death to reflection on what he had done. The centurion who supervised the execution felt there was a miscarriage of justice and said, 'Certainly this was a righteous man'.[1] 'The multitude that came together to this sight when they beheld the things that were done returned smiting their breasts.' It was beginning to look, even on the evening of the Crucifixion, as if a general resurrection of those very principles for which Jesus died had begun. Reason and Conscience, like voices of God, were making themselves heard in the garden in the cool of the day. According to later tradition, those responsible for the Crucifixion felt they were not finished with their savage work.[2] 'If the assassination could trammel up the consequence, and catch with his surcease, success',[3] all would be well, but there were stirrings and questionings that could not be laid or ignored. Have we evidence that anything more than a return to ethical sanity took place? Did the victim remain in the grip of death or did that vital and radiant Personality reappear, Victor through His defeat, and prove that eternal love is unconquerable?

There is no doubt that the records of the Resurrection are not very harmonious, but one point shines clear through all—that the writers are trying to describe something, to them, very real and unique and, when it happened, very unexpected. But we also know that what they try to express (and in some respects it is ineffable) has become an

[1] Luke xxxiii. 48. [2] cf. Matthew xxviii. 13, 15. [3] *Macbeth*, I. vii.

essential part of human history. We cannot run away from its consequences. It becomes the only adequate explanation of much that is noblest in mankind since. Yet when we try to say, or to listen to those who say, what happened at the tomb, we recognize that we touch mystery.

Dr. Grensted states the case very reasonably: 'There was a happening of the most definite and overmastering kind. There was, in other words, fact, with a place in history, and with supreme and creative consequences. And yet it is utterly impossible to give a direct and simple statement of this fact in terms which convey any concrete picture at all. The tomb was empty. There were certain appearances, and one final appearance which was remembered as specially significant. There was a moment when a new and overwhelming impulse came upon the little group of the friends of Jesus. . . . That there was a fact is clear, for these happenings changed the course of history. But, and more, the meaning of the fact is derived from Jesus.'[1]

We need not recapitulate all the various theories put forward to account for the belief that Jesus had risen—that Jesus swooned and came back to consciousness in the tomb; that the disciples, like men to-day, had a misleading tendency to see what they ardently hoped to see, or that a devoted band, influenced by the example of mystery cults, adopted the myth of a dying and rising god, to inspire loyalty to Jesus Christ. As Osiris in Egypt, Adonis in Phoenicia, or Attis in Asia Minor were believed to have come back from the underworld, bringing

[1] *The Person of Christ*, pp. 64, 65 (Nisbet & Co.).

immortal hope, so Jesus came back to re-inspire His devoted little flock.

Over against these and similar theories must be set the historic Christian Church, the dauntless courage and moral enthusiasm of the Christian disciples, the transforming power of the message preached, and its effect in religious and social ideals, and that at a time when the pagan world was in its most powerful and persecuting phase. It fails to satisfy us to say that its source was the resuscitation of a swooning man. It is contrary to the facts to suggest that the disciples had projected their hopes so eagerly that at last a hallucinatory vision of Jesus appeared to them. Every shred of evidence in the Synoptic Gospels goes to prove this, if it proves anything, that the disciples, women and men alike, so far from ardently hoping to see Jesus, fled in terror when an objective reality of some kind did present itself. The women went to complete His interment, not to hail His Resurrection. And so far as the men were concerned, the words of the women 'appeared in their sight as idle talk and they disbelieved them'.[1] This is the record in a tradition that grew up less than half a century after the events and it is more congruous to the facts that followed than the theory of Strauss, Renan, Harnack, or Loisy.[2] We need a cause for the ardent and triumphant primitive Church which is not subjective, much less morbid.

To relieve the strain on faith, Harnack thinks we may safely ignore the tomb and all the physical

[1] Luke xxiv. 11.
[2] For a good summary of theories, see Orr, *The Resurrection of Jesus Christ*, viii (Hodder & Stoughton).

happenings. The important matter, he argues, is the resurrection of truth and personal influence, and these have been secured to us in the Church for evermore. Faith in the truth, symbolized by the Easter story, is what is needed to regenerate mankind. 'Jesus Christ has passed through death' and 'God has awakened him to life and glory'. This is the 'Easter faith', but how it arose need not concern us too closely. Before we can divest the Resurrection of all its temporal and phenomenal conditions, however, we must answer one or two questions. If the word 'resurrection' means only a posthumous influence, or a joining of the choir invisible who live in lives made better by their presence, or a securing in time and the pages of history of moral ideals that tend to change the thought of mankind, then why limit the word 'resurrection' in the New Testament to Jesus Christ? Why not speak of the resurrection of James, who was slain with the sword, and of Stephen, who was stoned? These men, by their martyrdom, must have thrilled many a soul to nobler things, as indeed we seem to have proved to us in the case of Stephen and the young man, Saul.[1] The New Testament writers do distinguish clearly between the general 'resurrection at the last day' and the event at Joseph's tomb. However mysterious the event may have been, the disciples were convinced that they met and held communion with the same Personality with whom before the Crucifixion they had worked and talked, as their Master and Lord. It was unexpected and alarming, yet, when the surprise passed, it turned cowards into heroes,

[1] Acts vii. 58.

and baffled and forlorn men into the pioneers of a new world order. Let us turn to the most relevant passages.

The first Epistle of Paul to the Corinthians was written probably in A.D. 51, that is less than twenty years from the alleged date of the Resurrection. Few, if any, to-day doubt either the authenticity of this Epistle or the integrity of Paul's character. He was an instance of a man who, by birth, religious training, rare natural gifts, and ambition, was resolved to advance the interests of the old Jewish Church. He was 'exceeding mad' against and persecuted unto strange cities all opponents of the way of his forefathers. He had staked life, reputation, prestige, and eternal salvation on the old way, yet, because of an experience that he had at a particular time and place, the whole fabric of his life was shattered and lay in fragments around his feet. His own explanation of it was that he had seen the Lord. The One who met him said, 'I am Jesus whom thou persecutest'.

Just as at Joseph's garden, so on the road near Damascus we meet mystery. Psychological and religious experiences arise that remain only half-articulate. But since such events have happily persisted down history, we refuse to deny the reality of what happened to Paul because we find our medium of expression limited.

This same Paul less than twenty years later is called on to speak about the destiny of believers after death, to the Church at Corinth. As Greeks, they were disposed most probably to pantheistic stoicism and belief in the loss of personality in the

all-pervading Logos after death. At once he challenges so poor a conception of salvation. 'I would
have you know the gospel I once preached unto
you. . . . First and foremost I passed on to you
what I had myself received, namely, that Christ
died for our sins as the scriptures had said, that he
was buried, that he rose on the third day as the
scriptures had said, and that he was seen by
Cephas, then by the twelve; after that he was seen
by over five hundred brothers all at once, the
majority of whom survive to this day, though some
have died; after that he was seen by James, then by
all the apostles, and finally he was seen by myself,
by this so called "abortion" of an apostle' (1 Corinthians xv. 1, 3–9, Moffatt). Because of Christ's
organic relation to those who believe in Him, St.
Paul continues his argument: 'now if Christ be
preached that he rose from the dead how can certain
individuals among you assert that "there is no such
thing as a resurrection of the dead"?'

What Paul states in this paragraph amounts to
this: he rests his argument for the Resurrection of
all believers in Christ, with their full personalities,
on the ground that in the same manner Christ
Himself has been raised. Paul does not discuss the
nature of Christ's risen body, or the empty tomb, or
the visit of the women, but he is clear and unequi-
vocal that Christ as a vibrant Personality is alive
and has been revealed to and in himself. Next, he as
good as asserts that he can call living witnesses who
also saw Him: Peter, the twelve, James, 'over five
hundred brethren at once'. Some had since died,
but enough remained to whom the Corinthians

could refer. Then he reasons: If Christ did not rise, what have we to preach? Are we liars suffering hardship for our mendacious folly? What is the point of our ministry? So, whether at Pisidian Antioch[1] or Philippi[2] or Thessalonica[3] or Athens,[4] the burden of Paul's message is the same—God raised Him up from the dead.

Also if Christ is not risen what do we make of His death? This is the point of this chapter. Paul says: 'If Christ did not rise your faith is futile, you are still in your sins.' These are clear and consistent affirmations. Unless God has set His seal upon Christ Jesus and raised Him up again, there is no guarantee that all the gracious forgiveness that Jesus breathed with His dying breath represents the character of God. That Christ died to effect reconciliation and to restore the alienated is one of the cardinal truths in the primitive tradition, and that it is sealed to men in the Resurrection is also among them. While Paul was ridiculed and derided for this affirmation, it was never refuted, nor did it pass into oblivion like the story of the appearance of Zeus and Hermes to Philemon and Baucis, or the return of Adonis. Everything in the Christian message held together as an arch by its keystone, by the fact of the Resurrection. Indeed, unless we are prepared to go over to a materialistic monism, or, with Strauss[5] and many another since, regard the material universe as a closed system, into which no qualitative powers or forces can enter from the unseen, or regard all history as a great illusion, we not only believe in the

---

[1] Acts xiii. 30. [2] Acts xvi. 18. [3] Acts xvii. 3.
[4] Acts xvii. 31. [5] *Life of Jesus.*

possibility of the Resurrection, but feel the urgent need of such an explanation of the moral changes in men since the first century. We say this in presence of the retroactive forces at work in the world while these lines are being written. Unless Paul's words are true, we are left with a bigger problem upon our hands. 'Only from an intensely heated centre of burning zeal could this vast field of lava have been thrown out from a tiny country like Palestine to the limits of the Roman world.'[1]

The dynamic that created the Church, holds her on her way, renews the souls of men, raises their moral and social ideals, and fills them with an unquenchable hope, does not spring from the pathetic memory of the Crucified. It takes a risen Lord to create a risen Church. Through what transmutation, we repeat, Christ's body passed we shall probably never know. What happened in or at the tomb we shall probably never be able to do more than surmise. In what way the risen Christ made Himself known to the disciples or what was their experience we shall never be able to under-stand or articulate.

The man of science may say we are taking refuge in mystery. Not willingly, nor blindly, nor, we hope, timidly; but there are frontiers beyond which the apparatus of physical science is ineffective. We must leave room for *noumena* as well as phenomena, for being as well as becoming, for spirit as well as matter. Grant with the biologists and newer psychologists that there are 'emergences' in evolution when higher factors reveal themselves in lower

[1] Morison, *Who Moved the Stone?* p. 161 (Faber & Faber).

kingdoms and we see no solid reason for denying that in the Person of Christ is an emergence of the eternal Logos, and in the Resurrection a new emergence of Spirit in human history. If man is the crown of creation, why should not the New Man, raised into a new order of existence, be Head of a new order or community, the Church? This is Paul's conception of the matter and no word in modern science seems to contradict it or make it irrational.

When we pass to Peter, who, according to all the Gospels, was through the worst of the fray, we find the same unhesitating witness. Whether we can accept the words of Papias or not that the Gospel according to Mark is little else than Peter's reminiscences, we are convinced that Mark is written from a Petrine standpoint. Unfortunately, the vital account of the Resurrection in Mark is torn at verse 8 in the last chapter, but the story that seems to have come in the first instance to Peter from the alarmed women is important, especially when we put it alongside the speech delivered by Peter at the Feast of Weeks in Jerusalem. Writers have stressed the unreliability of the early chapters of Acts, but one point should be noted. The late Canon Streeter was at great pains to point out how careful Luke was to collect and collate and then submit his material to a first draft—a proto-Luke and a proto-Acts. In assessing the value of Peter's speech in Acts, we should bear in mind that both Peter and Luke were contemporaries and friends of Paul, and it seems utterly unlikely that a man in quest of data for history, as obviously Luke was, would miss his opportunity directly or indirectly of tapping Peter's resources, and recording the tenor of them with all fidelity.

What is the essence of Peter's testimony to the throngs in Jerusalem? Something has happened in the little community of disciples. It has become known outside. They gather mystified, and Peter finds in their question an opportunity: they had heard of Jesus of Nazareth. Many present knew of 'His mighty works, wonders and signs which God did by Him'. They also knew and witnessed His Crucifixion: 'whom ye by wicked hands have crucified and slain'. Since then has come the explanation of the events for which they ask. 'Him hath God raised up whereof we all are witnesses.' No one disputed a word Peter uttered. No one offered to confound Peter by leading the way to Joseph's tomb. Instead, many consented to the truth of Peter's words and asked: 'What shall we do?' Peter himself is a wonder, but the effect on many in the crowd is a greater wonder. As light broke on the meaning of their part in the Crucifixion, repentance followed and disciples multiplied. Christ is alive, calling men to forgiveness.

To the same effect is the argument in the First Epistle of Peter, a document that Dr. James Moffatt calls 'a pastoral letter sent by Peter from Rome, during the seventh decade of the first century'.[1] It grounds the Christian hope in the Resurrection of Christ from the dead (i. 21). 'God raised him up from the dead and gave him glory' (i. 21). 'Christ was put to death in the flesh but

[1] *Pastoral Epistles*, p. 87 (Hodder & Stoughton).

77

quickened in the spirit' (iii. 18). Conscience is quickened towards God through 'the resurrection of Jesus Christ, who is on the right hand of God' (iii. 21, 22). These and other statements in the Epistle are one with the truth proclaimed at Pentecost in Jerusalem. It is unnecessary to go through the other New Testament writings for similar affirmations. This has been done by other writers in books on the Resurrection. It is enough to see the conviction and certainty of those nearest to the events, to be persuaded that it was certainty of the risen Lord that drove them out as passionate heralds of a glorious fact, 'The Lord is risen indeed'.

What light then does the Resurrection shed on Christ's death? First of all, it brings God out unmistakably on the side of Jesus, or, conversely, Jesus is seen to be the revelation of all that God is. The kingdom has come. God has entered into history and, in a new way, revealed the powers of the world to come. Secondly, it shows that God has reversed the verdict of mankind on Jesus and in so doing condemned mankind, because the Resurrection is God's declaration of human guilt. Thirdly, Jesus was justified by His faith in the eternal goodness of God, when, in the last moments he cried, 'Father, into thy hands I commend my spirit'. He trusted in God. 'When he was reviled, he reviled not again, when he suffered he threatened not but committed himself to him that judgeth righteously' (1 Peter ii. 23). Fourthly, as at the Baptism and the Transfiguration, so especially by the Resurrection, God commends His Son to all the world as the Object of their imitation and trust. The Resurrection is God's 'Amen' to all Jesus was and said, and did. So far from being a deceiver or perverter, God declares that Jesus is the Way, the Truth, and the Life; or, as we might say, God sets His seal on His Son as the norm for humanity.

> None other Lamb, none other Name,
>   None other hope in heaven or earth or sea,
> None other hiding place from guilt and shame,
>   None beside Thee.

By thus exalting Him to 'his right hand' God sets Jesus as the criterion of judgement. Men can assess their moral worth here and now by making Christ and His way the test of their lives. The Resurrection shows what God's verdict on the nations is also. Guilt is stamped across five continents, since the principles of the men who crucified Christ are the driving force in those continents, but especially in Europe and Asia; and, finally, the Resurrection carries its pledge of assurance and comfort to a crucified Church and crucified nations that the end is not yet, that all that trust in God in the dark and dreadful day will be justified by their faith. A further coming of Christ is a moral necessity, how or when we know not, but He will come to judge the nations once more. Possibly this judgement has begun. Men are being forced even now to accept or deny the principles for which Christ died and rose again.

Chapter 5

ST. PAUL'S INTERPRETATION OF THE DEATH OF CHRIST

When we turn to trace the methods St. Paul used to expound and commend the Cross, two or three preliminary facts should be kept in mind. First, even in his most argumentative Epistles, such as Galatians or Romans, it would not be true to say that St. Paul was attempting a formal pronouncement on the meaning of Christ's death. In Romans there is the semblance of such an attempt, but it is introduced because he wants to prove that for Jew and Gentile alike the Cross is the wisdom of God and the power of God. He establishes general guilt and general spiritual impotence because he wishes to commend a general redemption. But his asides, his imaginary interlocutor, his answers, his spontaneous doxologies, his struggles with subordinate questions, such as election and predestination, show him to be engaged on a whole multitude of problems of which the Cross is one. This is peculiarly true of Galatians, where he is almost beside himself in his efforts to recover and restore his bewitched and misguided converts. But in every Epistle we are dealing with a great-souled, warm-hearted missionary to whom men and salvation come before systems of thought. His theology is subordinate to his gospel, and if he lapses into any formal statement it is to capture the unconvinced mind of some Jewish or Gentile hearer.

Secondly, while St. Paul regarded the death of Christ as the ground of his own forgiveness and redemption, he knew it was a problem, an offence, to his unconverted hearers, Jewish and Gentile.

To the Jew, the picture of the Crucified seemed a vile travesty of the Messiah. Only a minority in Israel had the spiritual insight or moral sympathy to enter into the later prophetic interpretations of the coming One. For one who dwelt in Second Isaiah there were a hundred who dwelt in the Second Psalm. Instead of preaching Jesus as a Leader and Commander, who took hold of the threads of national life, lifted the people out of defeatism, and restored national self-respect, St. Paul preached One who submitted to be crucified in unresisting weakness and repulsive shame. It took all the powers of St. Paul's masculine intellect, logic, persuasiveness, and divine inspiration to make Jesus reasonable as the Holy One of Israel. The word of the Cross was just foolishness.

Similarly, the way of the Cross was as stupid and unthinkable to the Gentile, whether Greek or Roman. The pagan in every man always resorts to physical weapons first. Even young students who know nothing about 1914, in their natural reaction, wish to try force on the pagan dictators of Europe; not yet realizing that no one permanently wins a physical victory, whereas the conquest of self-surrender abides. Even this last sentence will seem as sheer nonsense to some who may read it. It is no easier to present the way of the Cross to-day than in the first century. Yet the missionary can only commend his message in so far as he can in the first instance make it reasonable. Though the Christian gospel does not stand in the wisdom of men, yet it must be capable of rational presentation, and St. Paul strives to commend its truth to every man's conscience in the sight of God. How he presents the Cross to the Gentile world must be seen in his various letters.

Probably among devotees of the various mystery cults, who, by observation of nature, had conceived of an annual death and resurrection of their deity, did St. Paul find his most responsive hearers. These at least entered into the truth that life comes by death; and when they heard of Jesus and the Resurrection, they entered with more sympathy into the message than did the men at the Areopagus. Paul knew in himself the moral consequences of the death and Resurrection of Christ; they brought reconciliation, forgiveness, and peace, but while subjective evidence is good it must be mediated in terms that will capture those that are without.

A third fact to be borne in mind is the background of the Apostles' thought. This point is developed in the concluding chapter, but we may anticipate by reminding ourselves that his theological thought-forms are those of an educated Pharisee and his cosmological thought-forms are those of the first century. Conversion turns a man as he is to Christ, but we must not take even St. Paul's words too literally when he says, 'If any man be in Christ there is a new creation; the old things are passed

away, they are become new' (2 Corinthians v. 17).
Old moral evils—pride, self-will, and such like—are
passed away, but conversion, even of St. Paul, does
not recreate his forms of thought, his knowledge of
the universe around him, or his Greek vocabulary,
except in so far as his richer experience may require
additional means of expression. We have to take
the word of the Cross in Paul's own way or not at
all. When we try to enter into his interpretation,
we must keep our eyes also on the mentality of his
hearers, the Jews, whom he seeks to persuade.

His earliest explanation is based on the fulfilment
of prophecy. Whatever the Jews were, they were
a Bible-reading and a Bible-hearing people; but,
since men can read the scripture with a prejudice or
prepossession, they can wrest it to their own hurt.
St. Paul, however, finds a lever by which to raise
the Jews to God in their scriptures. He enters into
the meaning of vicarious redemptive suffering; it
was known to the prophets, it was known even in
St. Paul's own experience (cf. Philippians iii. 10),
but it came to full fruition in Jesus of Nazareth. So
in many of his sermons his argument is that the
Messiah must needs suffer, and that this is the view
forecast by men like Isaiah and Jeremiah. Paul
guides their minds away from the passages which
led them to think only of a military commander, to
those in which he appears as the suffering servant.
In such passages, St. Paul puts his finger on the
core of the new religion, and many Jewish hearers
responded to its appeal. For St. Paul, then, the
vicarious suffering of Christ was the way by which
sin could be borne and sinners reconciled to God.

It was the way of the greatest of the Jewish prophets, and it would be the way in which the Church would win the world in days to come.

But as we go on to ask more particularly at what point in his own life did the death of Christ impinge, we must note two points: (1) He stressed the death rather than the Incarnation. He obviously retained the idea of a sacrifice unto God, and the death seemed to express the fullness of that sacrifice as the life could not do. (2) In all his reflections on what Christ had done, St. Paul never thought in abstract terms. His mind was Semitic, not Hellenistic, and his use of terms is always vivid. His mind is full of clear images. Whether he actually conceived of the Law, Sin, Death, and Demons as distinct entities with a quasi-personality of their own, as he undoubtedly did so regard the Devil, or merely, as the writer in Proverbs (viii) has personified Wisdom, as abstractions is an open question. His mode of argument suggests that he did regard them as *stoicheia*, or elemental forces. They were enemies and must be dealt with by a stronger power than his own. By examining each of these factors in turn, we shall see how he came to regard Christ Jesus as his Redeemer.

First and most distressing in his thought came the Law. In every age this unhappy word seems doomed to ambiguity; so in Paul's day it had not a constant and stable meaning. Dr. C. Anderson Scott[1] has pointed out that at least three meanings are attached to it in the Pauline Epistles: first, the Apostle uses it to indicate 'a code of rules,

[1] *Footnotes to St. Paul*, p. 43 (Cambridge University Press).

commandments for life and for worship'; here it is a manual or personal *vade mecum* for worship and conduct. Secondly, it is 'a divinely appointed means whereby men, through obedience to its precepts might earn justification or salvation on the ground of merit'. This is the religious significance of the Law. And, thirdly, it is 'a symbol, almost a sacrament of the Jewish race'. It is regarded as a God-given copy of His own nature in which at all times He is present and by the observance of which we are assured of His favour.

It is in the second of these three meanings—the religious significance of the Law—that we find St. Paul's approach to the Cross. No one could have cherished a higher reverence for the Law than he. Its ideal was high, but in the freshness of his student youth this seemed only a glorious challenge. St. Paul was never at any time superficial; he was moved with deep moral sincerity and he was confident that with care, whole-hearted zeal, and self-confidence he could keep the whole Law and attain to a religious merit that would lead to his justification or acceptance by God. At this stage, his confidence in human nature was not shaken and he set himself no light task. Had he, like some of his contemporaries, ignored the inwardness of this divine law as it applied to motives, passions, intentions, and imaginations, he could have kept up his religious appearances and passed for a devout Jew; but Paul never trifled with anything, he was always whole-hearted and intense.

He had a most troublesome conscience; it called him continually back to his ideal, until his ideal, the Law, became a task-master and tyrant that made his life miserable. 'I was alive, apart from the law once'—in innocent childhood—'but when the commandment came' (as his criterion of conduct) 'sin revived and I died.' That brief sentence is packed with religious experience. This Law which at the outset he hailed so hopefully is becoming his enemy and threatens to crush him; instead of helping him to God, it exposes his moral weakness. With each fresh effort he makes to obey, its demands rise and his strength ebbs.

Long before he set out on the journey to Damascus, he was becoming alarmed about the success of his obedience to the Law. He felt his religious success was a great make-believe. The emotion of an inner conflict always tends to project itself on an object or person that seems a hindrance or a rival, and Jesus and the Christian disciples became the object with Stephen as the victim. Yet what can Paul do? Can he disown history, the Law, the Temple, the sacrifices? He is almost insane under what older theologians called 'religious conviction', and rather than admit defeat he embarks on a voyage of persecution going 'even unto strange cities'. Yet defeat he already knew. The Law ought to be obeyed, it is holy, just and good, but St. Paul has no moral strength to obey it. 'For the good that I would I do not and the evil that I would not that I do. . . . For I delight in the law of God after the inward man but I see a different law [principle] in my members, warring against the law of my mind and bringing me into captivity under the law of sin which is in my members. O wretched man that I am! who shall deliver me out of the body of this death?' (Romans vii. 19, 22–4).

It is at this point, as we shall see, that Christ's work comes into St. Paul's experience, but before this we must examine more closely his idea of Sin. Probably we do not misrepresent him if we say that he looked upon Sin as a universal, inherited, pervasive moral infection, a disease of humanity. It entered the human race through the offence of one; none have escaped; it saps all moral resistance to temptation and, worst of all, under certain circumstances, its presence and malignity may be unsuspected. While the spiritual patient is allowed to live according to the flesh and no high moral demands are made upon him, he may delude himself that he is strong and that all is well; but press the claims of our high calling of God in Christ Jesus, even apply the Law, challenge this diseased man to take up his bed and walk, to take his part as a true citizen in the commonwealth of God, and then comes the pitiful discovery, 'by the Law is the knowledge of sin'. The latent evil is revealed and man's moral helplessness is only too evident. St. Paul's usual word for this 'inbred sin' is *hamartia*, because it leads to moral failure, or missing of the mark. It is an alien intrusion that induces general paralysis. 'For until [i.e. prior to] the law sin was in the world, but sin is not imputed where there is no law, notwithstanding this death reigned from Adam to Moses . . . but the Law came in also that the trespass might abound' (Romans v. 13, 14, 20). Sin, then, is an alien, hostile power pervading man's entire nature, but only known in its full meaning and strength when the Law enters.

Be it noted at this stage that Paul regards the Flesh as the peculiar breeding-ground of Sin. No doubt he uses the word in a very comprehensive and not always uniform way, but he plainly means by the word 'flesh' that earthly part of us where passions and lusts are seated. As Dr. Garvie has said:[1] 'As a fact of experience, he was conscious of appetites, passions, desires, tempers, or ambitions contrary to the law of God, but so strongly en-trenched in his nature that he could not of his own will withstand, overcome, and repel them.' Yet we must guard against the notion that Paul looked upon the Flesh as the only source of temptation and evil, or as in itself incapable of redemption. His language in Romans vii savours of Manichaean dualism, but it is only apparent since he recognizes the sins of the spirit as well as of the Flesh and looks for the redemption of the body as necessary to a true personality after death. The hallowing of humanity in the Incarnation was a truth to which St. Paul was faithfully loyal. Beyond recognizing the flesh as lending itself in a peculiar way to sin and as a medium for all sorts of uncleanness, Paul does not go. The flesh is not neutral; it needs redemption, but it can with men, as with our Lord, become a medium of the Spirit of God.

To return to St. Paul's concept of Sin. It not only destroys all moral energy in the soul, but it incites man to resist and rebel against God. The mind or ego that allies itself with the flesh disowns

[1] *Studies of Paul and His Gospel*, p. 140 (Hodder & Stoughton).

the purpose of God, and through this rebellion and misery follow. Sometimes St. Paul calls this state of heart *anomia* (lawlessness) sometimes *parabasis* (transgression), but subjectively it alienates man from God and destroys all loving fellowship. Nowhere does St. Paul regard Sin as merely privative or the absence of goodness. It is active, virulent, disruptive, and begets a spirit of distrust and fear. The sinner shrinks from anything that would force him into closer relations with God, and death he ignores or abhors.

St. Paul further stresses the fact that there is a divine resistance against and condemnation of the sinner. If any one prefers to say 'resistance against sin in the sinner', we shall not quarrel, but we must remember there can be no sin without a sinner; and no sin without guilt, and guilt means that some one must accept responsibility for the guilty act. St. Paul's word to indicate God's resistance is *orgē* (wrath); it is always a saving, healthful fire coming to consume sin; it is a manifestation of love, as pain is a merciful protector, indicating, like an advance scout, the presence of the enemy.

We cannot see fully how St. Paul interprets Christ's work without observing, too, his idea about the *curse* that follows sin. In some passages, as Romans viii. 18–22, one would suppose he carried in mind the account of the blight that fell on the earth, as recorded in Genesis (iii. 17–19), but since his statement about the curse is set in a context where he is discussing the Law and actually quotes from Deuteronomy (xxvii. 26) 'cursed be he that confirmeth not the words of this law to do them', it seems certain that it is his favourite theme of the Law and not 'the Fall of Man' that is in his mind. The word he uses in Galatians iii. 13 is *katara* not *anathema* (curse), and the former word is less personal in its implication. It indicates a general deterioration in man, with its attendant miseries and distress when he fails to confirm every word laid down by God in the Law. Because the Law comes so much into prominence in this argument, some have thought St. Paul regarded the curse as applying only to the Jews, but his argument in Romans ii. 14, 15 about the Gentiles having a law of their own written in their conscience seems to include all within this common curse. How Christ is related to the removal of this curse will also come under consideration later.

There remains the question of St. Paul's belief about Demons, and, without taking this into account, it would be hard to understand some of his sayings about redemption. Under this word must be included all sorts of superhuman entities to which he refers particularly in Ephesians and Colossians. 'Put on the whole armour of God that ye may be able to stand against the wiles of the devil. For our wrestling is not against flesh and blood but against the principalities, against the powers, against the world rulers of this darkness, against the spiritual hosts of wickedness in the heavenly places' (Ephesians vi. 11, 12). Again, speaking of Christ, he says: 'Having put off from himself the principalities and the powers he made a show of them openly, triumphing over them in [the cross]' (Colossians ii. 15). Angels come to have a very evil character in

St. Paul and almost always appear as enemies from whom we need deliverance. 'Women must not be unveiled because of the lustful glances of the angels' (1 Corinthians xi. 10). Angels are not regarded by him as perfect beings, and he classes them with other evil powers. An angel from Heaven might preach an erroneous gospel (Galatians i. 7–8).[1] They can deceive the very elect. 'Satan himself masquerades as an angel of light' (2 Corinthians xi. 14, Moffatt).

All this conception of the unseen as peopled with hostile elemental forces, angels, and demons, St. Paul inherited from the current theology of the Pharisees of his day. We have already seen how he regards sin as spreading through the individual, then spreading from the individual through society, and then from the multitude to rulers in high places on earth. Now he carries the conception into a transcendental world in which this hierarchy of evil forces is resisting the dominion of God and seeking to encompass the destruction of man. Truly enough, they are creatures, limited in powers; and so, according to Romans viii. 38, they cannot finally separate the believer from the love of God, but call for circumspection on the believers' part and for those already in their toils, redemption.

But St. Paul looks upon Satan as the arch-enemy who has gained power over men, especially through the seduction of our first parents.[2] 'He it was who destroyed the Jews who murmured in the wilderness' (1 Corinthians x. 5). He it was who would destroy the flesh of the incestuous person, who, as

---

[1] Strachan, *The Individuality of St. Paul*, p. 61 (James Clarke & Co.).
[2] Cave, *The Gospel of St. Paul*, pp. 147, 148 (Hodder & Stoughton).

cut off from the Church would be again in the
sphere in which the Devil rules (1 Corinthians v. 5).
In his own 'thorn in the flesh', St. Paul saw the
work of a messenger of Satan sent to 'buffet' him
(2 Corinthians xii. 7). In all this we see the pessimism of the age into which Christ came, both in
Jewish apocalyptic and, may we add, in Hellenistic
thought also. It was an evil age, it was under the god
of this world, and St. Paul spoke not for Jews alone,
but for Gentiles. His most pungent words about
demons and sinful angels are addressed to the Gentile
Churches in Asia Minor. These then are some of the
conceptions in the background of St. Paul's mind
against which he sets the message of the Cross.

To that we now proceed. 1. All that Christ came
to mean to St. Paul and which he describes in such
words as *reconciliation*, *justification*, *propitiation*,
and *adoption*, began in his experience on the
Damascus road. He had striven to deny and to
stamp out the story of the disciples that Christ was
alive. Now he knows they have been proclaiming
a fact. As at the tomb in Joseph's garden, so here in
St. Paul's experience, as, indeed, we always find
when Christ enters a man's life, we touch mystery.
Whether in the first hour or days St. Paul grasped
the significance of his contact with and arrest by
Christ, he at least knew a moral revolution had
taken place. He had seen the Lord; this meant to
him three things. (1) He knew that Jesus had overtaken him in mercy as a Friend, and as He had done
with His dying breath on the Cross, so here He
covered St. Paul's bitterness and fiery hatred with
His unfailing forgiveness. 'I am Jesus whom thou

persecutest', is a message of entreaty and appeal, not of condemnation or retaliation. It completely broke St. Paul, for in his heart he was ripe for such a word. He expressed this tireless love in all his Epistles as 'the grace of our Lord Jesus Christ' and no man was more responsive to a kind word than St. Paul. (2) By this personal appearing of the Risen Christ and His offer of love, St. Paul knew that his old method of acceptance with God by personal merit was wrong; and his persecution of the disciples was at once futile and wicked. The heroic programme of the orthodox young Pharisee lay in fragments around his feet and, indeed, he had no mind to try to piece it together. Christ became the end of a great many things to St. Paul as well as the Law. (3) Best of all, as soon as he had admitted to himself and to his Lord that he was a beaten man and responded to the love offered to him, he became aware gradually of a moral revolution. He entered on a Christo-centric life, the conflict ended, the storm passed; light shined out of darkness, peace garrisoned his heart, power surged in his soul. One would need to con his Epistles line by line to find his interior biography as he wrote it. His old purposes, confidences, convictions, and ambitions were either purified or where necessary destroyed. He was in Christ and there was a new creation; he could do all things through Christ, who strengthened him. We do not need to remind ourselves that all he says at this stage is testimony to a new life and not systematic theology, but it began with the Resurrection rather than the death of Christ.

How did this experience of salvation come? It

was not by works of righteousness, but by His mercy He saved us. Christ became the end of the law for righteousness in St. Paul's life. The release of power by Christ swept away all impotence and slavery due to sin harbouring in the flesh. Paul writes of 'the exceeding greatness of his power to us-ward who believe, according to the working of the strength of his might which he wrought in Christ when he raised him from the dead' (Ephesians i. 19, 20). Paul now keeps the Law or, rather, rises above it because of this divine power.

2. But sooner or later Paul was compelled to rethink the meaning of Christ's sufferings and death. This may account in part for his journey to Arabia. He had, like so many of his Pharisaic comrades, dismissed the Crucifixion, even the very mode, as a proof of Christ's criminal folly; but, as we saw, the fact of the Resurrection shattered that delusion. God reversed man's judgement and, explain Christ's death as he might, St. Paul could not find its meaning as a penalty for sin.

3. The question of martyrdom, no doubt, flashed across St. Paul's mind. Some of the prophets and even Stephen had borne witness to truth at the cost of their lives. Jesus was later described as 'the faithful and true witness', but while this was true and all that was richest in martyrdom is present in Christ's death, St. Paul lays very little stress on this point. He says little of Jesus as the teacher or prophet. St. Paul has something more than the ideas of Jesus to proclaim, so we must press on.

4. It is in relation to God and sin and God's attitude to sin that St. Paul begins to study the

death of Christ. Agree or disagree with him, this seems to be St. Paul's path. He cannot get away from the sacredness of God's law; it is almost a copy of God's own being. It is so precious to God that He guards it by pains and penalties. As surely as God's approval rests upon the good man, so surely does God's resentment and resistance oppose the sinner. Sin must be punished. St. Paul believed that 'the anger of God is revealed from heaven against all ungodliness and unrighteousness of men' (Romans i. 18). He looks upon Christ's death as a sacrifice on account of sin in which Christ shares in this divine penalty because He has made common cause with sinners. Let us carefully observe that St. Paul never says that God punished Christ, or that Christ stood as a substitute, bearing the penalties due to all mankind in infinite woe in Himself. Such utterances have gone beyond what is written in St. Paul. But he is clear that by vicarious, suffering love, Christ so united Himself to our condition that He could not but feel something of the God-forsaken misery and horror of human sin due to God's antagonism towards it.

5. Another conception of St. Paul should be recognized. It is one that was more easily appreciated when the solidarity of society was stronger than it is to-day. Individual freedom has tended to make it unattractive. Paul regards Christ's death as a representative act, or, in the words of Dr. Peake, 'Christ's sacrificial work was a racial act'. The idea appeals to primitive peoples still where the clan is the unit and where a headman acts on behalf of the clan. His sin is their sin, his good work is their good

95

work. St. Paul believes that, as by the disobedience of the one the many were made sinners, even so through the obedience of the one shall the many be made righteous (Romans v. 19). By His Incarnation, Christ entered into our lot and, being the New Man from Heaven, He acted on our behalf. This interdependence of the human family we know to be true, and it is difficult to see how any one even now can undertake the role of deliverer and friend of the alienated and degraded without bearing shame and pain. So dreadful was this experience of Our Lord that on the Cross human sin and shame became more real than divine love. Paul goes to the verge of saying that Christ, by His identification with us, became a sinner, but his word is too guarded to be misunderstood. 'Him who knew no sin, he made sin on our behalf that we might become the righteousness of God in him' (2 Corinthians v. 21). This representative act does not work magically; it has meaning and value only for the penitent believer. It is appropriated and shared in by faith, so that a like death unto sin and resurrection to righteousness take place in each believer.

6. To return to the interpretation of Christ's work. St. Paul describes the necessity of suffering in his difficult saying in Galatians iii. 13: 'Christ redeemed us from the curse of the law, having become a curse for us: for it is written, cursed is every one that hangeth on a tree.' Here the curse, or moral deterioration due to sin is emphasized and, as we have already seen, it is, in St. Paul's mind, due to violated law. Also, no one could deliver men from this penalty without himself sharing in it. The

quotation, 'cursed is every one that hangeth on a tree', is used by Paul as a Rabbi for the benefit of his Judaizing opponents. How the mode of death could lessen or increase a curse is not easy to see. Crucifixion was the most shameful and terrible of all deaths. Possibly St. Paul did think it gave fullest expression to the degrading effects of sin. Anyhow, it is by His gracious self-identification with sinners that Christ redeemed men and so shared in or became a curse.

7. We have seen that, in at least one place, St. Paul regards Christ's death as a sacrifice to God: 'He gave himself up for us an offering and a sacrifice to God' (Ephesians v. 2). This raises the further question: What was the nature of the sacrifice? The mention of the word suggests placation or appeasement of an angry deity and, in support of this, the passage in Romans iii. 25, 'Whom God set forth to be a propitiation, through faith, by his blood', is quoted. (1) Since Paul had given up the Jewish Law and all the ritual ideas connected with it, he never thinks of Christ's death as something that God demands before He can forgive. Here, rather, in Ephesians v. 2, he is extolling voluntary, loving service and, because it is so exquisite in its effects, he presses it on his readers with his usual argument: 'even as Christ also loved you, and gave himself up for us an offering and a sacrifice to God for an odour of a sweet smell'. 'By giving himself for men Christ manifested supremely that loving will which is the will of God himself.'[1] (2) As to the passage in Romans

---

[1] Scott, *Ephesians*, p. 225 (Hodder & Stoughton).

iii. 25: volumes have been written on the word 'propitiation' and we can only try to summarize what is developed elsewhere. Unlike all pagan acts of propitiation, this is the act of God. He provides the *hilastērion*, or propitiation. Again the revisers and all recent translators of the passage place a comma after 'faith' and follow it with the words 'by his blood'. St. Paul never suggests 'faith in blood'. 'Faith is for him always faith in God through Christ.' He seeks to express the truth that divine forgiveness is revealed through an outpoured life even in blood on the Cross. That act, in all its comprehensiveness, is 'propitiatory' (which seems a better translation) where guilt and mercy meet; and, thirdly, all the claims of God in holiness and righteousness are fully sustained in Christ's obedience and devotion (cf. Romans iii. 26). No text in the New Testament has had more preconceived and inadequate theories of Atonement pressed upon it than this and it is only by patient rediscovery of St. Paul's own thought that we can distinguish between the foundation and the superstructures.

8. Lastly, we turn to St. Paul's idea of salvation by Christ from hostile spirits. His cosmology determines his interpretation. He conceives The Height and The Abyss as well as this earth as inhabited and governed by Beings, Elemental Forces, who, like man, have become alienated from God. 'The "things in heaven" clearly include the "Thrones, Dominations, Princedoms, Powers", those mythological beings who are always in the background of St. Paul's thought. . . . They not only had a place in Jewish thought of the time, as "angelic"

orders, but they were recognized in contemporary philosophy, both Platonic and Stoic, and so this mythology might pass in the first century for a statement of religious ideas in terms of "science". The Discarnate Intelligences were connected with the heavenly bodies, and thought to be agents of fate controlling human destiny.'[1]

St. Paul conceives of these 'principalities and powers' as alienated from God, enemies of men and making a concentrated attack on the incarnate Christ as man's deliverer. This, as we shall see, is the starting point of many patristic interpretations of Christ's death. It was on Christ's physical person that the assault was made. They actuated men like Pontius Pilate to encompass His death. But although the passage in Colossians ii. 15 is not free from ambiguity, Paul plainly regards Christ's death on the Cross as His moment of victory. It was in His flesh these hostile Forces sought to defeat Him. Temptations beyond our thought assailed Him; and, finally, acting through ignorant men, these discarnate spirits had Him crucified. This seemed their victory; it was actually their hour of defeat, because the garment of the flesh upon which they laid hold He shed off in death and rose in divine power Lord of all worlds. We shall see that this idea of the Cross as Christ's way to glory is taken over from St. Paul and expanded at length by the Fourth Evangelist. Probably the marginal rendering in the Revised Version of Colossians ii. 15 expresses St. Paul's idea most accurately, though we recognize that the grammar is capable of other

[1] Dodd, *Romans*, p. 185 (Hodder & Stoughton).

readings:[1] 'Having put off from himself his body, he made a show of the principalities and the powers, triumphing over them in the cross.'

One other point may be touched upon. St. Paul not only regards the discarnate entities as alienated and hostile; he is so confident of the power of redeeming love that he declares that Christ will reconcile these also to Himself. They may have been made to look foolish, and form, as captives, a triumphal procession at the Resurrection and Ascension, but they will become the willing captives under the thrall of His love at last. 'Through him' the Father will 'reconcile all things unto himself, having made peace through the blood of his cross; through him, I say, whether things upon the earth or things in the heavens'. The Cross is such a revelation of God's dauntless love that St. Paul can see no part of the Deep or of the Height where it will not ultimately reign. With this inspiring picture of the final victory of love we may leave St. Paul.

[1] cf. Scott, *Colossians*, p. 15 (Hodder & Stoughton).

Chapter 6

THE DEATH OF CHRIST IN THE SYNOPTIC GOSPELS

In any investigation of our theme in the Synoptic Gospels, we soon find that the emphasis comes to be laid on St. Mark. (1) This is admittedly the oldest gospel in our canon, and brings us nearer to the primitive gospel tradition and to the earliest reflection on the facts of the gospel. (2) As Dr. Vincent Taylor points out, 'most of the (passion) sayings are found in Mark and in the L tradition which is peculiar to Luke; no Passion saying can be traced to the M source and probably the same is true of Q.... These sources are, in the main, collections of ethical and religious precepts bearing on life and conduct; and it is not in such collections that we should expect to find sayings of Jesus relative to the Passion.'[1] (3) Matthew and Luke reproduce Mark very liberally in their Gospels. The late Canon Streeter held that Matthew worked with Mark before him as his framework, always following the Marcan order and inserting matter from other sources at clearly marked points. The whole of Mark, except fifty-five verses, reappears in Matthew. The passages of Mark absent from Luke are more numerous, but, as already seen,

[1] Taylor, *Jesus and His Sacrifice*, p. 79 (Macmillan & Co.).

except for the peculiar Lucan tradition (L), the important allusions to our Lord's passion and death are found in the Marcan sections. Since Mark records the earliest form of the tradition known to us we would expect to find more information about the way Christ was received or rejected. His death and Resurrection would be the essence of the earliest preaching. Afterwards converts would wish to know of His teaching and example. This is provided mostly in non-Marcan documents.

Again, we must distinguish between the sayings of our Lord concerning His passion and death and the use made of such sayings by Mark. We shall consider St. Mark's viewpoint first: The kind of material selected by the Evangelist and the amount of it leaves a total impression on the mind that the author was deeply concerned with the place that suffering must find in the life of a disciple of Jesus. He enlarges on the work and martyrdom of the Baptist, he preserves to us most of the sayings of Jesus we possess concerning His own sufferings and death, and he devotes almost a third of his Gospel to a detailed account of the trial and sufferings and death of Jesus. The absorption of the writer's mind with this whole matter can be seen by a patient study of the Gospel from this angle. Was there any reason in the historic conditions of the Church for such an emphasis? The conclusion to which most scholars have come is that Mark was originally written for Roman readers. A few argue for Antioch in Syria as the destination. From the point of view of Christian disciples and persecution, the difference between Rome and Antioch would be immaterial.

Each was a capital city—under the Emperor in one case, under a Roman governor in the other. What was done in the capital to-day would be done in Syria to-morrow.

Now, as few scholars will place the date of Mark later than A.D. 70 the impending shadow of persecution is not due to Domitian, but to the increasing sternness of Rome in repressing Jewish insurrections, in which Christians might easily become involved, and which culminated in the horrors of A.D. 70 under Titus, or to the earlier outbreak of insane persecution of the Christians by Nero in A.D. 64. Rome, as the destination of the Gospel and Nero as the sinister figure whose fury might spread throughout the provinces everywhere seem to give us the background against which the Evangelist sets his Gospel. As Dr. Bartlet writes:[1] 'It may well be that alike in aim and occasion Mark's Gospel was largely continuous with the Epistle of Peter, which was written probably about 63, to churches in Asia Minor, at a time when persecution was becoming more severe and menacing. The martyrdom of Peter and many others at Rome in 64 would create a fresh need for all possible means of assurance.' Dr. Bartlet continues: 'Such unexpected sufferings instead of an immediate share in Messiah's glory, were not really out of keeping with the promises of the gospel, and so with its truth. The best answer here was the example of their Lord and Saviour Himself on the lines already laid down in Peter's own epistle.' The kinship in thought in 1 Peter and in Mark is obvious. Of course, we do not

[1] 'St. Mark', *C.B.*, p. 38.

suggest that suffering, and courage to meet it, are
the only themes in Mark. We meet pronouncements
on such questions as divorce, the original divine
meaning of the Sabbath, and the significance of
certain food taboos. Yet it is true to say that the
emphasis is laid on persecution, and the spirit in
which it should be met as set forth in the conduct
of the Baptist and in the teaching, Passion, and
death of our Lord.

Before we are free to consider the statements of
Christ about His coming Passion and death we must
give at least a glance at the position adopted towards
them by the left-wing writers of the Form Criticism
school. Generally speaking, the basis of the Form
Criticism theory is this. Since literary criticism of
the Gospels had apparently exhausted itself and
become somewhat sterile, scholars sought to go
behind the earliest documents to that uncharted
territory between the Resurrection and the first
written record. Let us say between A.D. 33 and A.D.
65, though the figures are arbitrary. During this
period of oral tradition, what constituted the
message proclaimed? As yet there were no widespread, strong Christian communities. The work
was done by pioneers in new areas among Jewish
congregations in synagogues or among pagan
audiences in the market-places and highways. The
aim of the pioneers was to win converts to faith in
Christ and to re-create them in the life of Christ.

Can scholars get beyond guesswork as to what
constituted the staple of the *Kerygma*, or thing
preached? Two lines of evidence seem beyond
dispute: First, analogy from the mission field to-day

can hardly mislead us. Whether the missionary preached among Jews or among pagans, his aim was to convince his hearers that a Messiah Redeemer had come, to proclaim His character and purpose, to declare His rejection and Crucifixion, but, above all, to preach His Resurrection. On the ground of this Heaven-given seal, He ought to be received as Saviour and Lord by all men everywhere.

Secondly, this view is corroborated by some fragments of apostolic preaching in Acts ii, iii, and iv, and particularly by Paul in 1 Corinthians xv. 3–4, where he says: 'I delivered unto you first of all that which I also received, how that Christ died for our sins according to the scriptures; and that he was buried; and that he hath been raised on the third day according to the scriptures. . . .' The burden of the oral message was that Christ Jesus, a man approved of God by miracles and signs, had been rejected and crucified, yet raised up in power by God, and that repentance and remission of sins were preached in His name. So far there is general agreement, but the young communities of believers would find problems arising such as we have mentioned: What should be a believer's attitude to the Law? To Caesar? To the Jewish Sabbath? To clean and unclean foods? And so on. It would be in response to such questions that eye-witnesses and hearers of Christ would recall every apposite statement and these would quickly become stereotyped and fall into easily recognized groups such as 'pronouncements' and 'stories'. 'Such Sayings, Parables, and Paradigms are therefore directly connected with the life of the Church. . . .

This tradition was born of the desire to illustrate with examples the teaching of Jesus Christ, and to reinforce the exhortations to the Church, and to those who were becoming Christians, with the words of the Lord.'[1]

But the Form Criticism method while opening out new possibilities of thought about Gospel origins is not without its perils, and one is the temptation to refer every difficult saying attributed to Jesus in the Gospels, to a Christian community of a much later date and to make it a prophecy after the event. This way of disposing of difficulties we can appreciate when we remember that actually such prophecies after the event had been multiplied freely by writers of 'apocryphal' gospels in the second century. For dogmatic and sectarian purposes, sayings and doings are attributed to Jesus such as we find in the Gospel of Peter or the Gospel according to the Hebrews that reasonably warn us to examine every saying of Jesus in the canonical Gospels with care. Whether we can agree with the conclusions of left-wing writers like Bultmann or not, we are indebted to them for pointing out this danger. We pass presently to consider some of these sayings in Mark. We shall first, however, examine:

I. THE SIGNIFICANCE OF THE BAPTIST'S WORK IN THE SECOND GOSPEL.

Mark approaches our Lord's death as that of Messiah; this we shall see presently. He approaches it along the line of familiar Old Testament tradition.

[1] Dibelius, *Gospel Criticism and Christology*, p. 42 (Ivor Nicholson & Watson).

Messiah's appearance would be sudden, but not unheralded; the King would have his courier. Mark incorporates (without taking pains to cite his authorities fully) two statements concerning the forerunner—one from Malachi (iii. 1): 'Behold I send my messenger, and he shall prepare the way before me', and the other from Isaiah (xl. 3), 'The voice of one that crieth, Prepare ye in the wilderness the way of the Lord'. With these—the messenger and the voice—he identifies John. But when Mark proceeds with his record of John's ministry, he is so impressed with one aspect of it that it leads him into what we believe to be his predominant interest in the whole Gospel. It is the fact that has reappeared so often in history that truth's portion is the scaffold and upon the throne is wrong. John's part in the drama of redemption may be limited, but it is essentially one with that of Jesus. Matthew, following Q, expands this truth in our Lord's commentary on John before the multitude (see Matthew xi. 11). Mark develops, instead, the idea in Malachi (iv. 5) in which the messenger of Messiah is identified with Elijah. This was a familiar idea with the Scribes and was used by them apparently to belittle any pretensions of Messiahship Jesus might make. 'The scribes say that Elijah must first come', but, just as Jesus adapted to Himself the idea of Son of Man and of a Suffering Servant, so here he identifies the mission of Elijah and that of John. It is the continuity and completion of a sacrificial work of reform involving in Elijah's case persecution, in the Baptist's case martyrdom.

The parallel between Elijah's protest against 'the wickedness of the house of Omri' and the Baptist's against the house of Antipas, even between Jezebel and Herodias, was too obvious to escape the discerning eye. Though the narrative in 1 Kings does not tell how Elijah died, yet the story of his contest for an ethical monotheistic religion against a weak king and a remorseless vindictive queen passed into a national epic; it became a symbol of the eternal struggle between the flesh and the spirit, the Beast and the Lord's annointed. John met his Jezebel and his witness against a polluted court was in the spirit and power of Elijah. Though Mark skilfully defers the details of the Baptist's execution to a later stage, he unites John's ministry to that of Jesus at the very outset and he makes John's death the occasion of Christ's public ministry. 'After that John was delivered up Jesus came into Galilee preaching the gospel of God' (i. 14). The inference is that if men could not endure the courier, they are not likely to endure the King. Matthew's parable of the Householder (xxi. 33–42), which follows on a discussion of the Baptist's moral authority (xxi. 25), is another presentation and expansion of Mark's argument. This lesson for a young Church scattered over the Roman world under the shadow of persecution was bracing. Every follower of Christ must fill up that which is lacking in the sufferings of Christ if the redemption of mankind is to be realized. We do Mark less than justice unless we emphasize this point. We pass next to some of Christ's sayings concerning His death.

2. THE ARREST OF THE BRIDEGROOM.

In Mark ii. 20 we read: 'But the days will come when the bridegroom shall be taken away from them, and then will they fast in that day.' The plain meaning of the saying is that after a season of gladness in which Jesus unites to Himself a band of disciples whom we regard as the nucleus of His Church, the bride, He then foresees He will encounter hostility and a violent arrest. In that day 'the sons of the bridechamber will fast'. One of the objections to the authenticity of this saying is that Jesus did not encounter such conditions. While the Fourth Gospel does represent Him as forsaken by the multitude and as asking the Twelve if they also will 'go away' (John vi. 66), nevertheless, it is argued, it was at a much later stage than this that anything like defection or trouble arose. In other words, that Mark is guilty of an anachronism and the reason for the anachronism is to enhance the prescience of Jesus, and to show grounds why the Christ must suffer and die.

Several facts ought to be considered before we reject the saying or its setting. (a) It is easy to overlook the brevity of our Lord's public ministry and the rapidity with which feeling intensified for Him or against Him. The atmosphere was charged with emotion and every would-be Messiah received prompt attention and was quickly assessed at the popular estimate. This ministry was probably not more than two years, and to imagine that Jesus had to wait for the slow evolution of events before

He could sense resentment and hostility is to misread the facts. His was one of those dynamic personalities which soon attracted or repelled, and He never hesitated to press home His challenge—a very disturbing tendency where men are willing to listen, but not to act. (b) Again, Christ's reflections on national conditions, the truculence of the leaders, the fate meted out to the Baptist, the unreadiness of the leaders to recognize the divine mission of the Baptist, were facts that carried their own lesson. (c) Though this saying is associated with the problem of fasting, it is remarkable that in the paragraph immediately following, Mark introduces the incidents concerning plucking the ears on the Sabbath and the healing in the Synagogue and ending with the ominous words: 'The Pharisees went out, and straightway with the Herodians took counsel against him, how they might destroy him' (see ii. 23–iii. 5). (d) Further, 'The saying itself, too, stands in an integral connexion with the whole context in which we find it. It presupposes the bright conditions under which Jesus began His work; and cannot be ascribed to any later time without losing its force and appositeness. May we not conjecture that it affords us a glimpse into the mind of Jesus in that initial period when His horizon seemed quite unclouded. He was beset even then with a premonition of disaster.'[1] (e) Jesus began His ministry consciously offering Himself as Messiah to Israel, and the use of the term 'bridegroom' as a synonym for Messiah was familiar and current. It seems to have taken its

[1] E. F. Scott, *The Kingdom and the Messiah*, pp. 213–14 (T. & T. Clark).

origin from Hosea, where Yahweh as a Bridegroom 'allures' Israel and seeks afresh to make her His own (see Hosea iii). Nowhere is suffering love more vividly portrayed than in this prophecy, first of the prophet himself and then of his Lord, and nowhere, Isaiah liii excepted, would our Lord have found a background of thought more expressive of His premonitions than in this prophecy. Very early in His ministry He realized that His message of the Kingdom of God and eternal life would create opposition, and if He remained faithful to His message from the Father an attempt by violence would be made to silence Him. When He spoke, the cloud was not bigger than a man's hand, but it was visible to our Lord on the horizon.

3. 'HOW IS IT WRITTEN OF THE SON OF MAN?'

This statement is placed by Mark at the descent from the Mount of Transfiguration and is as follows: 'They asked him, saying, The scribes say that Elijah must first come. And he said unto them, Elijah indeed cometh first, and restoreth all things: And how is it written of the Son of man that he should suffer many things and be set at nought?' (ix. 11, 12). The point in this passage that creates a difficulty for some is the seeming irrelevance between our Lord's answer about the Son of Man and the disciples' question about the current statement that Elijah must precede the Messiah. Various attempts have been made to overcome the difficulty by transposing the order of the sentences; but the most satisfactory is that of the late Professor C. H.

Turner in his Commentary on Mark.[1] Writing on the whole passage he says, 'Sense and coherence are at once restored to the passage, if we may assume that the second question has got transposed to a wrong place, and that it should be brought back to its natural place in immediate sequence to the other question. "They kept that saying, discussing with one another what was this 'rising from the dead' and where did Scripture say about the Son of Man that He must suffer many things and be rejected" '.

Once this order is adopted the difficulty vanishes and two points emerge:

(a) To take the reply of Jesus first. We have seen how He identifies the Messenger of the Covenant and Elijah with the Baptist. The disciples put their question about the return of Elijah and He affirms that Elijah has come and suffered at their hands. Then comes one of those peculiarly self-revealing moments and to which Mark provides a parallel in x. 32. It is a moment when the consciousness of gathering hostility breaks the continuity of Christ's thought and speech and He passes by a quick transition from the Baptist's fate to His own. The saying is so psychologically relevant that it is wellnigh impossible it could be due to a later hand. If it be stated that nowhere is it written 'that the Son of man should suffer many things', we have to remember that as John becomes Elijah so the Son of Man and the Suffering Servant

---

[1] Gore, *A New Commentary on Holy Scripture*, Part III, p. 82 (S.P.C.K.). Turner adds: 'It is quite easy to suppose that words inserted between two short columns of a papyrus roll (the writing was always across, not down, the roll) intended to be inserted in the column to the left at [10], were, when the roll was recopied, erroneously inserted by the scribe in the column to the right at [12].'

are united by Jesus in Himself. In each case we might say 'it is the spirit that quickeneth. The flesh profiteth nothing'. Christ realizes in the travail and death of these forerunners that experience to which human sin and the divine will are leading Him. (*b*) Similarly, we can see that Mark with sure insight into the meaning of Christ's reply unites it to all that took place on the Mount of Transfiguration. All the Synoptists refer to the presence of 'Moses and Elijah'. Mark and Matthew say they were 'talking with them'. Luke expands from his source 'who . . . spoke of his decease which he was about to accomplish at Jerusalem' (ix. 31). It is not necessary here to offer any opinion on the phenomena on the Mount. The significant fact is that both the Marcan and Lucan tradition regarded the transfiguration events as intimately related to our Lord's death. While Luke gives the explicit statement just quoted, Mark, by placing his dialogue between our Lord and the disciples 'as they were coming down from the mount', proclaims the same idea.

4. A RANSOM FOR MANY (Mark x. 45).

This statement, 'For verily the Son of man came, not to be ministered unto, but to minister, and to give his life a ransom for many', has played such a great part, especially in the patristic doctrine of atonement, leading in some instances to repulsive images and pictures, that it suffers from the nemesis of abuse, and good reasons are eagerly sought for its rejection as non-authentic.

The introduction of the word 'ransom' (*lutron*),

found here alone in the Gospels and on our Lord's lips, is sufficiently remarkable to call for careful examination. Over twenty years ago Dr. Rashdall wrote: (These words) 'suggest a report coloured by the later doctrinal teachings of the Church',[1] and in 1937 Dr. Branscomb wrote: 'The verse can scarcely be attributed to Jesus.'[2] Many other names ancient and modern can be cited supporting this view. Quite frankly, Rashdall does not seem to have had his mind made up when he wrote on this text in the Bampton Lectures. He leans to the view indicated above, but always with reserve. Let us quote his own words: 'The hypothesis of a doctrinally coloured insertion is to my mind the most probable account of the words about the ransom. Still, I am far from denying that they may possibly represent a genuine saying of the Lord, and the question arises, what, if they are genuine, was their original meaning?' Assuming in this indefinite sort of way that the passage 'represents' a genuine saying of the Lord, the writer proceeds to expound its theological significance. This is not very satisfactory. If the foundation be insecure, why go further? It will make a real difference to interpretation if the words reflect the judgement or interpretation of a later generation rather than a conviction of Jesus that a death which He felt to be imminent would purchase freedom for sinners.

Branscomb rejects the saying as unauthentic because (1) in Luke we find another version of the

---

[1] *The Idea of Atonement in Christian Theology*, p. 29 (Macmillan & Co.).
[2] *The Gospel of Mark*, p. 190 (Hodder & Stoughton).

saying we find here, immediately preceding this text. Luke, however, concludes his group of parallel sayings with the words: 'But I am in the midst of you as a servant' (Luke xxii. 27). 'This ending is in line with the thought of the preceding verses, and it looks more original than the highly developed theological version of the same thought in x. 45.'[1] (2) The idea of Christ's death as a ransom is 'almost completely absent from the gospels elsewhere' and it formed no part of the teaching of Jesus. (3) Branscomb falls back on the idea that the thought is Pauline and gives parallel sentences from Paul. This mode of argument we have already seen reason to reject.[2] The arguments of other writers against the genuineness of the passage seem to be variations of these.

Is there nothing to be said for the defence? Admitting that the word 'ransom' is found here alone in the teaching of Jesus, it will, however, be difficult to deny that the ideas suggested by the passage and the offending word 'ransom' are present in other sayings that are admitted as genuine. We have seen them in the saying about the Bridegroom. The ideas in this passage (x. 45) spring from Isaiah liii generally, but in particular from v. 8, and we know that here Jesus found expression for an aspect of His ministry as Messiah. As Dr. Vincent Taylor says: 'A new idea is certainly introduced at the end, in the thought of a ransom given by the Son of man, but it cannot be described as irrelevant in a

[1] *The Gospel of Mark*, p. 190 (Hodder & Stoughton).
[2] For a clear statement of the anti-Pauline origin of the saying see article: 'Great Texts Reconsidered: Mark x. 45', in *Expository Times*, December, 1938, p. 107, by Professor W. F. Howard, D.D.

context which speaks of service, or impossible as a word of Jesus.'[1]

The question that scholars must decide is whether the word *lutron* or its equivalent in any other language was current when Jesus was teaching. The fact that an expressive word is found only once is not sufficient to condemn it as spurious. Jesus used thought-forms and metaphors from which writers would shrink to-day. We sometimes need to be reminded as we so often are concerning Paul that our Lord was not a systematic theologian, but rather a prophet using the language of poetry while at the same time achieving redemption by what He was and did. Any word that conveyed the truth to His sometimes dull listeners Jesus would use. One of the dangers of literary criticism is that its criteria in instances like this are often too subjective. If evidence were needed it is to hand in the formidable list of names given by Rashdall, for and against the genuineness of this passage (op. cit., p. 55). The statement that 'Luke's ending is more in line with the preceding ideas' is hardly convincing when we remember how Luke uses his materials. He usually tends to soften words and phrases that might seem offensive to his Gentile readers. To reduce the meaning of this saying, as Rashdall suggests, to 'if Christ did use it' He meant 'a physical deliverance from actual physical death', is almost bathos. At least it falls far below the moving conception in Isaiah liii, from which we believe our Lord took His starting-point. We see no reasons sufficiently convincing to reject the

[1] *Jesus and His Sacrifice*, p. 105 (Macmillan & Co.).

saying, and later we shall consider the import of the word 'ransom' as used by Jesus and His Church.

5. THE INSTITUTION OF THE SUPPER (Mark xiv. 22-5).

There is a clear discrepancy between the Synoptists and the Fourth Gospel regarding the day on which the Lord's Supper was instituted. The former represent it as being held on the day of the Passover, the latter as on the previous evening. Paul's view seems to agree with the Synoptists' when he refers to Christ as 'our passover sacrificed for us'. Before we decide—and the decision affects our interpretation of the Supper—we must bear in mind that during the week prior to the Passover feast anticipatory acts of worship had arisen in which the devout sought to enter, spiritually and ritually, into a fitting celebration of the Feast. We are familiar with the fact that such preparatory meetings were held by the devout for the Sabbath. What seems to have happened, then, was this: Jesus, eager to hold an intimate farewell, to win if possible, even yet, Judas Iscariot, and to witness to the disciples His faith in His own redemptive death, appoints such a meeting—anticipatory, in one sense of the Passover, but fulfilling it in another —with his disciples. Everything about this Supper was suggestive of the Passover. It was anticipatory of it. Its spiritual significance was one with the Jewish Feast and everything goes to show that the Fourth Evangelist is right in placing it on the evening before the great feast and not on the same day.[1]

Bearing these facts in mind, we proceed to

[1] John xiii. 1, 2.

examine the words of institution and their bearing on Christ's death: (*a*) 'He took a loaf, as they were eating, and when he had blessed, he brake it and gave to them and said, Take ye: this is my body.' This symbolic act, true in its manner to ancient prophetic usage, was a mode of preaching. In the Greek Church it is still known as the Drama of the Cross, and this symbolic significance is plainly stated in Paul by the added words, 'which is for you' or 'which is broken for you' (1 Corinthians xi. 24, mar., R.V.).

Underlying this act we have a twofold proclamation of vicarious sacrifice. The grain is crushed and loses itself in becoming bread. The loaf is broken and given before it can become strength to the one who eats it. But some modern writers[1] go further and affirm that it was in the breaking and in the eating that the sharing in the reality represented was made effective. That there is a truth in this seems certain, but also a great peril. The truth lies in the familiar fact that any truth becomes more deeply our own as we dramatize or in any way reproduce it in action. If in doubt ask the actor, teacher, or preacher. These tell you that in representing by word or action the truth to others it becomes vivid to themselves, representation becomes realization. The peril is that dull minds can rest in the representation as an end, or, worse still, the priest can come to control divine grace as a medicine man can 'make' rain by sympathetic magic. In view of the foregoing interpretation there is no need to labour the vexed question of *hoc est*

[1] e.g. Otto.

corpus meum. Transubstantiation and symbolism belong to different spheres of thought. Christ wished His disciples to know by what He did that so far from His death being an irretrievable disaster it would be laden with power and deliverance for all who entered into fellowship with Him.

The same in general is the meaning of the words concerning the cup: 'He said unto them, This is my blood of the new covenant which is shed for many.' From passages like Genesis xlix. 11, Deuteronomy xxxii. 14, and Ecclesiasticus xxxix. 26, we see the familiarity of Jewish thought with the metaphor 'the blood of the grape' (or vine); the wine-press was a symbol of sacrifice. Unless this is kept firmly in mind, it will be difficult to meet the criticism of writers like Klausner, Montefiore, and others, who maintain that, even symbolically, Jews would not use such words as 'this is my blood', because to Jews such an idea would be repulsive. But here, too, we miss the point unless we keep in mind the central reality that Jesus emphasizes. Sacrifice can bring life to others. The crushed grapes bring strength and inspiration. An out-poured life can save many. There is an allusive delicacy here that is at once arresting and yet, because of its meaning, inoffensive. Great truths can bear daring metaphors, and Jesus never hesitated to use them when men's dullness required it.

That this is the right road in interpretation is sustained by the introduction of the phrase, 'my blood of the covenant'. These words lift the subject into the context of an Old Testament incident in Exodus xxiv. 5–8. Moses reads the terms of a covenant between God and the people. The people proclaim their willingness to accept its terms, and then Moses sprinkles the people with part of the blood of the victims offered as burnt- and peace-offerings. The other part had been sprinkled God-ward upon the altar. Here was a covenant of mercy and of obedience sealed by sacrificial blood. Christ's sacrifice of Himself, He suggests, will bring a new, more inward relation to God, in which mercy will become an experience and obedience will be in the will and affections. It cannot come until He has surrendered Himself in death to God. The remainder of the phrase 'for many' is evidently an echo of Isaiah liii. 11–12. The underlying idea is the same, salvation through vicarious sacrifice.

6. THE CRY OF DERELICTION (xv. 34).

We must consider these words, not because they shed so much light on Christ's conception of His death as because they have been made the basis of theories that are singularly unsatisfactory. The words are: 'And at the ninth hour Jesus cried with a loud voice, Eloi, Eloi, lama sabachthani? which is, being interpreted, My God, my God, why hast thou forsaken me?' A familiar traditional inter-pretation has been that, since penal suffering is attached to all sin, and since all have sinned, God provided a substitute for sinners in Christ—in fact, made the sin of the world to fall upon Him so that in the act of inflicting the penalty God in His holiness could not draw near to His Son, but for a season was compelled to forsake him. Hence the awful cry on the Cross as the world's Redeemer was forsaken of the Father. This hardly misrepresents a crude interpretation that still lingers in some areas.

The difficulty of the words was recognized in the apostolic age, and various methods were adopted to obviate it. Luke and the Fourth Gospel omit the saying. Either it was not in their sources or they personally felt constrained to omit it. Codex D softens the words 'forsaken me' into 'reproached me', and the apocryphal 'Gospel of Peter' substitutes 'My power, my power, why hast thou forsaken me?'

Some modern writers have sought similarly to cut the knot. R. H. Lightfoot,[1] writing from the standpoint of form criticism, thinks the passion narrative was written for the edification of Christian communities, and holds that no Old Testament scripture so fully expressed the truth of Christ's sufferings as the Twenty-Second Psalm, which begins with these words. So that we should regard the cry as an Old Testament quotation placed on the lips of Jesus by a New Testament writer to convey some idea of what Jesus felt as He faced death for mankind.

In coming to a decision about the saying, the following points should be kept in mind. (1) The fact that a reading is theologically difficult is not a sufficient reason for its rejection. Textual criticism holds the opposite view that, other things being equal, of two readings in a manuscript the more difficult should be chosen. (2) There seems no more reason to believe that writers or compilers of the Gospels, half a generation later, should be more

1 *History and Interpretation in the Gospels.* See p. 157 ff. (Hodder & Stoughton).

familiar with the Twenty-Second Psalm and more likely to use it to express the experiences in the mind of Jesus than He was. No one disputes the fact that His mind was filled with Old Testament ideas and even phrases, and that in moments of spiritual crisis, such as temptation and conflict, He found expression for His faith or sorrow in the words of Old Testament scripture. (3) Branscomb,[1] Loisy, and others contend that, because the other incidents such as 'mocking', 'wagging their heads', 'thirst', 'piercing the hands and feet' are expressed by the evangelists in words from Psalm xxii, it is more likely that this opening sentence is due to them, too. They wish to tell of Christ's utter woe and so put on His lips the words, 'My God, my God, why hast thou forsaken me?' The answer here is the same: If Jesus was familiar with the Old Testament in its spirit and letter, as we know Him to have been, we are convinced that His quotation in His dying cry is as likely to have inspired the writers of the Gospels to continue to quote from the same source as that they put the Psalm, on Christ's lips, to give expression to what they thought of His sufferings and death.

How then are we to interpret these words? It is best to approach them, as far as we can, along the path of human experience. This will at least retain a sense of reality, and the continuity between Christ's sufferings and those of His disciples. Instances can be cited of saintly men and women who, through physical pain and exhaustion, entered upon a period, usually brief, of sheer desolation.

[1] *The Gospel of Mark*, p. 298 (Hodder & Stoughton).

The human spirit had not quite 'forsaken its house of clay', yet it was unable further to interpret life in terms of God and faith. In some instances, these very words: 'Why hast thou forsaken me?' alone express the sense of desolation. Because of this psychological fact, we lean to the view of McLeod Campbell that the cry of Jesus was in one sense an affirmation of faith. It was an assertion of confidence in God when His own condition, human wickedness, and the silence of Heaven seemed to belie it. This is the argument in Psalm xxii. (see verses 4–5); and Luke, though omitting these words, adds that Jesus said as He passed away, 'Father, into thy hands I commend my spirit'. The desolation was a transitory experience, due to physical conditions, aggravated by mental agony and woe, because of man's unspeakable sin; and an experience in which even the sense of the divine was eclipsed.

So far we may go, but to build up a doctrine of atonement that requires us to believe that at the moment when our Lord was supremely fulfilling His Father's will, God should, because of the load of sin Jesus bore, forsake Him and leave Him in eternal desolation, as He bears the penalty of human sin, is to go beyond Scripture and Christian experience. Dale, accepting one aspect of an argument in a sermon[1] by Stopford Brooke, seeks to find the clue to the mystery in Christ's identification with humanity. It was as one with humanity He felt the sin and the penalty, but this view will receive consideration later.

[1] See Dale, *The Atonement*, note G, p. 474 (Independent Press).

Chapter 7

THE DEATH OF CHRIST IN THE TEACHING OF ST. PETER

Our sources are the addresses of Peter recorded in the Acts, and the 'First Epistle General of Peter'. One preliminary question calls for attention. Do the words attributed to Peter in the speeches in Acts bear the marks of genuineness? Or has the author given us any guarantee that the voice is the voice of Peter? We cannot overlook Luke's literary method. Both the Third Gospel and the Acts forbid the idea of verbatim reports. He was a diligent note-taker and collector of facts, but the uniformity of style and the presence of favourite words show that he handled his material as an editor or historian with freedom and literary skill. We cannot look for the *ipsissima verba* of Peter in the Acts. Renan said that the closing chapters of Acts are the most purely historical of anything in the New Testament, while the opening ones are the least historical. What Bartlet says of 'Peter's Pentecostal Address' holds for the passages we are about to consider. 'It is too brief, too finished in form, to be more than a summary of Peter's address reduced to writing, from memory at a considerably later date. But in any case it carries us behind Luke's own standpoint to that of Judeo-Christian piety, before Stephen and Paul had introduced a new ferment into the conceptions of these early believers.'[1] The primitive view is present in regard to the Person of Christ and the meaning of His death. Jesus is 'a man approved of God unto you by mighty works, and wonders and signs which God did by him, in the midst of you, even as ye yourselves know'. We see this primitive element also in the apologetic as well as in the gospel that Peter offers to the Jews. These speeches give Luke's interest in the development of the gospel message and of the different methods of its presentation. Here we have 'an example of the most primitive preaching of the gospel to the Jews'.[2]

What, then, is the message of the Cross? It is most explicitly stated in the remainder of the passage partly quoted (Acts ii. 22-4): 'Him, being delivered up by the determinate counsel and fore-knowledge of God, ye by the hand of lawless men did crucify and slay, whom God raised up.' Here Peter first addresses himself to the shallow and facile rejection of Jesus because of the manner of His death. No words seem to have been more current on the lips of Jewish enemies than the passage in Deuteronomy xxi. 23: 'Cursed is every one that hangeth on a tree.' It was a proof-text to show that the Nazarene was an impostor, neither the promised Messiah nor even a prophet. He hung on a tree, and His Crucifixion demonstrated that He was God-rejected and God-accursed. So keenly did the hostile Jews press this argument, resting it on the

---

[1] 'The Acts', *C.B.*, p. 148; cf. Denney's *Death of Christ*, p. 76 (Hodder & Stoughton).
[2] Foakes-Jackson, *The Acts of the Apostles*, p. 14 (Hodder & Stoughton).

letter of the Torah, that the malignant party-cry was soon known to all believers and missionaries: 'Jesus is accursed' (cf. 1 Corinthians xii. 3).

To this probably impressive argument, when addressed to a popular Jewish audience, Peter addresses himself. He snatches his opponent's weapon and turns it against him. The ground on which the Jew rejects Jesus becomes the ground on which the Apostles base their claim. Jesus was not a miserable impostor whose guilt was revealed by the manner of His death. Even in His life He bore the divine approval by His works. This Man, because of what He was, is not to be judged by common catch-words even if from Holy Writ. His work and suffering, His humiliation and death, are the expression of the definite purpose and foreknowledge of God. Christ and His work belong to eternity. Whereas the Fourth Evangelist makes Jesus the central actor in the drama of redemption, choosing the moment and the place when He shall challenge and destroy sin, Peter carries the idea of the 'determinate counsel' back to God.

This raises afresh the perennial problem of human guilt on the part of those who crucified Jesus; but, taking the answer as a whole, Peter seems to hold that primarily God gave man moral freedom, foreknowing he would abuse the gift and fall into sin. This, He anticipated and met by an atonement even before man sinned. Christ's death has a significance that lies deeper than its manner. By it, in its most shameful form, Christ pierces to the depths of man's sin and destroys it. The Cross is the battleground and, though crucified in the flesh, Christ is unbroken and victorious in spirit. 'It was not possible that he should be holden of death.' This Peter shows to be plain when the God, under whose condemnation He is alleged to have fallen, reverses man's verdict, and raises Him from the dead. These Jewish opponents are confronted by the empty tomb, by the fulfilment of prophecy, and by the gifts of the Spirit, all of which are worse than meaningless if 'Jesus is accursed'.

Here most writers of the Abailardian school would stop and say that Peter had proved his point. Christ's death was a tragedy, but one that God over-ruled and turned into a revelation of grace. But students who relate this death to 'the determinate counsel' of God, see in it the expression of a divine necessity, something that the moral relations of God and man require, and due to causes more remote than priest or ruler. Denney, for instance, says that 'the idea that the cross *in itself* is nothing but a scandal, and that all the New Testament interpretations of it are but ways of getting over the scandal, cannot be too emphatically rejected . . . the gospel would never have been known as "the word of the cross" if the interpretation of the cross had been merely an apologetic device for surmounting the theoretical difficulties in the conception of a crucified Messiah'.[1]

Peter, rather, lodges the Cross in the eternal counsel and purpose of God. Whether it yields to a rationale, completely satisfying or not, at least we must avoid shallowness and triviality. What do

[1] *The Death of Christ*, p. 78; cf. Lidgett, *The Spiritual Principle of the Atonement*, p. 222 (Epworth Press).

we mean by conceiving Christ's work as 'a divine necessity'? Not that God lay under any extraneous constraint that diverted Him from His divine purpose, and led Him to act in a manner contrary to His will, else the throne of the universe had come under control of another power. But God, being in His moral and fatherly nature what He is, at once seeking to redeem and establish sons in righteousness or to grant what we may call an ethical forgiveness, required and provided an atonement in Christ. Unless and until this is recognized, any writer cannot be said to have done full justice to the theology of the New Testament.

In his appeal in ii. 38, 'Repent and be baptized every one of you in the name of Jesus Christ unto the remission of your sins', Peter throws the emphasis, not so much on what Christ did for man as upon the individual's response and identification of himself through repentance and faith with Christ. That which God provided and Christ revealed can become effective in the sinner when he responds in thought and action to Christ, and stakes his life on what is offered. Peter's speech in the home of Cornelius (x. 39–40) is to the same effect, except that it also seeks to obviate the Jewish difficulty about Messiah hanging on a tree. It then passes on to show that God embraces Gentiles as well as Jews in His determinate counsel and welcomes all God-fearers and workers of righteousness in every nation. Peter's chief contribution, then, in Acts is that behind the apparent or historical causes of Christ's death lay a moral necessity in the purpose of God to give Jesus as a sacrifice for human sin.

THE FIRST EPISTLE OF PETER.

From our study of the historical background of
Mark, it will be seen that we accept the genuineness
of this Epistle, but something must be added in
support. Moffatt, indeed, in his most recent commentary, assumes the genuineness of 1 Peter without
seeking to prove it.[1] Among scholars who accept
it also are Ramsay, Adeney, Dr. J. V. Bartlet, and
Zahn. Those who reject the Petrine authorship,
usually do so on three grounds: (1) First, that no
imminent persecution, such as is hinted at in the
Epistle, can be located within the Apostle's lifetime.
The nature of the persecution, however, is not
represented as general. It is rather impending and
is the kind of situation that could easily have
developed into the outburst against the Christians
under Nero. 'The storm of the Neronian persecution had not yet swept over the Church at Rome,
and no persecuting policy against the Church had
been accepted by the magistrates in Asia Minor.
Not a word is found in the Epistle about men
shedding their blood or laying down their lives for
the gospel . . . but they were called upon to face
violence, slander, the severance of social and family
ties, worldly ruin.'[2] (2) That the Greek of this
'beautiful epistle' is beyond the powers of a Galilean
fisherman, or, in Moffatt's terse words, 'Is it
credible that a Galilean fisherman who left out
his H's (that, we are told, is what Matthew xxvi.
73 implies) should after middle life, and in the
midst of absorbing occupations, have learned to

[1] His arguments will be found in his *Intro. to the Lit. of the N.T.*,
pp. 331–8.
[2] Chase, 'Peter: First Epistle', *H.D.B.*

write scholarly Greek like this?'[1] But in v. 12 the author declares that 'by Silvanus, our faithful brother as I account him, I have written unto you briefly', and this entirely agrees with Peter's usage of giving material to others and entrusting its literary form to them.[2] (3) The third objection is to the 'Paulinisms' that are found in almost every chapter of this Epistle.[3] These, it is argued, came not from Peter, but from some one on better terms with Paul than Peter is represented to have been in Galatians ii. 11 and Acts xv. 39; some protagonist of Paul who wished to insinuate his ideas among the Judeo-Christian party. This was a favourite field of thought fifty years ago with F. C. Baur and the Tübingen School. It is not so impressive to-day. If Silvanus was a personal friend of Peter and Paul alike, having co-operated with both in 'the work', and if Peter dictated in substance his ideas to Silvanus, leaving the form to his amanuensis, we need not be surprised if we find traces of Paul's interpretation of the gospel in this Epistle.

Moffatt probably represents the thought of most British scholars when he says, 'Instead of 1 Peter representing a diluted and faded Paulinism, it denotes an attitude influenced but essentially uncontrolled by the special ideas of Paul's theology. The latter's faith-mysticism, his conception of justification, and his eschatology, are absent from this writer's pages, which reflect the outlook of a primitive Christian who had breathed the messianic atmosphere of the better Judaism, not the definite

[1] See Moffatt, *I.L.N.T.*, p. 334.   [2] See Eusebius, *E.H.*, iii. 39.
[3] cf. Bennett, '1 Peter', p. xxiii. *C.B.*

soteriological standpoint of one trained in rabbinic and Hellenistic modes of thought'.[1]

What then has this Epistle to say concerning the death of our Lord? Its aim is manifestly practical, not doctrinal. Such doctrine as exists is derived and not original. The author's mind is steeped in Old Testament ideas, and Old Testament thought and language provide him with a medium for his message. There are two leading ideas in the Epistle, viz. the pre-existence of Christ and God's eternal covenant with man. These ideas are regulative and underlie his allusions to Christ's death.

His first allusion in i. 2 to Christ's sacrifice is in the words 'elect . . . unto obedience and sprinkling of the blood of Jesus'. Here we have unmistakably an Old Testament idea and one which arose in our study of the Lord's Supper in Mark xiv. 24. It is more than probable that we have a reminiscence of that momentous hour in Peter's own experience in the Upper Room. We need not therefore repeat what is already written, except to say that as the blood ratified the covenant between God and Israel, so Peter would remind us of a new covenant in Christ's blood, and that all who are sprinkled by it are pledged to obedience, not to Law but to Jesus. Man's relation to God is based on Christ's sacrifice, and faith in Christ's redemption is unreal unless it is followed by a ready response to His will.

In i. 11, Peter introduces the somewhat unusual idea that the Spirit of the pre-existent Christ went beforehand and enabled the prophets to see that redemption could only be accomplished by sacrifice

[1] *I.L.N.T.*, p. 331.

such as would be consummated in Messiah. The general idea of the Spirit's activity in the prophets revealing Messiah is found in Barnabas v. 6, 'the prophets receiving grace from him prophesied of him', but Moffatt thinks that the 'messianic woes' of Mark xiii. 8 are in the writer's mind. Of course the cry of Moses in Exodus xxxii. 32, that forgiveness may come to sinful Israel if it be at the cost of his own communion with Jehovah, may also have prompted this idea.

In i. 19 the emphasis is laid on the efficacy of Christ's death because of the sinlessness of the One who dies. Here two points demand attention. 'The blood of Christ' means all that Christ was and did for sinners in His life and death; and the preciousness of it lies in that He alone offered to the Father a life of unqualified obedience in which every phase and aspect of the Father's will was realized and satisfied. We are redeemed from our futile manner of life, not by anything extraneous or material, but by the outpoured life of one who cleansed the conscience and vitalized the whole man by His risen power.

In ii. 21–4 we have a contrast between Christ as an Example and Christ as Sin-bearer. Peter begins with the challenge of Christ's character and conduct in presence of His enemies. 'Christ also suffered for you, leaving you an example that ye should follow his steps.' The imitation of Christ has always had a necessary place in Christian theology, since by the struggle to be like Him we develop a conscience of sin; but Peter passes rapidly to the truth that effective imitation is a mirage until sin is dealt with. Sin must be borne and borne away. The soul must be emancipated before the imitation becomes possible. Human effort must be perfected in redemption. 'Who his own self bare our sins in his body on the tree, that we having died unto sin might live unto righteousness.'

The only remaining relevant passage is in iii. 18, in which the challenge to suffer is varied from the foregoing. Christ resisted sin and denied its claims even when that required His life. Die He would, but sin He would not. In the final act of death, He completed for ever His conquest. (The reading 'died' instead of 'suffered' is well sustained.) But the death He died was also to emancipate sinners. Christ also died for sinners once the righteous on behalf of the unrighteous, that He might bring us to God. His sacrifice is ultimately to restore fellowship between God and men.

Chapter 8

THE DEATH OF CHRIST IN THE EPISTLE TO THE HEBREWS

THE approach to the meaning of Christ's death in this epistle is decidedly unique. Though the ideas are often Pauline, yet the mental background of the writer is quite different. To see this it will be necessary to glance briefly at the questions of authorship, people addressed, and aim of the writer.

So far as the author is concerned, what Origen wrote about A.D. 225 still holds good: 'Who wrote the Epistle to the Hebrews, God only knows.' Paul, Barnabas, Luke, Clement of Rome, Apollos, Priscilla and Aquila have all been cited as the author. A recent theory will suffice to show how far the solution has got. Dr. Badcock suggests that the Epistle is a composite work written in Caesarea 'by St. Paul, St. Barnabas, St. Luke, and Philip the Evangelist. The voice is the voice of Barnabas the Levite, but the hand is the hand of Luke, to whose style it shows a marked resemblance. . . . Philip may account for likeness to St. Stephen's speech and behind all is the mind of Paul'.[1] If, however, the name is unknown, the cultural and religious qualities of the man are plain. He was a

[1] *The Pauline Epp.*, p. 198 (S.P.C.K.).

Jew who found life eternal in Jesus. His underlying idea, as we shall see, is that Jesus is *Christus Consummator*. He is the fullness and perfection of the Law, the priesthood, sacrifice, and all ritual shadows.

In his effort to express this evangel, he does *not* establish contrasts between Christ and the Mosaic Law, except indirectly. This point needs close attention. Instead, he uses the Platonic forms of thought and is more akin to Philo than to Paul. He conceives of the universe as a world of shadows expressive of divine reality, 'the very truth of things, all that is meant by God'. Or, in the words in Aurora Leigh, he would say:

> And verily many thinkers of this age,
> Aye, many Christian teachers, half in heaven,
> Are wrong in just my sense, who understood
> Our natural world too insularly, as if
> No spiritual counterpart completed it,
> Consummating its meaning, rounding all
> To justice and perfection, line by line,
> Form by form, nothing single nor alone,
> The great below clenched by the great above.

All earthly things related to religion, as priests, sacrifices, and temple, have their divine counterpart. His philosophical lineage is indicated in one small matter. He never quotes from the Hebrew, but always from the Septuagint version. Professor T. H. Robinson says: 'We need not assume that he read Plato or others of the well-known Greek philosophers; he may have absorbed their teaching at second-hand, but he was certainly familiar with the writings of the Jewish-Alexandrian philosophers, and knew the Wisdom of Solomon, and also probably Philo. His treatment is certainly of this school and there is nothing in the Epistle which tends to throw doubt on its Alexandrian provenance. This does not mean that it was necessarily written in Alexandria or to an Alexandrian group, for every type of thought spread widely over the world.'[1] This writer then proceeds to commend the Christian gospel as the revelation of 'the world to come' (ii. 5) but the world to come is, paradoxically enough, present, a kingdom within a kingdom. Our world is but its copy and the two orders of things exist side by side, a higher and a lower, the pattern and the copy.[2] All this is applied to religion, and much in the Epistle can only be understood if we approach it from this view-point.

As to the people addressed: the title, 'To the Hebrews', though found in very early MSS., is no part of the Epistle, and sheds little light. It is an inference from the matter in the text. Writers like E. F. Scott, James Moffatt, and F. D. Narborough argue for a Gentile Christian constituency, chiefly on the ground that the Epistle is in elaborate, literary Greek, makes no distinction between Jews and Gentiles, and does not even mention the Law. But to represent the Epistle as a philosophy of the Christian religion, designed to meet intellectual difficulties only, is much too general.

The Epistle is written *ad hoc*. Whether we decide on Rome, Antioch, Alexandria, or Jerusalem, the important fact is that a party within the Christian

---

[1] *Hebrews*, p. xvi (Hodder & Stoughton).
[2] cf. Peake, *Hebrews*, pp. 16–17 (Nelson).

Church are disturbed; their anchor is dragging, they are being moved away from their original confidence and hope and are failing to associate themselves with the new Christian community (x. 25). The author is moved with a deep concern for them that is not compatible with calm philosophical reflection. He even warns them that defection from Christ puts them beyond the pale of repentance. He pleads with them to 'suffer the word of exhortation'. Those addressed seem to have been Hellenists who were losing their grasp on the realities of the gospel in Jesus Christ, and were being attracted by the more impressive, sensuous rites of Jewish orthodoxy.

Here as in Galatia a Judaizing party is at work, and this points to a group of Hellenistic Jewish Christians in Jerusalem. They cling to the Temple and the Jewish cultus so ardently that they are losing the substance for the shadow. They are going back to the weak and beggarly elements of the world. The writer, with deep conviction, presses on them the necessity of a courageous choice. 'Let us catch the spirit of the ancient heroes, let us be warned by the secularism of Esau, let us run with patience the race set before us, looking unto Jesus the Pioneer and Perfector of our faith.'

To sum up, we see a group of Jewish Christians, familiar with Alexandrian culture, now in Jerusalem, urged by the Judaizing party to place their confidence afresh in the venerable Jewish cultus rather than upon Jesus Christ. To these the author writes with anxiety, in 'the purest Greek in the New Testament', pressing the authority, supremacy, and finality of Jesus Christ.

Passing to the nature of the message: one point to be observed is that the allusions to Christ's sacrifice and death are not only important, but sustained by illustrations from his Platonic philosophy. The central idea is the perfection of Christ in every aspect of His redemptive work. There are fourteen references to perfection in the Epistle, each reference being related to our Lord or to the way in which He brings things or persons to perfection. A few examples will be sufficient: 'To make the author of their salvation perfect through sufferings' (ii. 10). 'Having been made perfect, he became unto all them that obey him the author of eternal salvation' (v. 9). 'Christ having come a high priest of the good things to come, through the greater and more perfect tabernacle' (ix. 11). In these and similar instances the word 'perfect' or the phrase 'to make perfect' means to make complete in the sense of finality. Nothing more is needed or can be added. The ideal or pattern is reached, the type is consummated in the antitype. Christ cannot be increased or superseded. He is greater than the prophets (i. 1), than the angels (i. 4), than Moses (iii. 3), than all preceding High Priests, who are transitory through death (vii. 23–24), than all preceding sacrifices that must be repeated because of their moral inadequacy (x. 1). He offered one sacrifice for sins for ever (x. 12). His coming means the removing of those things that can be shaken so that the things which cannot be shaken may remain (xii. 27). The only one who bears any similarity to this perfect and final Saviour is the legendary figure of Melchizedek, who 'was flung upon the stage of history without the least hint as to his forebears', yet who was a priest and king, had power to bless faithful Abraham, and to whom Abraham paid homage. But even Melchizedek was 'made priest after the law of a carnal commandment', but there ariseth another Priest who is made 'after the power of an endless life'.

With this general conception of Jesus as the fullness of divine reality and perfection in mind, we consider some of the main ideas in the Epistle bearing on our Lord's atoning work. First, the writer lays stress on the part played by the Incarnation in atonement. This is so prominent that writers like Westcott, F. D. Maurice, and others have tended to shift the centre of gravity from the death to the life of Christ.

This distinction between atonement by His life and by His death we believe to be artificial and psychologically unreal; like the reformers' distinction between the active and passive rightousness of Christ. Christ's sacrifice began when He took upon Him the form of a servant, and continued until He cried 'it is finished', and died. So the authors of the Litany seem to have believed when they wrote, 'By the mystery of thy holy Incarnation, by thy holy Nativity and Circumcision, by thy Baptism, Fasting and Temptation, Good Lord deliver us', as well as 'By thine agony and Bloody Sweat, by thy Cross and Passion . . . Good Lord deliver us'. Christ's work, like Christ's person, is a unity and His sacrifice is continuous. The living sacrifice is consummated in death. The meaning and fullness of the final sacrifice is revealed in the earthly life.

The writer to the Hebrews finds the necessity of the Incarnation in the work Christ came to do. 'For verily not of angels doth he take hold, but he taketh hold of the seed of Abraham. Wherefore it behoved him in all things to be made like unto his brethren, that he might be a merciful and faithful high priest in things pertaining to God, to make propitiation for the sins of the people' (ii. 16–17). Similarly, in x. 5 we read, 'When he cometh into the world he saith, Sacrifice and offering thou wouldst not, but a body thou hast prepared me'.

The writer does not discuss nor exclude the idea that the Incarnation might have taken place even if man had not sinned. We know how much the Incarnation has meant to the human race in revealing the ideal to which God wishes His sons to be conformed. We also know how by His Incarnation Christ has revealed the possibilities that are latent in human nature. He has shown that not only is there no antagonism between matter and spirit, but that human nature is capable of being a medium of divine revelation. God is willing to use our nature as a means of making Himself known in redeeming love.

But for the writer the Incarnation is the inevitable path to reconciliation or 'propitiation'. Man, as he knows him, is a sinner, and all latent possibilities must remain latent until the problem of sin is resolved. To present the example of the Perfect man without at the same time a Deliverer is only to mock us.

This raises the question of the way of deliverance. It is always the work of a priest to mediate and act on behalf of the people. As the prophet speaks to men on behalf of God, so the Priest speaks on behalf of men to God. But the value of his work depends on his own character. What if he too is a sinner? What if he has no moral standing in the presence of God? He cannot in himself or by his offering challenge men's consciences, or give them a sense of sin above his own, much less lead them in to God. Here the writer proceeds to show in Christ the ideal priest. He is of men but above men. He comes to His task in all points tempted like as we are, yet without sin. He is not ashamed to call us brethren, yet He is the only begotten Son. 'Every high priest taken from among men . . . is compassed about with infirmity, and by reason thereof is bound, as for the people, so also for himself, to offer for sins' (v. 1–3), but when we consider Jesus 'such a high priest became us, holy, guileless, undefiled, separated from sinners, and made higher than the heavens, who needeth not daily, like those high priests, to offer up sacrifices, first for his own sins, and then for the sins of the people: for this he did once for all, when he offered up himself' (vii. 26–7).

It is not our task to attempt to refute the charges brought against the moral perfection of Jesus. These, based on various grounds, are recurrent in every generation.[1] It is only necessary to say here that the writer to the Hebrews entertains no such thought. Christ's perfect manhood is equated by His divine nature so that this 'sinless root', this great High Priest advances to His work in all the

---

[1] cf. Dr. Lidgett's valuable chap. ii, pp. 23–32, in *The Spiritual Principle of the Atonement* (Epworth Press).

limitations of our human nature, yet so unique in inner harmony with God, in unclouded purity, that He acts vicariously, quickens men's consciences by His life, and purges their consciences by His death. What He was gave redeeming value to what He did.

The author further sets in contrast the sacrifice of Jesus and that offered by Jewish priests. The primary idea in sacrifice is self-giving to God of one's property, service, or person. The moral value of any sacrifice is determined by the measure in which the worshipper bestows himself. Sacrifice and offering that barely engage a thought from the giver, that are the overflow of wealth, or the unthinking concession to a usage, or a sop to satisfy a dishonoured deity, called down the maledictions of the great prophets.[1] Such sacrifices priests were continually required to offer, but with what moral results? 'The law having a shadow of the good things to come, and not the very image of the things, can never with those sacrifices which they offered year by year continually make the comers thereunto perfect. For then would they not have ceased to be offered. . . . For it is not possible that the blood of bulls and of goats should take away sin' (x. 1, 2, 4). The world waited for a conscious, voluntary, moral sacrifice of one whose sacrifice was a perfect fulfilment of the Father's will and whose offering was spirit and life even Himself. Or, as Peake put it, 'He offered no brute beast as His sacrifice, no irrational unconscious victim. He, God's eternal Son, was Himself the victim whom He offered, in

[1] e.g. Isaiah i; Amos.

loving sympathy for His brethren, in loyal obedience to the Father's will. The sacrifice of such a Person, offered in such a spirit, released the most potent spiritual energies'.[1]

So essentially personal and spiritual is this sacrifice that Rashdall denies there is any other meaning of an expiatory kind in Christ's death save that of a fully surrendered will. He says, 'Whenever the writer attempts anything like an explanation of the way in which Christ's blood has a redeeming or saving effect, he immediately becomes quite ethical, rational, and spiritual',[2] words with which we may agree. The essence of all sacrifice is the outpoured life, and only in Christ's do we find that in perfection. His was spiritual, holy, vicarious, complete, such a sacrifice as men had barely envisaged in the earlier so-called sacrifices in the Temple.

Another idea in Hebrews is worthy of attention —the atoning work continued by Christ in heaven. The writer considers that reconciliation is still required and can be accomplished in the world to come. The idea is Pauline. Christ must 'reconcile all things unto himself. . . . Whether they be things upon the earth or things in the heavens' (Colossians i. 20). Accordingly, when the writer to the Hebrews conceives of Christ's work, it is not as finished on the Cross. He falls back on his Platonic conceptions of a dual world and conceives of Christ in His risen personality passing through the veil of his flesh into the ideal sanctuary in heaven. It is

[1] *Hebrews*, p. 19 (Nelson).
[2] *The Idea of Atonement in Christian Theology*, p. 157 (Macmillan & Co.).

the true sanctuary made by God. The tabernacle of Moses and the temples of Solomon and Herod passed away. The things that can be shaken are removed that the things which cannot be shaken may remain. There in that true sanctuary, Christ as priest for ever, continues to pour Himself out an eternal sacrifice in Eternal Spirit on behalf of all rebellious forces in the universe and for us men and our salvation. 'Having then a great high priest, who hath passed through the heavens, Jesus the Son of God, let us hold fast our confession' (iv. 14). 'We have such a high priest, who sat down on the right hand of the throne of the Majesty in the heavens, a minister of the sanctuary and of the true tabernacle, which the Lord pitched and not man' (viii. 1, 2).

His ministry as priest on our behalf is unique. His understanding of men by His earthly experience is not lost. He has taken to heaven more than 'a human brow'. He has carried our humanity into God's presence and by His sympathy and full understanding of everything in men except sin, He is able to bestow on us mercy and grace to help us in time of need. 'None of us is a complete man; there are aspects of human feeling of which each of us is incapable. Our imagination too is restricted and with the best will in the world we find it difficult to share in the sorrows and trials even of those whom we love most. So it comes to pass that we cannot sympathize fully with our brethren, for every one of them has a weakness somewhere which does not apply to us, just as we have failings and difficulties which no other human spirit can

fully share.' Only One has been in all points tempted
like as we are and can enter into the struggle of the
human heart.

Lastly, as there is a perfect sanctuary, priest, and
sacrifice, so there is a better covenant. It is unnecessary to detail the account of the covenant
given by Moses once more.[1] It was set forth by
God through Moses and was assented to by the
people and sealed by blood sprinkled first God-ward
on the altar and then on the people. Even this
covenant was faulty. It indeed showed God's grace
in His willingness to be found under certain conditions, but it was extraneous, it failed to provide a
dynamic for high aspirations, it overlooked the
individual, and it could only meet man's religious
needs at a primitive and tribal stage of development.
Jeremiah under the emergence of individualism
and a keener sense of personal responsibility had
expressed discontent with it by saying, 'Behold,
the days come, saith the Lord, that I will make a
new covenant' (Jeremiah xxxi. 31–4). But even
Jeremiah's need remained unfulfilled until the
individual conscience was reached and cleansed by
the blood of Jesus. God's claims are deepened. His
terms are inward, piercing to the thoughts and
intents of the heart, but man's response now comes
from a redeemed personality, a reinforced will and a
heart filled with the Spirit of Christ. It is a new
covenant ratified by blood that cannot pass away.

These seem to be the leading ideas in this Epistle
bearing on the meaning of Christ's death. Dr.
A. B. Bruce thought that the entire teaching of the

---

[1] Exodus xxiv. 6–8.

Epistle might be regarded as a reply to three difficulties felt by Jews in accepting Christ. 'The superseding of an ancient divinely appointed religion by what appeared to be a novelty or an innovation.' 'The humiliation and sufferings of Jesus regarded as the Christ.' 'The absence from Christianity of a priesthood and sacrificial ritual.'[1] To these, we believe, the points we have just considered constitute an answer and they may again be expressed in the two words, *Christus Consummator*.

[1] *The Epistle to the Hebrews*, p. 11 (T. & T. Clark).

Chapter 9

THE DEATH OF CHRIST IN THE JOHANNINE WRITINGS

1. THE FOURTH GOSPEL.

BEFORE we can appreciate his views on our Lord's death, it is necessary first to get the perspective of the writer. This writer we shall continue to call John, without accepting the traditional view that he was the son of Zebedee. By almost general consent, it is agreed that this Gospel was not written earlier than the last decade of the first century. Some would bring it into the second century. It was written by one who reflected on the person and work of Christ as they had been tried and proved in Christian experience. For six or seven decades the Christian community had been learning the latent meaning and power of the gospel. It had changed some of its grounds of interpretation. The eagerly looked-for second advent of Christ had not been realized. The transplanting of the gospel out of a Jewish environment, social, intellectual, and religious, into a Hellenistic atmosphere had involved enormous readjustment of thought and interpretation.

In its march into new territories, where ancient, if somewhat decadent, religions existed, it had to

147

answer such questions as: What is the relation of the Christian message to other beliefs? Can it assimilate to itself anything that may be true in such systems and by the unerring Spirit of God eject anything that is only error? Has it a natural vigour that will prevent it, in contact with other faiths, from being lost in a syncretism or will it regulate and subsume all that is true without yielding to any? Or must the gospel stand apart from all religions and philosophies in a proud intolerance and isolation?

Again, is the Kingdom of Christ a thing of vaster consequence in the world order than was represented by the Christians of Judea, or even by St. Paul in his earlier letters? If the Jewish forms of thought and mode of religious interpretation are not only alien to the Hellenistic mind but also inadequate to give full expression to the content of Christian experience, must not some other religious categories be adopted to communicate to Gentile minds the full significance of Christ and His work?

These and kindred questions were agitating the minds of Christians in Ephesus, Corinth, and the towns of the Lycus Valley at the end of the first century, as they continue to agitate the minds of cultured Indian or Chinese Christians in the twentieth century. Unless this fact is kept in mind, the contrast between the presentation of the gospel in the Johannine writings and that in the Synoptic Gospels will present an insoluble problem. We must, as Dr. Garvie says, bear in mind in reading the Fourth Gospel the difference between the time *about* which and the time *in* which this Gospel was written. We must also distinguish between the gospel as a living organism that can flourish in any soil and the gospel as an exotic that can grow only under the local conditions of a particular country or race.

Coming to details, we can see that the Fourth Evangelist had at least three classes of people in mind whose prejudices he seeks to allay and whose faith in Christ he seeks to win. (*a*) First, there was a vigorous and hostile faction of Jews, towards whom he uses no soft words. (*b*) Next, he reasons indirectly with a sect composed of followers of John the Baptist. (*c*) Thirdly, some of the epistolary writings seem to suggest that ideas more fully developed by the second-century docetic gnostics were already making themselves felt. The allusions to these groups or classes will arise later in this study. Everything goes to sustain the view that the Gospel and Epistles were written in Ephesus. The evidence for this view must be sought elsewhere.

An additional word is needed for the sake of clarity on the difference between the aim of St. John and the Synoptic writers. Whereas the aim of the latter, particularly Mark, is, as we have seen, to provide facts for missionary propaganda about the life, death, and resurrection of Christ, and in so doing to restrict observation and reflection to a minimum, in the Fourth Gospel the record that in any way approaches to a 'life' of Christ is subordinated to interpretation. The writer almost overshadows the historic facts by their meanings. Such items of history as he uses become merely lenses in his stereoscope through which he sees eternal vistas and meanings.

Not Bethlehem, Nazareth, or even Calvary fill the background of his mind, but the eternal purpose of God and the white light of eternity. This contrast is not fanciful. While St. John handles historic incidents with reverence and at times deliberately corrects the Synoptic writers, yet his aim is not history, but the religious meaning Christ has given to history. Professor Bacon writes:[1] 'Interpreters have frequently employed a very appropriate analogy of Xenophon's descriptive *Memorabilia* of Socrates in comparison with the dialogues of Plato. In the form of introductory narrative, briefly describing significant scenes in the life of Socrates, followed by interlocutory discourse developing a given subject, Plato succeeded in conveying to the Greek-speaking world a conception of the inner sense and value of the great master's philosophy in his own apprehension.' The Synoptists, we may say, are our Xenophon and St. John is our Plato. All living truth is growing truth, and an interpreter, like an artist with his brush, may give us more of the eternal significance of the subject than the chronicler or historian, who merely gives a mechanical picture, so to speak, with his camera.

John's aim is to interpret the significance of the life, death, and resurrection of Christ as he sees them in the mellow rays of eventide and to transmit this to the people of Asia Minor. The opening words, 'In the beginning was the word', are integral

[1] *Hibbert Journal*, October, 1926, p. 116.

to the whole Gospel. He writes with the light of eternity falling across his shoulder. Christ's incarnation, sacrifice and death, are all seen *sub specie eternitatis*.

Of the evangelist himself it may be said that it was his to show, as no other New Testament writer does, the meaning of Christianity as life eternal in the Spirit. For him, as for St. Paul, manifestation of the Spirit of God, whether in prophets or in the nation or in Jesus Christ, is a *kenosis*, a humiliation; the medium, whether it be a phrase or a creed or a person, obscures as well as reveals, though it reveals as well as obscures. He that is sent is never as great as He that sent Him. Hence we come on such phrases as 'It is the spirit that quickeneth, the flesh profiteth nothing; the words that I speak unto you they are spirit and they are life' (vi. 63).

Unless we keep this mode of interpretation in mind, we shall miss St. John's approach to Christ's death. It is nothing material or external that gives it value, but instead the spiritual principle of a surrendered life. If he writes about the soldier piercing the side of Christ and that forthwith there flow water and blood, these suffice to stir his thought on spiritual renewal and reconciliation. Jew that he is, he had caught, nevertheless, something of the Platonic way of interpretation, only where Plato would put Ideas, St. John puts the Spirit of Jesus Christ.

One other word needs to be added. We shall do St. John less than justice if we represent him as eviscerating history of all significance. Indeed, it was this tendency he had to combat in Asia Minor. Just as modern science and philosophy cannot bear (to use the words of Dr. Gerhard Kittel) 'the scandal of particularity',[1] so neither could the Hellenistic mind easily brook it in the end of the first century. This was the cardinal weakness of docetic gnosticism. It had no feeling for the worth of history. Religion was offered as an escape from the ugliness of life, and life and its material conditions were a mortuary from which the soul should escape.

Not a trace of such doctrine is found in John. In his defiant affirmations that the Son of God is come in the flesh, as well as in his details concerning the Crucifixion, we find ourselves in the hands of a teacher who challenges a vague theosophy and asserts that it was part of Christ's mission to come by water and by blood. 'Every spirit which confesseth that Jesus is come in the flesh is of God, and every spirit which confesseth not Jesus is not of God' (1 John iv. 2–3).

We gather these introductory words to a close by quoting a paragraph[2] from Mr. G. H. C. Macgregor: 'If the Christian message was to live for a new age it must be reinterpreted in new terms. To understand Christ, it was necessary not only to know the actual facts of His life and teaching, but also to take into account the great religious movement to which those facts had given impulse. Hence, almost unconsciously, John alters the perspective of the earlier Gospels and, looking at Jesus

[1] *Mysterium Christi*, p. 31.
[2] *The Gospel of John*, p. xxvii. (Hodder & Stoughton.)

across the intervening years, reads into words and incidents the point of view of his own later age.'

What then are the leading ideas in these writings concerning the meaning of Christ's death? They may be summarized under four heads: (1) The general idea of sacrifice; (2) Christ's sacrifice as voluntary; (3) Christ's sacrifice as vicarious; and (4) Christ's sacrifice as creative.

(a) *Sacrifice*. Although recent writers have tended to regard this Gospel as primarily concerned with such ideas as the relation of God to man, essential mysticism, or Christianity in Platonic moulds, yet we miss much unless we catch the undertone of sacrifice throughout its pages. Sin is a stern reality. It leads, John teaches, to moral blindness and obstinacy; regeneration is a necessity; therefore to win an obstinate and unbelieving world and at the same time maintain perfect loyalty to the Father's will can only involve humiliation, suffering, and death for Jesus. Early in the Gospel this idea is introduced; not to mention phrases in the prologue such as 'the light shineth in the darkness and the darkness comprehended it not', or 'He came unto His own and His own received Him not', we find it in the allusion to the Baptist. John does not recount the story of the Baptist's martyrdom, but no one can miss the implication of these words: 'On the morrow he seeth Jesus coming unto him and saith, Behold the Lamb of God which taketh away the sin of the world.' We are not concerned here with the Baptist so much as with the ideas incorporated by the Evangelist in his Gospel. 'The idea of Christ as a lamb seems to be jointly derived from the sacrificial ritual and from the "servant" passage in Isaiah liii, and therefore includes the threefold idea of patient submission, vicarious suffering, and redemption from sin.' Christ, to destroy sin, must bear it. He will not overwhelm His enemies by violence, but save them by identification with their lives and by bearing their sins. It is an ethical redemption. The word *airein* (to bear) means not only to bear, but to bear away;[1] reconciliation will be in righteousness.

The same idea is developed in chap. x, with the additional truth that the motive of sacrifice is divine love. 'The good shepherd layeth down his life for the sheep; he that is a hireling and not a shepherd, whose own the sheep are not, beholdeth the wolf coming and leaveth the sheep, and fleeth, and the wolf snatcheth them and scattereth them. . . . I am the good shepherd' (vv. 11–14). Divine love is neither daunted by threats nor repulsed by enmity. Love impels Christ to lay aside not alone His garments, but even His incarnate self to rescue men who cannot save themselves. A hireling does not understand love, therefore he does not understand sacrifice. He expects his wages, while Jesus expects a cross.

The same general idea of sacrifice reaches its crucial expression in the somewhat difficult words in xi. 50. Caiaphas is distressed over the unreadiness and impotence of the Sanhedrin in presence of the raising of Lazarus and its influence on the multitude. Christ must be executed. 'Nor do ye take into account that it is expedient for you

---

[1] cf. Westcott, *in loco*, vol. i, p. 40.

that one man should die for the people, and that the whole nation perish not.' The explanation offered in the following verse (51) seems too prosaic and commonplace to be other than the work of a redactor. It quite misses the Evangelist's point. Caiaphas had spoken better than he knew. Saul is among the prophets; an eternal principle that life comes by sacrifice is here enunciated by a man who believes neither in angel nor spirit![1] It is a literary masterpiece to be set beside the evangelism of Pilate as he cries, '*Ecce homo*' (xix. 5). So in various other passages the same idea of redemptive sacrifice is set out and any exposition of this Gospel that overlooked this truth would be less than adequate.

(*b*) *Voluntary Sacrifice.* Another central idea that for various reasons tends to be obscured is the voluntariness of Christ's sacrifice. One of the reasons is the stress laid in some sentences on the Father's action in determining Christ's work. Over a dozen times we have such phrases as 'God . . . gave his only begotten son' (iii. 16); 'God sent his son' (iii. 17); 'he whom God sent' (iii. 34); 'the Father which sent me' (xx. 21). So much emphasis is laid on the Father as the determining source, anointing the Son for His task, that the co-operative activity of the Son and the unity of the Godhead are obscured. The impression left is that it was the Father's to command and the Son's simply to obey. The sovereignty of God overshadows His Fatherhood. Only a little examination is needed to show that this misrepresents the teaching of John. As

[1] cf. Howard, *The Fourth Gospel in Recent Criticism and Interpretation*, p. 189.

Dr. Vincent Taylor points out,[1] 'The Evangelist believes that the course of events, including death itself, lay entirely under the sovereign control of Jesus. Three times He speaks of His "hour" (vii. 30, viii. 20, xiii. 1), and twice he refers to Jesus as "signifying by what manner of death he should die" (xii. 33, xvii. 32). This point is of interest, because in the sayings ascribed to Him, Jesus is also represented as speaking of His "time" (vii. 6, 8) and of His "hour" (xii. 23, 27, xvii. 1)'. Throughout this Gospel Jesus is seen as master of His destiny. He chooses the time and place in which to give Himself up to fulfil His mission. If He was sent by the Father, He so completely accepts the Father's will that He acts as if it were His own. There is no tension between His will and the Father's, though the outworking of the divine will may mean 'strong crying and tears unto Him who was able to save Him'. Christ is the embodiment and revelation of all that moves within the Godhead. Strictly, we know nothing about God until He is revealed to us in Christ and His work. This entire unison between the Father and Son is expressed incidentally in chap. iv. Jesus catches a vision of a needy world ready to respond to the divine invitation as He talks to the Samaritan woman. 'In the meanwhile the disciples prayed him saying, Rabbi, eat. But he said unto them, I have meat to eat that ye know not of. . . . My meat is to do the will of him that sent me and to accomplish his work' (vv. 31, 32, 34). So completely and joyfully did He offer Himself to do the

[1] *Jesus and His Sacrifice*, p. 22 (Macmillan & Co.).

Father's will in the Father's love that it became a secret of His passion and strength. In this obedience to the divine will, the flame of love and fellowship burned ever higher. 'Therefore doth the Father love me because I lay down my life that I may take it again. No one took[1] it away from me, but I lay it down of myself. I have power to lay it down and I have power to take it again. This *commandment I received of* my Father' (x. 17–18).

Too frequently the words 'no one' have been referred to Herod or Pilate or some earthly enemy of Jesus. If this were all that is intended by the words, it would be a mere truism. Jesus only needed to avoid Jerusalem and no one would have taken His life from Him. It is an allusion, delicately expressed, to His harmony with the Father. He is under no constraint save that of a common love with the Father and a perfect acceptance of the Father's will.

Another expression of His voluntary surrender to His mission is found in the account of the feet-washing (xiii. 1–15). This is John's substitute for the institution of the Lord's Supper, unless chap. vi be intended to express the Evangelist's doctrine of sacramentalism. In spirit this event and that of the Lord's Supper are one. Macgregor thinks[2] we may explain the omission of the Supper 'by John's desire to detach his sacramental teaching from any

[1] N.B.—Read the aorist, *ēren*, 'took', which is followed by Westcott. He adds: 'The work of Christ, the Incarnate Son was, so to speak, already accomplished when He came. This work was imposed by no constraining power at first (took) but was to its last issue fulfilled by the free will of Christ Himself in harmony with the will of the Father' (*Gospel According to St. John*, vol. ii, p. 61).

[2] *The Gospel of John*, p. 273 (Hodder & Stoughton).

historical occasion and to attach it to the eternal realities of spirit'. As we saw, every symbol in the Supper stands for life through sacrifice. Here among a band of men, forceful in pressing their rights, stands one who as Master and Lord might pre-eminently assert His claim. 'Ye call me Teacher and Lord and ye say well, for so I am' (xiii. 13). Yet when supper is in progress He rises, puts on 'the apron of humility' and as the voluntary slave He washes their feet. The act is so gracious, so self-abasing, that its spirit consumes 'the filth of self and pride' in the self-seeking and assertive disciples. The deliberation with which the Lord rose from supper, laid aside His garment, took a towel and girded Himself, poured water into a basin, began to wash the disciples' feet and to wipe them with the towel, is so expressed in this series of sentences that it is worthy to stand beside the words already quoted: No one taketh my life from me. I have power to lay it down of myself.'

(c) *Vicarious Sacrifice*. But few words are required to indicate the fact that Christ's death is for others. Nowhere do we find any hint that the Cross was the scandal to the Evangelist that it was originally to Paul. But two points should be noted in this connexion. (1) The sin that requires atonement is not treated by John in the Hebraic, but rather in the Hellenistic sense. It is not conceived as moral failure, lawlessness, or transgression in the Pauline manner, but as life's great negation. It is darkness, blindness, falsehood, death. It is that ignorance of God that means death. This privative aspect of sin is so marked that it has led writers like

Reitzenstein and Bultmann to conclude that we have here a strong tincture of Persian or Mandaean dualism. Into this suggestion we cannot go, save to quote the words[1] of a prominent British scholar in a letter to Professor W. F. Howard: 'I feel that Reitzenstein and especially Professor Bultmann are on a wrong track and that the Fourth Gospel is not derived from Mandaism or pre-Mandaism.' (2) Nevertheless, the heinousness and alienating power of sin are never far from the Evangelist's thought. The Lamb of God is needed to bear them away and the Sin-bearer is made to say to His enemies concerning Himself, 'Which of you convicteth me of sin?' His work is always for others, and if He is lifted up from the earth He will draw all men unto Himself (xii. 32).

(*d*) *Creative Sacrifice*. The idea that death is the way to life is, of course, not peculiar to this Gospel or even to the New Testament. It is too obvious to escape the thought of men everywhere. Not only the grain of wheat must die in reproduction, but many sub-human creatures continue the species by actual death and people are alarmed still, and rightly, at the annual maternal death-roll. Every gift we enjoy, whether it be comfort from a cheerful fire, or food for our table, or personal and national liberties is purchased with some one's sweat and blood. *Mors janua vitae*. So in this Gospel the law of higher life through death is set out by a simple analogy. Every nobler form of being presupposes the loss of that which precedes it. The analogy in xii. 24, 25 is this: Except a grain of wheat fall into

[1] Howard, *The Fourth Gospel in Recent Criticism and Interpretation*, p. 25.

159

the earth and die, it abideth by itself alone, but if it die it beareth much fruit.

Here is a sharp contrast between the vitalizing and creative value of true sacrifice in which lesser values are surrendered for higher and ultimate values and the perverted, sadistic notion of suffering and renunciation as ends in themselves. This latter view besmeared pagan thought and found its way through un-Christianized thought into the Medieval Church. The worshippers of Baal cut themselves with lances. Gotama's renunciation was purely negative to end in a dreamless sleep, and the fanaticism of St. Simeon Stylites only showed the excesses to which blind emotion could carry men.[1] The expansion of the analogy in John xii. 24, 25, which is apparently taken from Mark, shows that one may make his choice and live on a low plane for lower ends or he can fling away his immediate rewards at great cost and, rising on his dead self, not only enter into life himself, but open the gate of life to others. As in the parallels in the Synoptists, the word for 'life' in each case is different. He that loveth his life (*psyche*—the temporal life) loseth it, and he that hateth his life (*psyche*) in this world shall keep it unto life (*zōe*) eternal.

'Eternal life' in John means a condition of the soul due to its obedient, believing relations with God. We shall find the same idea recurring in 1 John ii. 17. 'The world passeth away and the lust thereof, but he that doeth the will of God abideth for ever.' The idea of the grain also passing through

---

[1] See Inge, *Christian Ethics and Modern Problems*, chap. iii (Hodder & Stoughton).

gloom, corruption, and death to reassert itself in multiplicity of life is so vivid that nothing can be added when the thought is applied to suffering, gloom, and death in Jesus only to end in resurrection and eternal life. John regards the Cross as Christ's path to glory. 'The hour is come that the Son of Man should be glorified.' The harvest of His passion will be gathered. The inquiring Greeks are a kind of first-fruits, and if Christ be lifted up He will draw all men unto Him. Godet remarks that in these truths we have the condemnation of Jew and Greek. The Jews, ordained to be God's missionaries to the world, clung to self-interest and isolation and lost soul, home, and nationality. The Greeks were also condemned, 'for what was Greek civilization but human life cultivated from the view-point of enjoyment and withdrawn from the law of sacrifice'.

2. THE EPISTLES.

In the First Epistle we have an elaboration of some of the leading ideas in the Fourth Gospel and their application to the needs of the readers. Bennett[1] accounts for the emphasis on the Incarnation by the presence in Asia of docetic gnostics. But the death of Christ is also considered, and we shall confine ourselves to three points in this respect alone.

1. *The relation of Christ's death to the removal of sin.* It is true that he here refers to the sanctification of believers. 'If we walk in the light as he is in the light, we have fellowship one with another, and

---

[1] *General Epp.*, p. 82.

the blood of Jesus his Son cleanseth us from all sin' (i. 7). By the phrase, 'the blood of Jesus', we are to understand all that life of Jesus, in its total ministry, offered in healing, teaching, revealing, suffering, and finally outpoured in death for men. It is a convenient symbolic sentence but always representing a life fully devoted to God and the salvation of men. The relation of that death to sin in believers is effected by acceptance of the continuously revealed will of God. 'If we walk in the light' we walk in God. We share the purpose of Christ. We die to sin. We are cleansed in our desires. Further, this moral purity, and fellowship with God, carry with them a renewed social order. Men have 'fellowship one with another'.

In his exposition of these words, Denney[1] criticizes Westcott for distinguishing between 'the life Christ laid down' and 'His life liberated and made available for men', in his commentary on the Epistles of St. John. Denney refers to the idea as 'a strange caprice', 'a groundless fancy', &c., yet one is compelled on examination to agree, not with Denney, but with Westcott. By His act of dying, Christ did liberate and make available for men life in an altogether new and fuller way. It is a familiar fact among ourselves that the influence and power of a good man are multiplied a hundredfold by his death. All that was obscured by the idiosyncrasies in his personality is revealed. Men see the principles for which he stood and perchance suffered and have a new constraint to take up his fallen banner. But by His death Christ went much further; in His

[1] *The Death of Christ*, p. 272 (Hodder & Stoughton).

spirit He becomes available to all and can even come and abide in men.

2. *John's assertion of an objective element in Christ's death*. In ii. 2 and in iv. 10 he introduces the word 'propitiation'. but a variant from that used by St. Paul. It should provide us with the right clue to the meaning of the word if we remember the persistent emphasis in this Epistle on God's nature as love. That is the fundamental and ultimate essence of the divine nature. Findlay[1] distinguishes between the word propitiation (*hilasterion*) used by Paul and the word (*hilasmos*) used by John. '*Hilasterion* is the more concrete expression construed as accusative masculine—"a propitiatory person", "in a propitiatory character"; *hilasmos* the more abstract—"a means of propitiation", one in whom propitiation is realized.' It is the latter word that confronts us in this Epistle, and it means an agency or power that breaks down the barrier that sin interposes between God and man, enabling God again to enter into fellowship with him.[2] It is contended by writers like W. E. Wilson[3] that this propitiating agency has nothing to consider or act upon except man's stubborn will and sin. But the context of these quotations will not bear such a view. The propitiation is 'Jesus Christ the righteous'. If God is essentially love, that word has a vigorous ethical meaning. Love is seen only in purity, justice, and righteousness and until unrighteousness and sin are condemned and all moral

[1] *Fellowship in the Life Eternal*, p. 123.
[2] cf. Driver, *H.D.B.*, vol. iv, under 'Propitiation'.
[3] *The Problem of the Cross*, p. 160 (Jas. Clarke).

virtues are honoured in a perfect life, to proclaim forgiveness would only amount to an immoral amnesty. Salvation is the deliverance of men from every form of evil into the glorious liberty of the children of God. Christ upon His Cross breaks down the barrier of sin by condemning it, by resisting it unto blood, and by honouring the Father's will in His own perfect self-sacrifice. The propitiation is in holiness and righteousness. No question of placating the Father arises, but divine concern that forgiveness shall be ethical does arise. In the second passage (iv. 10) this assertion that 'all things are of God' is clearly made. God sends Christ into the world to embody before men what He wishes His sons to be. Such a mission would be costly, since men would not receive Him. Yet even the cost did not deter the Father or the Son. 'Herein is love, not that we loved God, but that he loved us and sent his Son to be the propitiation for our sins.' God is not the subject of propitiation, but there is that in God which must be recognized and honoured if forgiveness is to raise sinners into a life of righteousness.

3. In v. 6 there is an enigmatic passage about the manner in which Christ came to do His work, viz. 'by water and blood'. The sentence is written to protect believers from docetic error. This variety of gnostic doctrine admitted that Jesus came as a man to John's baptism, and there the Christ united with Him and remained in Him until the eve of the Crucifixion. Cerinthus (c. A.D. 100) held that the Christ could not be subjected to such shame and humiliation as Jesus suffered on the Cross. As to

Paul in his earlier years, so to Cerinthus the Cross was a scandal and incredible. John rejects the gnostic error and states that the Conqueror of the world came by blood as well as baptism. He sees the hallowing of pain and sorrow for others in the Cross. This seems more faithful to the context than the theory that John wished to emphasize the two sacraments of baptism and the Lord's Supper as Denney, Sir Edwyn Hoskins, and others seem to hold. There is little or nothing in the Second and Third Epistles of St. John that is apposite to our study. They contain practical counsels for problems in Church life.

Chapter 10

THE DEATH OF CHRIST IN THE PATRISTIC WRITERS

It is impossible to feel the full force of the argument in most of the patristic writers unless we see the position of those against whom they wrote, for the patristics are polemical as well as constructive. The common enemy was gnosticism, and the doctrines of many gnostics are so remote from our ways of thinking that an effort is required to assess them at their true value. Harnack describes the gnostics as the first theologians, and no doubt at systematic thought they aimed. One virtue their labours possessed: they forced the Church of the second century to think out the implications of the person and work of Christ.

Gnosticism traces its origin to Iranian dualism, and that, as is well known, is a dualistic interpretation of the universe. Two Eternal Beings are at work—one the God of light, life, joy who alone is pure spirit and the source of what is spiritual in man. The other is the demon of darkness, creator of matter, and source of all evil passions, disease, and death. Between these there is eternal conflict.

By the first century of our era, after passing through a variety of forms, this philosophy had united with various Eastern cults and fragments of

Jewish theology (which it had influenced at and after the exile 586–537 B.C.) and formed a syncretism. At first it was a spiritual movement, existing side by side with genuine Christianity as this gradually crystallized into the Old Catholic Church, and then it incorporated and used parts of the Christian message to further its own development. So much was originally in common between the two that this was easy. The early Christians took over much Old Testament doctrine and with it some Iranian ideas.

Gnosticism sought salvation and looked for a Saviour-God; it had a highly developed doctrine of demons from whom men needed deliverance; it was a religion of the spirit over against ritual and legalism. Many of the gnostics, like Marcion, hailed Paul as a heaven-sent Emancipator who repudiated the flesh, legal modes of deliverance and all forms of Jewish struggle towards righteousness.

It is when we come particularly to gnostic beliefs about matter that we touch the theme germane to our subject. The age-long question, Whence evil? had challenged the mind of the great Iranian thinker and all those who were in any sense his followers, and this is the gnostic's answer. Evil and matter are synonyms; life belongs to spirit, death to matter, 'to be carnally minded is death, to be spiritually minded is life and peace'. Since matter is alien to God and springs from another creative centre, God cannot under any circumstances come into contact with matter.

This notion strikes at the root of the Christian doctrine of incarnation. The good God cannot send his eternal son to be made flesh and so to come under the power of the Demiurge; this would mean the conquest of good by evil. By various subterfuges and ingenuous suggestions, the gnostics sought to relate the only-begotten Son to men as redeemer, such as the notion that He assumed only the appearance of a body, that He descended only on Mary's son at the Baptism and forsook Him on the eve of the Passion and so on. Into these we need not enter.

One point, however, requires attention. The Fathers were driven by the current cults and half-Christian beliefs to concentrate their thoughts on Christology rather than on atonement. Yet, as we shall see, soteriology enters, because once views on the person of Christ became clarified His redeeming work also came into view; Christology and redemption are bound together; the nature and value of the work of Christ are determined by what He is. If Christ was not genuinely human, then doubt is cast upon man's capacity to receive God or to enter into fellowship with Him. If there is no hallowing of humanity in Christ or consecrating of the social order, gnostic pessimism must settle upon the Church. This world is evil in its origin and irredeemable in its process. Human flesh is only worthy of contempt either through harsh asceticism or gross libertinism.

The spiritual man who attains to gnosis thinks himself as related to and part of the good God and Father of Jesus Christ, but this clog, this prison house of clay, this evil body he learns to regard as something to be despised; it is a body of humiliation, misery, disease and death. It would be impossible, thought the gnostic, for the Son of God to come in the flesh. It was against a background of thought such as this that the Fathers wrote, and their writings can only be understood over against it.

It will be impossible to examine every writer, but the most important seem to be Irenaeus, Tertullian, Origen, Athanasius, and the two Gregorys.

Irenaeus is the pioneer in a constructive reply to the docetic gnostics. Whether his mode of reasoning always appeals to us or not, he deserves the honours of a pioneer. Though he does not despise philosophy, yet he leans mostly on the authority of the New Testament writings. He uses their metaphors consciously as metaphors, a practice not maintained by all his successors. He begins his task with the question put by Anselm nine hundred years later, 'Why did God become man?' and proceeds to establish the necessity of the Incarnation. Unless the Incarnation had taken place, there could have been no atoning work. God alone has power to deliver men from sin, death, and the Devil. If it is impossible for God to become man, the whole question of salvation falls. The fact of history contradicts the gnostic theology; however the origin and nature of evil may be interpreted, 'the Word became flesh and dwelt among us'. 'That Word', Irenaeus continues, 'was made flesh in order that He might destroy death, and bring man to life, for we were tied and bound in sin and live under the dominion of death.'

When he passes to the manner of redemption, it must be admitted he too often carries analogies to the point of absurdity and falls into poetry rather than the language of theological science. Following Paul, he argues that as sin came by a man's act of disobedience, it was both appropriate and necessary that sin should be destroyed and life restored by a man. It was by the fruit of a tree that man fell into sin and death, so it is fitting that man should obtain salvation from a tree (the Cross); it was by a woman (Eve) that the misery began, so it is right that by a woman (Mary) the Redeemer should come; and so on.

But Irenaeus does not rest here. He seeks to express a truth that finds corroboration in the ever-growing complexity and interdependence of society, viz. the organic unity and solidarity of the human race. If it be a fact that 'the Word was made flesh', then the incarnate Son takes up into Himself the experiences of the human race. Each phase in man's long story is epitomized in Christ. The story of the temptation, the struggle between the flesh and the spirit, the sufferings in the struggle are subsumed, only with this difference that while the human race fell in the first assault and came under the dominion of the Devil, sin, and death, Jesus withstood the assault and returned victorious to God. Though we cannot press the words of Irenaeus into anything like complete consistency, yet he seems to have in mind some such summary of man's moral history in Christ as biologists find in the various embryonic phases of pre-natal life. He uses the word *anakephelaiōsis*, or recapitulation, to express his meaning. It is certainly vague and, worse still, he seems to regard words like 'renovation' and 'restoration' as synonyms. Yet he grappled with a profound truth.

Christ as man and within the limitations of man experienced temptation, but went forward and realized the goal of human nature. In Him we see the meaning of humanity, its possibilities, and its entire renovation. 'He became what we are that we might become what He is.' Beyond this Irenaeus did not go, but it may be pointed out here that some of his disciples carried this truth to the point of exaggeration and drew two illegitimate inferences. (1) That as man's sin is always attended with penalty, and since Christ took perfect human nature upon Him, so He mysteriously bore within Himself the penal sufferings of the entire human race. Irenaeus suggested the idea, but did not develop it. It stands condemned because it impugns the righteousness of God. If Christ suffered the penalty attaching to the sin of the human race, how then can God ask a second penalty from unbelievers? (2) The idea of man being raised to divinity or 'deification' also grew to a point of fanatical exaggeration, but this we may defer until we come to the writings of Origen.

So far we have seen in Irenaeus the emphasis on the necessity of incarnation and that any theory that denies it makes nonsense of Christ's redemption. We now note particularly how he develops the idea of redemption. Man is a slave under sin and death and the Devil; 'to whom we yield ourselves servants to obey, his servants we are to whom we obey'. Man has come under a definite relationship to the Devil, and Irenaeus recognizes that in any redemptive action the Devil must be taken into account. God can assert his omnipotence and coerce the Devil or He can persuade him (*secundum suadelam*). The latter method alone is worthy of a great and magnanimous God. Now, the argument leads us into deep waters and further away from the New Testament. The much-quoted passage in *Against Heresies* that contains the essence of the argument is this: 'He who is the Almighty Word and true man, reasonably [*rationabiliter*] redeeming us by His blood, gave Himself as a redemption for those who were led into captivity. And since [the Devil] unjustly ruled over us by an apostasy [i.e. by leading Adam to apostasize] and whereas we by nature belonged to Almighty God, alienated us contrary to nature, making us His own disciples, He the word of God, powerful in all things, and not failing in His own justice, behaved justly even as against the very apostasy; redeeming what was His own from that apostasy, not violently, inasmuch as that apostasy dominated over us from the beginning—not insatiably seizing on what was His own, but by way of persuasion, as it beseemed God to get what He wanted by persuasion, and not by employing violence; so that neither should the law of justice be violated nor the ancient creation of God perish.'[1]

Again, 'For if man who had been created by God that he should live, losing his life and injured by the serpent who had corrupted him, were not any

[1] v. 1.

more to return to life, but were wholly abandoned to death, God would have been conquered, and the wickedness of the serpent would have overcome the will of God. But since God is unconquered and magnanimous, He showed Himself magnanimous with a view to the reproof of man, and the probation of all, as we have already said: but through the second man He bound the strong and spoiled his vessels, and evacuated death by giving life to the man who had been subjected to death. For Adam was first made a vessel for his [the Devil's] possession, whom he both held under his power [that is to say he unjustly brought transgression upon him], and by pretending to offer him immortality, made him subject to death. For promising that they should be as gods, which it was not in his power to secure, he produced death in them: whence also he who had carried off man as a captive was justly recaptured by God: while man who had been led captive was loosed from the chains to which he had been condemned'.[1]

Again we find Irenaeus using phrases such as 'the magnanimity and persuasion of God towards the devil' that easily provoked the inference that the Devil had acquired a vested interest in man, and that God gave him compensation on winding up the estate. The Devil, however, pressed for too high a satisfaction by encompassing Christ's death and this in turn gave God a just opportunity to take away from Satan all rights and control over man. Here we are offered religious myth resting on a small foundation of Hebrew tradition and

[1] III. xxxii. 2.

interest flags as we try to follow the theory. In a passage quoted above, however, we learned that 'Christ gave himself a ransom for those who had been carried into captivity'. This thought is Marcan and not only carried weight in the primitive Church but, as the late David Smith pointed out, the conditions in the Roman Empire made the metaphor arresting. 'In the remoter regions unrest was still rife, and the disturbing forces were brigandage and rebellion. The mountains were infested by robbers who sallied forth from their fastnesses, and plundered travellers and held them to ransom; and there was ceaseless commotion among the subject tribes, and the victors demanded ransom as the price of their prisoners' release.'[1]

Let us look then more closely at what it was from which man was redeemed. It was not so much from the guilt of sins, such as figures so largely in Latin theology. There is relatively little about the forgiveness of sins in Irenaeus but much about the destruction of man's sinful nature, and the communication of new life. 'They that fear God and believe in the advent of His Son, and by faith establish their hearts in the spirit of God, are justly called men and spiritual and alive unto God, who have the spirit of the Father, who cleanses man, and exalts him to the life of God.' It is not personal pronouncement of divine forgiveness by a dishonoured God that we find, but rather the infusion of new life in the corrupt soul by the spirit of God. In another passage the personal relations, however, appear. 'Men', he says, 'were by nature

[1] *The Atonement*, pp. 61, 62.

sons of God, because they were created by Him, but according to their deeds they are not His sons. For as among men disobedient sons, disowned by their parents, are indeed sons according to nature, but in law have become alienated, since they are no longer the heirs of their natural parents, so with God, they who do not obey Him are disowned by Him and cease to be His sons.'[1]

Irenaeus continues to argue on this basis that as man and God are now enemies a *reconciliatio* is needed and shows that God Himself provides the reconciliation. 'He had pity on men, and flung back on the author of enmities the enmity by which he [the Devil] had purposed to make man an enemy to God; He took away His enmity against men and flung it back and cast it upon the serpent. So the scripture says: I will put enmity between thee and the serpent, and between thy seed and the seed of the woman; he shall bruise thy head, and thou shalt watch for his heel. This enmity the Lord recapitulated in Himself, being made man, born of a woman, and bruising the serpent's head.'[2] Christ redeemed man from bondage to a sinful nature and from a sense of alienation due to disobedience, but He also paid the ransom to the Devil by which man was set free from his thrall.

Irenaeus is concerned to emphasize the point against the gnostics that this concession to the Devil was not by way of divine justice but by magnanimity. The world and man belong to God. God is supreme and any authority the Devil has over men is due to the fact that he is a liar or deceiver, a

[1] *Heresies*, iv. 41, 2–3.　　　[2] *Heresies*, iv. 40, 3.

rebel and a tyrant. No trace of dualism is tolerated.
But what has the death of Christ to do with redemption from the Devil? This, that as reconciliation is
effected by the obedience of Christ in His entire
life, and consummated in His death, so the Resurrection and Ascension are the seal and sign to men
that through death Christ destroyed him that had
the power of death, that is the Devil, and delivered
all them who through fear of death were all their
lifetime subject to bondage.

'The Resurrection is for [Irenaeus] first of all the
manifestation of the decisive victory over the powers
of evil, which was won on the cross; it is also the
starting-point for the new dispensation, for the gift
of the Spirit, for the continuation of the work of
God in the souls of men, "for the unity and communion of God and man".'[1] 'The passion of Christ
brought us courage and power. The Lord, through
His passion, ascended on high, led captivity captive,
and gave gifts unto men, and gave power to them
that believe in Him to tread upon serpents and
scorpions and upon all the power of the enemy—
that is, the prince of the apostasy. The Lord
through His passion destroyed death, brought error
to an end, abolished corruption, banished ignorance,
manifested life, declared truth, and bestowed incorruption.'[2] The value of the Atonement then lies
in the obedience of Christ. The Incarnation is the
necessary condition. The Death is the degree of
perfection and the Resurrection and Ascension are
the seal of divine approval and authority.

[1] Aulén, *Christus Victor*, p. 48 (S.P.C.K.).
[2] *Heresies*, ii. 20–3.

Tertullian.

Dr. Glover reminds us that the popular mis-conception of Tertullian's character and work among English readers is due not a little to the caricature of him sketched by Gibbon and to a sonnet on 'the stern Tertullian' and 'the unpitying Phrygian Sect' by Matthew Arnold. That he was tempestuous at times and gave no quarter when certain Christian principles were at stake is true, but a little examination of the man and his work will reveal a great soul of rugged mould and a tender heart. His temperament, his age, and his opponents should never be forgotten when his work is considered. He is the Paul, the Luther, or Carlyle of his day—fierce yet gentle by turns.

Nowhere is his tenderness seen more fully than when he writes on the Incarnation and all that it means in the hallowing of human life—the hallow-ing of infancy, the sacredness of motherhood, the immanent intimacy of God in nature. One passage on the Incarnation, as paraphrased by Glover, in which he replies to the views of the gnostic Marcion must be quoted: He has described Marcion's contemptuous picture of Bethlehem and the Nativity and continues: 'Do you think nativity impossible or unsuitable for God? Declaim as you like on the ugliness of the circumstances; yet Christ did love men (born, if you like, just as you say); for man he descended, for man he preached, for man he lowered himself with every humiliation down to death, and the death of the cross, yes he loved him whom he redeemed at so high a price. And with man he loved man's nativity, even his flesh. The conversion of men to the worship of the true God, the rejection of error, the discipline of justice, of purity, of pity, of patience, of all innocence—these are not folly, and they are bound up with the truth of the gospel. Is it unworthy of God? "Spare the one hope of all the world, thou who wouldst do away with the disgrace of faith. Whatever is unworthy of God is all to my good." The Son of God also died. "It is credible because it is foolish. He was buried and rose again; it is certain because it is impossible." And how could all this be if his body were not true? "You bisect Christ with a lie. The *whole* of him was Truth." The gospel narrative from beginning to end implies that Christ's body was like ours—"he hungered under the devil, thirsted under the Samaritan woman, shed tears over Lazarus, was troubled at death (for the flesh, he said, is weak) last of all, he shed his blood". How could men have spat in a face radiant with celestial grandeur? Wait! Christ has not yet subdued his enemies that he may triumph with his friends.'[1] So far the Incarnation.

When we turn to his treatment of sin, we must bear in mind that Tertullian is a Latin lawyer, who brings the legal quality of his mind to sin and redemption. Rashdall seems to exaggerate when he says, 'Not merely the scheme of the atonement, but all the relations between God and man, put on the character of legal transactions'. This is hardly true, yet we may agree that Tertullian's pages bristle with phrases like 'debt', 'satisfaction',

---

[1] *The Conflict of Religions in the Early Roman Empire*, pp. 340–1 (Methuen & Co.).

'guilt', 'merit', 'compensation'.[1] God, for him, was undoubtedly a Lawgiver and Judge whose rewards and punishments were heaven and hell. The Christian was a military citizen who fought for the King and against the King's enemies. As Harnack says, Tertullian was called on 'to combat all gnostics, opportunists, and worldly minded clergy'. As for Paul, Luther, Calvin, Knox, the kingdom of heaven called for violence.

Two terms are commonly attributed to his pen— *vitium originis* and *satisfactio*. By original sin he means more than an inherited bias to evil. What he does mean is not very obvious. He uses Irenaeus' term 'recapitulation', only he stresses this rather in relation to Adam than to Christ. Men are so bound together by descent that the act of the first man and its consequent guilt are communicated to all Adam's posterity. Men share the guilt in the Fall; and secondly, from the same primal fall there has spread universal corruption.[2] Man's fall and guilt are the cause and condition of incarnation and sacrifice. Had there been no fall there would have been no incarnation. When Tertullian comes to explain the nature of atonement we meet the same disjointed utterances that we meet in all evangelical writings where exhortation and appeal, apologetic and warning take the place of system building. Sometimes he stresses the saving work of the Incarnation, sometimes the example of Christ, sometimes the instruction, sometimes the fulfilment of prophecy, sometimes the death.

[1] *The Idea of Atonement*, p. 249 (Macmillan & Co.).
[2] *Adv. Marcion*, vol. ii, p. 15.

We are justified in saying that he never separated the work of Christ prior to the Cross, and the death from each other. The 'satisfaction' rendered to God is, strangely enough, not made by Christ, but by the penitent believer. In his tract on Penitence he says: 'Thus they who through repentance for sins had begun to make satisfaction to the Lord will through another repentance of their repentance make satisfaction to the devil.' Again: 'For repentance is the price at which the Lord has determined to award pardon: He proposes the redemption of release from penalty at this compensating exchange of repentance.' Again: 'How absurd it is to leave the penance unperformed and yet expect forgiveness of sins!' [1] Tertullian so stresses separate virtues and obligations in isolation, because the moment so required it, that others who followed could quote him as maintaining contradictory beliefs. This tract on Penitence had its value when under persecution many lapsed and again sought to be restored, but Cyprian makes it a quoin in building a legalistic theory in Latin theology, and through Cyprian the way is prepared for Anselm's doctrine in the eleventh century.

In regard to man's bondage, Tertullian follows Irenaeus almost word for word, sometimes developing an idea or metaphor. By obedience to the Devil, man has become the Devil's property and is subject not only to the prince of devils but to all evil spirits and demons, too. The path of redemption was the converse of that of the Fall. As the Devil sowed the seeds of doubt and disobedience in Eve's mind so

---

[1] *Concerning Penitence.*

God sowed the new seed of His holy Son in Mary's body and destroyed sin.[1] From all this it will be seen that cogent reasoning or a comprehensive system resting on clear principles is not to be sought in Tertullian. He used the only mind he had, moulded by Stoic thought and Roman law; he contends earnestly for the faith as he sees it in a time of great peril, he emphasizes a strenuous morality which in his own person he carried to extreme lengths, but unconsciously he was moving away from the free grace of God in the Cross to a doctrine of personal merit that did great disservice to the purity of the gospel in following years.

[1] *De incarne Christi*, vol. xviii, p. 2.

Chapter 11

THE DEATH OF CHRIST IN THE PATRISTIC WRITERS (*continued*)

Origen.

In Origen we meet a man of spacious, masculine, adventurous mind. Harnack affirms that orthodox theology never advanced beyond the boundaries of his scheme. His conceptions of Christ and His work were related to God, the Devil, evil spirits, the sentient creation, and man. The tranquillity in the State during the early part of his life gave him opportunity and his innate passion for ordered thought induced him to toil unweariedly as a dogmatic theologian. The Neoplatonism of Plotinus and the daring speculations of the gnostics, especially the Valentinians, stirred his mind to great flights of speculative and constructive thought. He saw Christ, the creative Logos, as Lord of all and he claimed the fullness of Greek culture, Roman civilization, Jewish revelation and Christian experience for the Christian Church.

Barring St. Augustine, he was the greatest patristic theologian. But all his Christian dogmatics he rested on the Old and New Testament. He had no apprehension of historical development in God's self-revelation, held that salvation really consisted in a restoration of man to the original sinless condition of Adam and that every part of

Scripture is an inspired communication to man. This led him as it led Marcion and many another since into exegetical difficulties; but, just as Greek moralists had tried to escape from the moral crudities of Homer by the method of allegory, so Origen succeeded to his own satisfaction with the same instrument in the Old and New Testament. This makes some of his exegesis unreal to the modern student.

When we turn to his theology, we find that he first discusses the nature of revelation. Briefly stated, God has made Himself known in conscience, in the Law and the Prophets, and in the Incarnate Word: This self-manifestation will be perfected at the second advent, when the divine purpose in all its full redeeming scope will be revealed. Though we must refer to it later, Origen is a universalist; not only men, but angels, demons and the Devil himself will finally come under the sway of redeeming grace. This revelation of God in the second advent he calls the eternal gospel.

His finest work is done in his writings on the Incarnation, both in his commentaries and Homilies. What the light of conscience and the Law failed to do was done by the incarnate word. Man could not rise, but the Son could stoop. 'The Word and Wisdom of the Father assumed the form of a servant in order that by His obedience unto death He might teach the art of free obedience to those for whom there is no other road to blessedness. This is the fuller revelation of the gospel—a revelation adapted to the various needs of the different orders of rational creatures from the highest angel down to the lowest demon. To all men burdened with this corporeal nature the word has at length visibly appeared to bestow on them redemption and eternal blessedness according to the measure of their receptivity.'[1]

Origen's conception of the Person of this Redeemer would not satisfy strict trinitarians. He says the Logos is of the same nature as the Father, and though of 'distinct mind', is inferior to and created by the Father. This creation is eternal; though what was in Origen's mind when he combined this adjective and noun we do not know. Later writers tried to avoid the difficulty by substituting the word 'generation'—eternal generation. Rashdall says that at this stage Origen 'halts between Ditheism and Monotheism'. He was innocent of the demand for cosmic unity presented by modern science, and more under the animistic idea that a personal spirit can become incarnate than any one can be to-day.

He thinks, too, of the Logos as uniting Himself to all good men in all ages and nations, but Jesus is the supreme incarnation because His will is in entire surrender to the Logos. 'The Logos was united and made one with the soul of Jesus in a far higher degree than any other soul, seeing that He alone was able completely to receive the highest participation in the true Word and the true Wisdom and the true Righteousness.'[2] The only New Testament saying that comes near to this is in 2 Peter i. 4: 'Through these ye may become partakers of

[1] Fairweather, *Origen*, p. 179 (T. & T. Clark).
[2] *Contra Celsum*, vol. ii, p. 39.

the divine nature.' Origen seeks to explain the union between the Logos and the human soul of Jesus, but, as Harnack says, in so doing 'all conceivable heresies are touched upon but guarded by cautions'.[1] The human soul is the medium of union; it can assume a human body and it can receive God. As a piece of red-hot iron has heat residing in the iron and the iron in the heat, so the soul dwelt in the Logos and the Logos in the soul. But this holds true for redeemed sinners also who believe; they, too, can as cold metal receive the divine warmth and be raised to deification. Sometimes Origen writes of our Lord in such a way that His true humanity seems to have vanished; sometimes the Logos seems to him impersonal, at other times personal spirit. When He is personal, we find him toying with an unsatisfactory monotheletism. In his adventure we find him in spheres where only a humble agnosticism is fitting. His great merit is that he holds unequivocally to the human and the divine natures in One for whom he coined the name 'the God-man', but his great defect is in his interpretation of the Incarnation. As for most, the well was deep and he had nothing to draw with.

When we turn to his ideas about the mode of redemption, no doubt can remain. He says bluntly that the teaching and example of Jesus, because of their revealing power, are as significant in atonement as the death. The death only fulfils and perfects the life; it also fulfils prophecy, displays divine love, self-sacrifice, and humility. The Cross crystallizes in one act all that preceded it. As a

[1] *Outlines of Dogma*, p. 164.

modern writer puts it, so would Origen: 'The cross is the outcome of His deepest mind, of His prayer life. It is more like Him than anything else he ever did. It has in it more of Him.'[1]

On the man-ward side, Christ's death redeems by its moral influence. Sin is largely an intellectual difficulty. In his Commentary on Romans (v. 10), he writes: 'Not without cause did [St. Paul] say this: "*Reckon* ye yourselves to be dead unto sin" [*exestimate vos mortuos esse peccato*] which is better expressed in the Greek "*Reflect* that ye are dead unto sin" [*cogitate vos mortuos esse peccato*]. For the thing of which he speaks lies rather in thought and reason, since this sort of death must be understood to lie not in actual fact [*in effectu*] but in the region of thought. For he who reflects or reckons in his own mind that he is dead, does not sin: for example, if desire for a woman carries me away, or cupidity for silver or gold or land, and I put myself in mind that I am dead with Christ and think of that death, forthwith the desire is extinguished, and sin is put to flight.'[2] Knowledge of the love of Christ shed abroad in the heart, which will make one ready to die for Christ, and faith in Christ who died to sin are the double elements in salvation. (See on Romans v. 8.)

But there is also an objective aspect of Christ's death, and in a double sense. Despite what Rashdall has written to the contrary, it seems impossible to be faithful to Origen and represent him as denying a propitiative element in Christ's work. Origen

[1] Glover, *Jesus of History* (S.C.M. Press).
[2] See Rashdall, *The Idea of Atonement*, p. 265 (Macmillan & Co.).

does not say what it was in God that required propitiation—righteousness or honour or governmental authority or what—but on Romans iii. 23–25 he writes: Paul 'had something more sublime, and declares that God set Him forth a propitiation through faith in His blood, by which, indeed, *He would make God propitious to men* by the offering of His own body'. The same idea is repeated in his comments on John xiv, and in his Homily on Leviticus ix. It would have been gratifying if he had expounded the word 'propitiation', but he leaves us to guess his intention. Dr. Lidgett is justified in saying that Origen was less guarded than St. Paul in making God the object of propitiation.[1]

But if vagueness attaches to his exposition of 'propitiation' none attaches to his exposition of 'ransom'. As seen already, Origen regards the entire universe, visible and invisible, as interrelated and originally good. With the fall of the Devil and the Angels, a new problem arose. The Devil carries his warfare into the human family, and by subtle enticement draws man under his power. Origen will not agree with Irenaeus and Tertullian that the Devil possessed any acquired rights in men, so that Christ did not pay any account due to Satan.

Christ indeed was a 'ransom' in the sense that only by His surrender of Himself to Satan could He emancipate man and destroy both Satan and sin. Writing on Matthew xvi. 8,[2] Origen says: 'But to whom did He give His soul a ransom for many? Surely not to God. Could it be then to the evil

---

[1] See *Spiritual Principle of the Atonement*, p. 433 (Epworth Press).
[2] Tome iv, 27.

one? For he had us in his power, until the ransom for us should be given to him, even the life of Jesus since he [the Devil] had been deceived and led to suppose that he was capable of mastering that soul, and he did not see that to hold Him involved a trial of strength greater than he was equal to. Therefore also death, though he thought he had prevailed against Him, no longer lords it over Him. He having become free among the dead, and stronger than the power of death, and so much stronger than death, that all who will, amongst those who are mastered by death, may follow Him, death no longer prevailing against them. For every one who is with Jesus is unassailable by death.'

Without doubt, Origen uses the word 'ransom' here in the metaphorical sense in which the word is used to-day to indicate the costly sacrifice that must be made to liberate those who are in bondage to any curse; though there is small doubt that the Devil meant much more to Origen than a personification of evil.

The stress then is laid by Origen on man's deliverance from the Devil by the incarnation and death of Christ. But in concluding, it may be pointed out that in a very Platonic manner he reasons that man's character is made or unmade by his own acts. 'A soul in which dwells impiety, injustice, folly, luxury, and all the multitude of evils to which it has made itself the minister and slave—if this soul, returning to itself, again opens the door of its mind to piety and the virtues, will not piety entering in forthwith dethrone impiety?' (Comm. on Romans ii. 1). While Christ redeemed us from the dominion of Satan, yet we work out our own salvation by the practice of good works which destroy the evil.

Athanasius.

Athanasius is usually associated in public thought with Christology and not with the meaning of Christ's death. This is due to the part he played, mostly behind the scenes, at Nicaea. But no greater mistake could be made. It was his concern for redemption that made him so uncompromising a champion of the deity of our Lord. It is admitted that in intellectual calibre and constructive ability, his mind is far removed from that of Origen, but he had a gift unsurpassed to meet the crisis in theology in the fourth century.

His greatness, to use Harnack's phrase, 'consisted in reduction'. He had the discerning eye for the few central principles without which there could be no genuine Christianity. Abundance of ideas of second or third-rate importance prevailed, some scintillating with suggestion, but the profusion was bewildering rather than helpful. One has only to think of the variety of attempts to explain the Person of Christ to see how much the mind of the Church needed guidance. The action of Athanasius has been compared to that of ecclesiastical architects in the same century 'who, confronted by a number of models in ancient architecture, laid hold of one of them, the Basilica, and transmitted it alone to the Middle Ages'. The dignity, strength, and beauty of the Basilica became a governing model at a time of confusion. So in theology the conception of Christ and His work corresponded to the Basilica. 'Both were happy simplifications from a wealth of ideas—reductions which concealed full and varied contents.'[1]

The Arians and semi-Arians forced the issue and on two grounds—first, their optimism about the moral sufficiency of human nature, and, secondly, their conception of Christ. To the Arian He was an abnormality, neither God nor man. He came nearer to a Greek demi-god than to anything else. Though He was before all worlds and time yet He was created. There was when He was not. He is not coeval with the Father and He is not Creator.

As has frequently happened, these theories accompany each other. If man can become his deliverer, a humble estimate of Jesus often follows; if man is overcome by sin and moral paralysis, the distressed soul is concerned to know more about the possibilities in Christ Jesus. So it was at Nicaea. The Arians were shallow in thought and in experience. Athanasius takes a grave view of man's moral condition. God threatened sin with death. The stark reality of sin needs no proof. So also God's threatenings are not vain. The doom of death has fallen in part, but it must fall on sin, directly or indirectly, in full. For such distress, the 'creature' of Arius is not adequate. Only a divine Saviour, the Logos, could deliver. The nature of His sacrifice is determined by His person; hence Athanasius is greatly concerned to give full expression to the essential deity of our Redeemer. The diphthong (*homoousios* or *homoiousios*), which seemed such a trifle to Carlyle, meant life or death to Athanasius.

[1] Harnack, *History of Dogma*, vol. iii, p. 144.

His Christology may need to be overhauled to-day; yet he would be the first in such an attempt to say that if the eternal deity in flesh is kept before the eyes of a needy world the form is secondary. He conceived of the Logos as coming to earth and assuming the body of Jesus. A *psyche* Jesus had, but not a *pneuma*. In the place of the *pneuma*, or spirit, entered the Logos, and as such He took the place of our Lord's intellect.

These are his own words: 'For the Logos, knowing the corruption of men could not be undone unless at all costs there was a death, and it was not possible for the Word to die, being immortal and the Son of the Father, for this reason He takes to Himself the body that can die, so that this body participating in the Word who is above all, may become liable to death on behalf of all, and, on account of the indwelling word, may remain immortal, and that in future the corruption may cease in all by the grace of His resurrection. Whence, as a victim and a sacrifice free from all blemish, carrying unto death the body which He took unto Himself, He made death to disappear in all His likes by the offering of an equivalent. For the Word of God being above all, presenting His own temple and His bodily organ as an equivalent for the life of all, fittingly discharged the debt which was owing to death: and thus the incorruptible Son of God, dwelling with all through that which was like them, fittingly clothed all with incorruptibility in the promise of His resurrection.'[1]

We may lawfully conclude from these words that

[1] *The Incarnation*, vol. ix, p. 1.

the incarnate Logos met the penalty of death that attached by God's decree to human sin; that the value of this death as a penal substitute is sealed by the Resurrection—in rising again, our Lord triumphed over all the power of death; that having risen Christ leads believers in the grand return to God, and that by incarnation of the Logos a union of God and humanity is for ever established. Since Christ is united to humanity by incarnation, so all died in Him and all rise through Him.

Other points of a secondary nature in Athanasius' interpretation of Atonement are that forgiveness is manifested rather than conditioned by Christ's death. The great blessing on which he lays such stress as coming by the death of Christ is immortality or incorruption. Only the Logos who created man and bestowed on him the divine image could restore that image when lost. By incarnation, the Logos reinstated the divine image perfectly in the body of Jesus, and the gift of incorruption is evidenced by the Resurrection. In view of these points it is true to say of Athanasius, as of the Alexandrian theologians generally, that the Incarnation and the Resurrection receive more emphasis than the death. Propitiation scarcely appears, neither is there emphasis on law, guilt or forgiveness. Man by sin has lost fellowship with God, and Christ in His Resurrection life is able to bestow on believers the medicine of immortality.

Gregory of Nyssa.

Gregory of Nyssa, one of the four great Cappadocians, receives less respect for his treatment of the

Atonement than he deserves. The reason is this: He allowed himself to indulge in crude metaphors and, more serious still, as he developed his theme, especially in his *Oratio Catechetica Magna*, he hardened his metaphors into cold and literal prose. But, apart from this defect, his treatment of redemption is serious.

He conceives of the Godhead as triunity, and stresses this fact as essential to a full salvation. God is Creator, Redeemer, and Sanctifier. Only a Creator could restore a created one. No creature can rise above itself and become its own Saviour any more than water can rise above its own level. Gregory is emphatic that a man must be born from above. In this part of his theology it is evident that he has Arius in mind, and much of what he writes is identical with that in his older contemporary, Athanasius.

When he comes to the meaning of Christ's death, he follows the Greek tradition. Christ's death is a ransom; and here he wishes his words to be taken at their face value. Some one pays, some one is paid, and something is paid. The imagery in his mind is slavery. That institution provides him with his mode of interpretation. It is not the imagery of prisoners captured in war and held to ransom, but of slaves either born in slavery or sold into slavery. Sometimes, however, he speaks as if men by their eagerness for the pleasures of sin sold themselves to the Devil. He gave them the pleasures, but when the pleasures ceased the sinners had become his property. At other times he speaks of the Devil, by deceit, luring men to their doom by the pleasures of sin; and so strongly does he express this that man's moral responsibility is reduced to zero. Thus in his *Oratio* he says: 'For the Devil brought deceit for the destruction of [human] nature.'

The outline of his soteriology is this: God's essential goodness and wisdom move Him to seek to restore the sinner. Because all His attributes are perfect, what He purposes He can accomplish. Not even man's freedom can ultimately thwart God according to this optimist. The Scriptures, he declares, teach 'the complete annihilation of evil' and the Devil will come under influences that will lead him to repentance (*Oratio*, p. 26). But justice belongs to the being of God, and it would be unjust even in God to go to the owner of a slave, for which the owner paid good money, and by violence tear the slave away. It would be just, however, to pay fair compensation, a ransom fixed by the slave-owner.

This suggests that Satan deserves and is about to get his ransom price, but Gregory pauses to ask a far-reaching question. How did the Devil actually make man his slave? The answer to this will determine our understanding of God's approach. The naked fact is that Satan, as an ambitious, self-assertive, proud monarch, was restless until he ruled over creatures that belonged to God. Man may have played into his hands, but the cause of all evil, natural and moral, is the Devil, and the chief weapon in his armoury is deceit. He deceived the woman, and through her Adam by transgression fell.

The characters in the drama narrow down to

two—God and Satan. Man, the deluded, paralysed victim, scarcely comes into the scene. When the Devil is challenged to release the slaves, he puts up his price. Alone among the sons of men stands the wonder-working Jesus of Nazareth. Gregory enlarges on His unique influence, power, and miracles. The Devil recognizes a challenge to his authority in Jesus and so would accept Him as the ransom price, knowing full well that if he got Jesus under his control his supremacy over One so unique would enhance his prestige and glory. 'What would he have accepted in exchange for the thing which he held, but something higher and better, in the way of exchange, that thus, by an exchange of the less for the greater, he might foster his own special passion of pride' (*Oratio*, 22). To conquer One who could work such wonders would make Satan's name resound through earth and heaven.

At this stage Gregory, with real insight, dilates on the moral ignorance of Satan. Since only the pure in heart see God, it is plain that the Devil, sodden with pride and ambition, has no eyes to discern God even when He appears in Christ. He discerns only what is fleshly. He sees the man Jesus as one of the sons of men, even though a wonder-worker. This blindness to Christ's divinity is not God's act, but due to Satan's nature. God's goodness, wisdom, and justice are revealed and sustained in Christ's Incarnation; but, unable to see this, the Devil eagerly grasps at Christ, and God gives Him into Satan's power as the ransom for the Devil's slaves.

Here with great dramatic skill Gregory displays

what he does not hesitate to call the 'divine deceit' of the Devil. The latter made his bargain and believed he was gaining ascendancy over his only human rival, Jesus, but, instead, he found concealed beneath the flesh, the Immortal Son, the Fountain of Life, the Source of Immortality. 'For the Devil wrought deceit for the destruction of nature; but He who is at once righteous and good and wise used, for the salvation of that which was destroyed, *the invention of deceit*, benefiting by this means not only that which was destroyed but also him who had wrought the destruction against us' (*Oratio*, 26). God is seen by Gregory as the great Angler. Christ's deity is the barbed hook concealed from the wary Leviathan by the fleshly bait of Christ's humanity. 'In order to secure that the thing offered in exchange on our behalf might be the more easily accepted by him who demanded it, the Deity was hidden under the veil of our nature, that so, as is done by the greedy fish, the hook of Deity might be gulped down along with the bait of the flesh, and thus, life being introduced into the house of death, and light shining in darkness, that which is the contradictory of light and life might vanish away; for it is not in the nature of darkness to remain when light is present, or of death to exist when life is active' (*Oratio*, 24).

In all this, however, God had not acted unjustly. It is by the law of retribution that this just judgement falls on the Devil. He sowed the wind and reaped the whirlwind, though, as already seen, even the Devil's eyes may be opened and salvation may ensue.

Such in outline is the theology of the Cross in Gregory, but one or two general reflections may be made upon it. Quite unlike the Latin theologians, Gregory lays small emphasis on man and man's condition. The divine 'transaction' takes place almost over man's head and, while he is the beneficiary in God's saving act, it is done so much apart from man's concurrence or response as to become extraneous and mechanical. Christ's relation to mankind is not stressed and moral conditions come into a subordinate place.

Again, while Gregory stresses the freedom of the human will, he passes, by an easy optimism, to a belief in the restoration of all souls to God, without offering any solution of this perennial problem. He consciously or unconsciously reduces religion and ethics to naturalism. 'When in the course of long periods of time the evil of our nature, which now is mixed up with it and has grown with its growth, has been expelled, and when there has been a restoration of those who are now lying in sin to their primal state, a harmony of thanksgiving will arise from all Creation, as well from those who in the process of purgation have suffered chastisement as from those who need not any purgation at all' (*Oratio*, 26). Finally, in Gregory the emphasis falls on the Incarnation and the Resurrection, because, first, he wishes to stress the infusion of deity into human nature and, secondly, because he has no interest in the death of Christ as a sacrifice, oblation, or satisfaction for the sins of the world. 'The great service to Christian theology rendered by Gregory was to keep alive the Origenistic protest against the horrible eschatology which was already becoming dominant in the Western Church, and to reaffirm with even increased emphasis the fundamental truth that the only way in which sins can be forgiven is by the sinner being made really better.'[1]

Gregory Nazianzus.

This writer, who was also contemporary with Gregory of Nyssa, contributes one point only of sufficient concern to detain us, but a point of profound significance. He turns later thought away from the prevailing idea that Christ's death is part of a treaty with the Devil, and to some extent shakes theological confidence in the 'ransom' view of the Cross. He considers that the Devil is only a usurper and robber; and that God should enter into negotiations with him would be to imperil the moral character of God, and to admit that the Devil has acquired some kind of moral rights in man. This would shatter the supremacy of God and the righteous government of the universe. Nor, again, is Christ's death a ransom paid to God, inasmuch as men are not held as slaves by God, neither are they His captives held to ransom. When Abraham was about to make his great sacrifice on Moriah, says Gregory, God would not even let the blood of Isaac be shed as an offering to Him; much less does He require the blood of His Son. Christ came and died to reveal God as a man among men and to win men to Himself because of their understanding of Him.

[1] Rashdall, *The Atonement*, p. 308 (Macmillan & Co.).

A sentence from his *Theological Poems* will suffice to show the new path he was opening up: 'If any one asks to whom was the blood of God poured out? To the evil one? Alas! that the blood of Christ should be offered to the wicked one! If you say, To God? How should that be when it is to another that we are enslaved?' He then pays lip service to the ransom theory, but proceeds to restore its metaphorical meaning and to suggest that the redemption is from powers of evil latent in our own breasts. Lastly, he so stresses the manner in which Christ entered into man's fallen condition to become his deliverer that it is not too much to say that Gregory Nazianzus anticipated the modern theory of atonement by sympathy. It is also true to say that this diversion of thought from the imagery of slaves and slavery and from ransoms gave a restored spirituality and experimental reality to Christ's work, though the full outworking of it had to tarry for centuries.

Chapter 12

AUGUSTINE AND ANSELM

THE theology of St. Augustine is the outcome of his moral struggles and his spiritual pilgrimages. His sanguine temperament, his fiery passions, and his perverted will deeply influenced his interpretation of the work of Christ. Unlike the Eastern Fathers, he never appreciated the wonder of the Incarnation. He knew of the flesh as a base tyrant rather than as a medium of divine revelation. The flesh was the seat of sin, particularly that pervasive sin of concupiscence. Though he read and understood his Plato in a Latin translation, he remained unconvinced of the supremacy of reason. In the struggle with the flesh, he found that reason could only 'see and approve the better' but was impotent when the will, swayed by the passions, rose up in revolt.

The Incarnation took place not to enable man to see God's ideal and perfect design for men, but from the sheer necessity of man's need. 'If man had not erred the Son of God had not come.' This brings us to the first point to be borne in mind; there is no genuine consistency in Augustine's doctrine of atonement. At times he seeks the clue in his own struggles and deliverance. At times he looks wistfully to a sovereign law that should control the rebel

in his soul as Roman law ruled over rebels in the
State, and at times, with due deference to what was
thought and written about Christ's death in the
300 years preceding him, he falls back on the
Greek theory of ransom paid to the Devil. But if a
student compares the *Confessio* with the *De Trinitate*
he will note, what time has already shown, that the
fervour and conviction of the heart are revealed
in the former while the less moving results of a not
too-confident mind are found in the latter.

Augustine may be looked upon as a half-way house
between the Greek Fathers and Anselm. He is not
so confident about Satan and his conquest over and
rights in man as, say, Irenaeus. There is no doubt
he held to the reality of the Devil and his influence
over men, but the Devil and his angels were also
known in his own heart. Lust, envy, selfish ambition, and moral enslavement were part of a hierarchy about which he could have no doubt. When
it came to theology he was unable to reconstruct
a system that would express more clearly what he
felt. So we get the two volumes named, that on
the Trinity in which the ransom theory finds its
customary expression, and that on the struggles and
deliverance of his own heart which is deeper, more
universal, and consequently more treasured, in the
Confessions. In the *Confessions* deep calleth unto
deep.

The ransom theory of atonement did not remain
wholly unmodified in his writings. It had given
a regnancy to Satan that imperilled the supreme
sovereignty of God. Augustine's revised philosophy
led him to correct this. After floundering for years

in Manichaean philosophy, he rejected it root
and branch. No satisfactory interpretation of the
universe could be found that divided it equally
between the God of light and the demon of darkness.
'God is the one absolute substance, the *Summum Ens*,
the eternal ground of all created reality.' Account for
the principle of evil how we may, we are on surer
ground with Plato's unifying metaphysic than with
the dualism of the Persian Mani.

The Devil, Augustine argued, did not gain a
victory over man and take him captive. Man
sinned against a holy God, and God sentenced him
to punishment. The Devil was the lictor who
inflicted God's strokes on the sinner, but the Devil
had no more ownership in or dominion over man
than a jailer has over the prisoners under his
control. Men are God's creation, God's subjects,
and by redemption God's sons. But even the Devil
is entitled to a subordinate authority and can
demand a ransom. Augustine will not go so far as
to say that the Devil was an obedient jailer carrying
out the laws of God, but rather the Devil seized on
such power as came his way and asserted such
authority as he could.

It is in his treatment of the ransom paid that
Augustine shifts the emphasis from God the Father
to the Incarnate Son. It was as Son of Man that
Christ came and delivered men from Satan. 'The
Devil held our sins [i.e. as the ground of his
dominion over us] and through them deservedly
planted us in death. He, who had no sins of His own,
dismissed them, and yet was undeservedly conducted
by him to death. That blood was of so great worth

that no one clothed with Christ ought to be detained
in the eternal death which was his due by him, who,
even for a time, slew Christ with undeserved death.
What is therefore the justice wherewith the Devil
was conquered? What but the justice of Jesus
Christ? And how was he conquered? Because he
found nothing worthy of death in Him; yet slew
Him. And surely it was just that the debtors whom
he held should be dismissed free, on believing in
Him whom, without any debt incurred, he slew.
This is why we are said to be justified in Christ's
blood. The innocent blood was poured out for the
remission of our sins' (*De Trin.*, xiii, C. 14).

Put into less literal English, his argument is this:
By our submission to sin we voluntarily yielded
ourselves to the Devil, and to death. The eternal
Son came voluntarily as man and by triumphant
resistance to sin destroyed it, but not before the
Devil encompassed His death. Augustine also
introduces the metaphor of the mouse trap, Christ's
flesh being the bait, but the divinity being the
deadly spring that snapped on Satan. All who
unite themselves to the risen Christ share in His
victory over the Devil and sin, and so by His death
or innocent blood our sins are remitted. This
victory over the Devil was just. Satan assailed
Christ as a man but found that he was in conflict
with a powerful and righteous God. Augustine
leaves it to us to infer that if the Devil did not
discern the one with whom he had to do, that was
due to his own moral blindness, and God's justice
abides.

But Augustine regards Christ's sufferings as God's

punishment of sin, and he seeks to support this
view by saying that as sin entered the human race
vicariously so the penalty that God must attach to
sin can be borne vicariously by the second Adam.
Universal guilt he seeks to prove by the solidarity
of mankind. We were all in Adam's loins when he
sinned and show our origin by perpetuating his
sinful character and conduct. The destructive
power of Adam's sin, like a leprosy or cancer, has
consumed the original divine image in man. It
is gone. Man is totally corrupt, and unless he is
elected by the sovereign will of God to re-creating
grace and life eternal he remains dead and damned.
Because some show no sign of renewal while others
are transformed, Augustine is driven to the belief
that God in His own divine counsels determines to
draw some to Himself and to pass by others.

Augustine is not happy over this dark mystery
and seeks to vindicate the ways of God and the
character of God to men by saying that evil is
negative and that God is not the cause of any
positive misery or evil. His theodicy can hardly be
said to be satisfactory.

When we turn to his grounds of salvation, despite
what he has said about Christ's work in *De Trinitate*,
we are disappointed. The way of salvation is based
on sacramental mediation of grace in baptism and
the Lord's Supper. Grace or 'the divine influence
in the soul', as he describes it, becomes impercep-
tibly materialized and it is communicated by certain
mechanical acts.[1] It is first bestowed on the child's
soul in baptism—an unbaptized person is dead to

[1] cf. *De peccatorum meritis*, i. 19.

God and without hope—and it continues to be ministered at the altar. Since this resolves the work of Christ into the mystery of magic, we need pursue the inquiry no further.

Anselm.

By the eleventh century, thought and sentiment had undergone drastic change regarding Christ's work. Revolt had set in against the degrading idea that God, for any reason whatever, had entered into commerce with the Devil or that Christ had been deposited as the ransom for which Satan would set sinners free. The whole mythology of the Greek fathers lost its appeal. It was unscriptural, it was an abuse of metaphor, it belonged to a crude and primitive fancy, and, worst of all, it imperilled sound views about the unity, sovereignty, and moral character of God. Some hint of a nobler approach to the meaning of Christ's death is found in St. Augustine and that hint was seized and developed in a very remarkable classic, *Cur Deus Homo* (Why God became Man), by Anselm.

As a reverent son of the Church, this scholarly Italian, who was educated in Normandy and exercised his arch-episcopal functions in England, paid tribute to 'what has been said by the Holy Fathers on this subject'. But in his famous dialogue between Boso and himself he quickly shows how complete is the change in his approach to the meaning of Christ's sacrifice. His interlocutor is made to re-state in the clearest terms the interpretations of the Greek Fathers, and Anselm then proceeds to expose their weaknesses.

On one point we must enter a word of caution. Anselm never pretends he can unfold the meaning of the cross in terms of reason. Boso is his mouthpiece in saying, 'Just as the right order requires that we should believe the deep things of the Christian faith before we presume to discuss them by means of our reason; so exactly does it seem to me to be culpable carelessness, if after we are settled in the faith, we do not seek to understand that which we believe'.[1] The true order is *credo ut intelligam*. The Church promulgates the dogma, it is the task of Reason not to criticize, much less to refute it, but to understand it. It cannot be said that Anselm always quite succeeded in acting on his profession. He certainly moved forward from many views of his predecessors.

These facts must be borne in mind if we would understand his approach to the subject. Nowhere does he attain to the New Testament conception of God as Father, nor did the idea of the divine Father suffering to restore sinners once enter his mind. His experience as a boy in the home in Aosta left an abiding scar on his soul. While his devout mother 'used to talk to her child as mothers do about God', he had a father whose harshness drove him from his home and for ever perverted for him the true meaning of the word father. It suggested to him arbitrary domination, and a haughty sensitiveness to real or imaginary affronts. We do not overlook the fact that the Fatherhood of God had receded generally into the background of Christian thought,

[1] Bk. i, chap. ii.

but nothing in the character and conduct of Anselm's father tended to restore it.

A second determining factor was the prevailing influence and fashion of chivalry. In coarse and violent days, the emergence of orders of knights who vowed to 'do chivalry' towards all women, little children, the helpless, and the frail was much to be esteemed. But the blot on the escutcheon of chivalry was its puerile and petty sensitiveness about personal prestige, prerogatives and honour. To allow another to say an insulting word, to express contempt, or impugn one's integrity was to be less than a worm and no man. Every insult demanded satisfaction or else the one insulted lost caste in society.[1] Anselm spoke the language of his day and applied the conception to God. God, too, has a supreme majesty, prestige, and honour. 'I am the Lord, that is my name, and my glory I will not give to another' (Isaiah xlii. 8). And if God be insulted He would be less than deity if He did not demand satisfaction.

This dangerously anthropomorphic view of God determined Anselm's definition of sin. Ultimately sin is insult. 'To sin', he says, 'is nothing else but not to repay God one's debt. . . . Whoever renders not unto God this due honour takes away from God that which is His. . . . Nor is it enough only to repay what was abstracted, but he ought for the insult done to return more than he took. If one injures another's dignity, it is not sufficient that he rehabilitate that dignity unless he restore something

[1] David Smith cites the classic description in Scott's *Peveril of the Peak* chap. ix.

to give pleasure to the injured in proportion to the injury of the dishonour done. Each sinner ought to repay the honour of which he robbed God; and this is the satisfaction which every sinner ought to make to God.'[1]

Elsewhere he says: 'Nothing is less tolerable in the order of things than that a creature should rob his Creator of the honour due to Him and not repay Him that of which He robbed Him. . . . If nothing is more great or good than God, nothing can be more just than that which preserves His honour in the disposing of events, even the supreme justice which is nothing else than God Himself.'[2]

From this several points become clear. First, all future approach to the meaning of Christ's death will be with an increasingly God-ward reference. It is towards something in God, call it honour, justice, integrity, law, or what else. The meaning of atonement lies in man's relations to God and man's discharge of obligations to God. Heaven not Hell is the venue. Again the moulds of thought are taken from Anselm's study of Lombard law. At every point we hear the jargon of the court house. At one time he conceives of sin as a civil offence requiring civil damages that can be paid by the offender. At another as a criminal offence requiring sentence of death. Again, as with Dr. Dale last century, he is so concerned with justice or the fulfilment of the eternal laws of righteousness that he creates a kind of *alter deus* that must be recognized and satisfied, though he does say that the supreme justice

[1] Bk. i, chap. xi.　　[2] Bk. i, chap. xiii.

is nothing else than God Himself. Further, it is this stress on justice as the cardinal and fundamental quality in God, that tends to an artificial conflict between the attributes of God. Justice demands satisfaction; so mercy arises with gentle but earnest entreaty and pleads against justice on behalf of the sinner. Here abstract qualities are torn away from the perfect Personality of God, and gradually, as certain hymns of a pseudo-evangelistic type represent, God the Father is the guardian of justice and Jesus Christ represents eternal mercy.

The stress laid by Anselm on the satisfaction of God's honour is carried to a degree. That God should be robbed of His honour is impossible, it cannot be. Either the sinner offers freely what he owes to God or God will recover His honour in another way from an unwilling sinner. 'Either man of his own free will exhibits that subjection to God which is due from him, whether by not sinning or by making amends for his sin, or else God subjects him to Himself by tormenting him against his will and by this means shows Himself to be his Lord which the same refuses of his own will to acknowledge.'[1]

This brings Anselm to the work of Christ. The position is this: God's honour stands insulted by man. God's integrity requires action. Man acting conjointly with the Devil has stolen what belongs to God. Sin is now insulting theft. Man has no power even if he had the desire to restore to God that which he has stolen. He is destitute of the

[1] Bk. i, chap. xiv.

qualities most prized of God, justice and obedience.
Only One who is more than man can repay man's
debt. He must be divine. Yet no deity or arch-
angel can pay man's debt. It must be paid by man,
the debtor.

On the ground of this moral necessity, Anselm,
in bk. ii, chaps. v–vii, shows the importance of the
Incarnation. In some manner God must come to
the rescue and help man to pay his debt. The
eternal Son becomes man and as man fulfils all
His own obligation to God. But God's abundant
munificence must make recompense to His well-
beloved and perfect Son. What can God give Him?
Already Jesus says, 'All that the Father hath is
mine'. Direct recompense cannot be made, but it
can be made indirectly. Here emerges that doctrine
of merit that has played, be it said with all plainness,
such a pernicious part in both Roman and Protestant theology. The recompense which Christ
merited but could not receive, having all things,
can now be transferred to sinners. Boso says,
'Certainly I take it to be just and necessary that
any one to whom the Son might wish to give should
be recompensed by the Father; since both the
Son may give what is His own, and the Father can
only repay to another what He owes'. To which
Anselm replies, 'To whom could He more fitly
assign the fruit of, and recompense for, His death
than to those for whose salvation . . . He made
Himself man, and to whom (as is said) He in dying
gave the example of dying for righteousness' sake?
In vain, however, would they be imitators of Him
if they were not sharers in His merits. Or whom

could He more justly make heirs of a debt due to Him of which He Himself had no need, and of the overflowings of His fullness than His kindred and His brethren, whom He sees burdened with so many and great debts and wasting away in the depths of misery; that what they owe for their sins may be remitted to them, and what on account of their sins they are in need of may be given them?'[1]

This is the core of Anselm's thought on Christ's work. On the positive side it reasserts the majesty and holiness of God. He is God alone, and God over all, blessed for ever. No conception of forgiveness that disregards the moral integrity of God is sound. God's redemption of sinners is rooted in righteousness, and the social consequences of the Cross can only be righteous when this view is upheld. We imperil society when we lose a sense of the holiness and righteousness of God. The Christian Church can never forget Anselm's contribution to this great truth. The defects in his teaching are his misinterpretation of God by thinking of Him in terms of a medieval baron who is over-concerned with his own prestige. Indeed, in bk. i, chap. vii, he appeals to the *lex talionis* as the ground on which God may advance to smite the sinner who has insulted Him. Obviously thought here has got away from Him 'who, when he was reviled, reviled not again; when he suffered, threatened not; but committed himself to him that judgeth righteously' (1 Peter ii. 23).

And finally as Dean Rashdall pointed out,

[1] Bk. ii, chap. xix.

Anselm, following 'a bastard Platonism', tended to make abstract ideas into concrete entities. He speaks of Christ's work for 'humanity' and the transfer of Christ's merit to 'humanity', as if 'humanity' or 'human nature' had an existence apart from individuals. Similarly, he speaks of God's justice and honour requiring to be satisfied, as if there were something other than God our Father who acts with a justice and glory worthy of His own nature. The personal relations between God and sinners are obscured, if not ignored. As to the imputing of Christ's merit or righteousness to sinners, a point made much of by the early reformers, it needs to be considered with caution. It can easily cut the nerve of all effort to enter into an experimental righteousness. Atonement becomes a commercial transaction in which bankrupt sinners have lodged to their credit the superabundant wealth of Christ's merit, or the recompense paid to Him by the Father.

But when the speculative idea of transferring merit from the holy to the unholy entered the Church, we know that it developed into the idea of transferring the merits of saints, due to works of supererogation, to sinners. There is a further sense in which by repentance and faith a mystical union is established between the believer and Christ and men become members of His spiritual body. Then, in the wealth of character, 'Jesus and all in Him is mine'. But Anselm never developed this idea; and resting on his theological presentation of merit many a man since the eleventh century has sheltered himself without any moral effort behind the statement, 'I plead only the merit of Christ'. We are, however, under heavy obligation to Anselm for raising the work of Christ into its noble relation to God.

Chapter 13

THE MORAL INFLUENCE SCHOOL

Abailard.

THE theological works of Abailard are not extensive. Unfortunately one of his more valuable writings, *An Introduction to Theology*, has perished; but we have his *Commentary on Romans*, in which we see much of his teaching on the Cross. His main task lay in the realm of ethics. In a volume, *Scito te ipsum*, he comes to the question of sin and forgiveness. Out of his ethical problem arises a theological problem and it is this that brings him within our purview.

Is or is not God free to forgive a sinner? Is there any other factor such as Satan, or divine honour, or law, or justice that must first be considered and satisfied before God can forgive and bring the sinner into fellowship with Himself? Abailard's answer is 'None'. All mediators, substitutes, and deliverers are due to the ingenious activities of men's minds. These thoughts had been incubating in his mind for years as a student, but they emerged fully developed by a particular circumstance. He was forty-six years younger than the great Anselm, so he came to Laon to attend Anselm's lectures. Anselm was a Platonic realist. Every class-name or 'universal' represented an eternal reality from which each 'particular' drew its meaning. Over against all particular men is yonder the eternal archetype, man; class-names represent realities. Abailard was a nominalist and he held that class-names or universals are only convenient abstractions for purposes of thought, a sort of counters in conversation or writing. Apart from particular men there is no abstract 'humanity', just as apart from particular righteous men there is no abstract righteousness.

As we have seen, Anselm based much of his argument about the work of Christ on what He had done for humanity. Christ had rendered satisfaction to God on behalf of humanity. In the lecture-room Abailard the student challenged Anselm the lecturer as to what this abstraction 'mankind' or 'humanity' meant and, driving home his nominalist shafts with great force, he shook the lecturer, drew many of the students away from him and opened a rival school at St. Genevieve. Shortly after he was appointed to the chair at Notre-Dame. Abailard held to the ground that all questions of sin and forgiveness are purely personal. On the human side, it is a question of repentance and a turning of the heart and life to a pardoning God. The gospel is simple and must be cleared of all the cumbrous machinery of the realists.

Wherein, then, lies the meaning of the work of Christ? In this: That something is required to stimulate the guilty sinner and rouse him to a sense of sin. St. Paul said, 'By the Law is the knowledge of sin', but Abailard said, 'By Christ is the knowledge of sin'. It is only as men see the perfect that they repent of the imperfect; as they see eternal love, that they turn away from sin to God.

Consequently Abailard shifts the emphasis from the death on the Cross to the full revelation of divine love in the Incarnation, in the infancy, youth, manhood, word, and deed of Jesus. We are saved by the knowledge of eternal love in Christ Jesus. The Cross is only the utmost consummation of that love. 'I think', he says therefore, 'that the purpose and cause of the Incarnation was that He might illuminate the world by His wisdom and excite it to the full love of Himself.'

In his *Commentary on Romans* he says: 'We are justified and reconciled to God, because by the singular grace which God has manifested to us in giving us His Son, who assumed our nature, and, having become man, persevered even unto death in instructing us by His teaching and example, God has more closely attached us to Himself by the bonds of love, and because true charity, fired by such a gift of God's grace, cannot shrink from any suffering for His sake.'[1]

Again, speaking of Christ's death as a ransom, he says: 'How cruel and unjust it appears that any one should have demanded the blood of the innocent as any kind of ransom, or have been in any way delighted with the death of the innocent, let alone that God should have found the death of His son so acceptable, that through it He should have been reconciled to the whole world.' 'It seems to us, however, that we are justified by the blood of Christ

[1] Quoted from Dale, *Atonement*, p. 285 (21st Edn.; Independent Press).

and reconciled to God in the following way. His Son took our nature and *persevered in instructing us both in word and deed even unto death*. This was the singular grace shown us, through which He more abundantly bound us to Himself by love; so that, set on fire as we are by so great a benefit from the Divine grace, true charity should fear nothing at all.'

He continues the same argument in various forms, but the essence of the matter is that love kindles love, while fear begets fear and distrust. 'Every man is also made juster, that is to say becomes more loving to the Lord, after the Passion of Christ than he was before, because a benefit actually received kindles the soul into love more than one merely hoped for. Our redemption, therefore, is that supreme love of Christ shown to us by His passion which not only frees us from slavery to sin, but acquires for us the true liberty of the sons of God, so that we fulfil all things not so much from fear as from love of Him who exhibited so great favour towards us, that favour than which, as He Himself attests, none greater can be found. "Greater love", He says, "hath no man than this, that he lay down his life for his friends."' God is a free, loving Person who seeks to restore sinners into fellowship with Himself. His laws and honour are not His first concern, but sinners. Towards them in Christ Jesus, He displays a love that melts the frozen hearts of men, and kindles instead a fire of ascending love in their souls.

Abailard's interpretation was soon attacked. Bernard of Clairvaux could write very tender hymns, but the author of *Jesu dulcis memoria* vehemently championed the cause of Anselmic orthodoxy and, at the Council of Sen in 1141, accused Abailard of Pelagianism. Pelagius at the beginning of the fifth century was so repelled by the low morality of the monks in Rome, and even more by their feeble apology about the 'weakness of human nature', that he adopted as his maxim, 'If I ought, I can'. He stresses, perhaps over-stresses, the moral resources of human nature. 'The body must not be crushed, but governed' was another of his ethical maxims. All this tended to throw less stress on the depravity of human nature, and the work of Christ, and more on a humanistic optimism about self-recovery.

Bernard's Christology was centred on the Christ suffering on the Cross. Abailard kept his eye on man's response to divine love, as seen in the man Christ Jesus. It was a question of emphasis rather than denial, and Abailard was not a Pelagian. His treatment of man is too slight to know how far he differed from Augustine and leaned towards Pelagius. His significant contribution to soteriology is the immediacy of God's saving relation to sinners and the response awakened in men's hearts by the visible demonstration of divine love; in John's words, 'We love because he first loved us'.

Besides the charge of Pelagianism, Abailard was also accused of making the Atonement wholly a subjective matter. Before concluding this brief survey, it is interesting to note how greatly Abailard's views have come into favour during the present century. The trend of interpretation is largely along his path. It is increasingly felt that man is the problem and not God or divine justice or law. In his Bampton Lectures for 1915, the late Dr. Rashdall found himself in a congenial atmosphere in expounding Abailard; and, in an appreciation of Abailard's mode of approach to the death of Christ, concludes with these words: 'To see a living and permanent meaning in the doctrine of the Atonement, it is not necessary for us to enter into elaborate or *a priori* reasons for the death of Christ. It is enough to recognize that that death came to Him in the discharge of His Messianic task, and that He faced it from the motive which inspired His whole life—love to His Father and to His brethren. That is enough to enable us to say with Abailard that the death of Christ upon the Cross was an essential part of the Incarnation, "the purpose and cause of which was that He might illuminate the world by His wisdom and excite it to the love of Himself".'

But probably the most conspicuous living champion of the position taken by Abailard is Dr. R. S. Franks. Both in his *magnum opus*, *A History of the Doctrine of the Work of Christ*, and in his Dale Lectures,[1] *The Atonement*, he espouses this view. In the latter volume he rejects the description of Abailard's theory as subjective. 'It would be more correct to speak of the experiential theory; since the term "experience" implies both object and subject and the relation between them.'[2] It is not our duty here to go into this interesting and illuminating development of Abailard's views at this stage. It is enough to note that after men had sought the rationale of

[1] 1933 (Oxford University Press). [2] *The Atonement*, p. 4.

the Cross in deliverance from Satan, next in deliverance from an angry God, Abailard said, Why not seek the clue to the meaning in the effects on man? If we come to understand anything by what it can do, why not find the meaning of Christ's death in its effect on sinners? 'God commendeth His own love toward us, in that, while we were yet sinners, Christ died for us' (Romans v. 8). Since Wesley and Schleiermacher, since the inauguration of the new psychology and the stress upon experience, the path opened by Abailard has become increasingly popular. We shall consider three representative writers, viz. Schleiermacher, Maurice, and Bushnell.

Schleiermacher.

Schleiermacher's name must be included in the list of those who interpreted Christ's work in terms of its influence on man. His theology is grounded in his philosophy. The former is treated in *The Christian Faith* and the latter in *The Addresses*. He began his labours by a sharp attack on the prevalent rationalism that had invaded both Lutheran and Calvinistic theology after the first rapture of the Reformation had passed away—the period of Protestant Scholasticism. Rationalism put a part for the whole and, as Kant pointed out, it expected the intellect to pierce realms of reality too far beyond its ken. Reason with its 'dry thinking' was supposed to provide the soul with all its necessary aliment, mostly served as 'a mess of metaphysical and ethical crumbs'. Upon all this he heaps contempt. 'You are, without doubt, familiar with the history of human follies, and have run through the different fabrications of religion, from the meaningless fables of savage nations to the most refined Deism, from the raw superstition of our own folk to the badly compacted fragments of metaphysics and ethics which they call rational Christianity and you have found them without rhyme and reason.'[1]

Because the intellect skirmishes over a part of personality and fails to reach truth, we have credal differences and dogmatic controversies, wars over shadows. Man's deepest longing is to effect a union between the universal and the individual life, between universal and individual reason. His contemporary, Schopenhauer, sought to find this deeper synthesis in the will. This also, for reasons into which we need not go, Schleiermacher rejected.

Where then can that contact with eternal reality be found which we call religion? In human feeling. The secrets of the universe are revealed in feeling. It is the grand medium of revelation. Here religion abides and reigns in its own right. 'If only man's sense for the profoundest depths of his own nature is not crushed out . . . religion would, after its own fashion, infallibly be developed.'[2] These profoundest depths are below cognition, volition and feeling. They belong to the elemental stuff of our nature where God and man meet. He writes: 'But in order that you may understand what I mean by this unity and difference of religion, science, and art we shall endeavour to descend into the inmost sanctuary of life. There alone you discover the

[1] Chapman, *An Introduction to Schleiermacher*, p. 59 (Epworth Press).
[2] Addresses, p. 144.

original relation of intuition and feeling from which alone this identity and difference is to be understood. But I must direct you to your own selves. You must apprehend a living movement. What you are to notice is the rise of your consciousness and not to reflect on something already there.'

This leads him elsewhere to define religion: 'The contemplation of the pious is the immediate consciousness of the universal existence of all finite things in and through the Infinite and of all temporal things in and through the Eternal. Religion is to seek this and find it in all that lives and moves, in all growth and change, in all doing and suffering. It is to have life and to know life in immediate feeling, only as such an existence in the Infinite and Eternal. It is a life in the infinite nature of the whole, in the One and in the All, in God, having and possessing all things in God, and God in All.'[1]

It will strike the most casual reader that we are here on the verge of pantheism. The ground work of religion is to be sought by psychological introspection, by inward and downward glances. In 'the inmost sanctuary of life' we must discern that infinite universal spirit or absolute, revealing itself in each particular, and each particular is to be seen in and through that universal spirit. There we do not know, but feel reality in a mystical union. At once we breathe the air of nineteenth-century Romanticism, of Goethe and Schiller, of Wordsworth and Scott. The edge of rational criticism is

---

[1] Oman, *Schleiermacher on Religion*, p. 36 (Kegan Paul, Trench, Trübner & Co.).

turned, divine revelation is not regarded seriously, and salvation must come from the states of a man's own consciousness. Attempts have been made to represent 'feeling' in Schleiermacher's writings as if it meant nothing more than the emotion that accompanies the exercise of faith in the living God, and probably sentences could be culled from his writings that would support this view. But, to quote the late Professor Mackintosh,[1] 'The crucial question: Is feeling for him merely a subjective state, or is it the emotionally coloured apprehension nominally called faith, grasping a self-revealed God? cannot be answered with any degree of assurance. To the end his language is equivocal'.

What part, then, can Christ and His work be found to play in Schleiermacher's system? Though he leaves us with a depersonalized God and turns prayer into a 'bathing of our spirits in the world spirit', yet with some inconsistency he proceeds to speak of the way in which God communicates with men in great personalities. Here the Moravian pietist breaks away from the pantheistic philosopher and speaks the more orthodox language of Canaan.[2]

To him Jesus of Nazareth is everything. He writes: 'When in the mutilated delineations of His life, I contemplate the sacred image of Him who has been the author of the noblest that there has yet been in religion, it is not the purity of His moral teaching, which but expressed what all men who have come to consciousness of their spiritual

---

[1] *Types of Modern Theology*, p. 95 (Nisbet & Co.).
[2] Oman, p. 246.

nature have with Him in common . . . that I admire;
and it is not the individuality of His character, the
close union of high power with touching gentleness,
for every noble, simple spirit must in a special
situation display some traces of a great character.
All those elements are merely human. But the truly
divine element is the glorious clearness to which
the great idea He came to exhibit attained in His
soul. This idea was, that all that is finite requires a
higher mediation to be in accord with the Deity,
and that for man under the power of the finite
and particular, and too ready to imagine the divine
itself in this form, salvation is only to be found in
redemption.'

It is clear that Schleiermacher's conception of
redemption is Johannine rather than Pauline. Sin
is privative rather than positive. It is due to man's
finitude rather than to personal transgression.
Indeed, it would be difficult to graft Schleiermacher's shoot on St. Paul's doctrine. Human
weakness and ignorance he recognizes as clearly as
Socrates, but he is strangely lacking in the Hebraic
conception of moral responsibility to the living and
true God, of guilt and forgiveness, of the necessity
for a divine initiative to remove that guilt. Sin
seems to mean the unsubdued animal nature, 'the
unspiritualized brute' or a profound discontent in
man because his ideals are negatived by his mortal
limitations.

Christ's redemption consists in leading men out
of the darkness and unreality of the cave of nature
into the light of Deity. 'As Saviour, our Lord has
on men two kinds of effect. In the first place, He

takes up the sinful into the power of His God-consciousness, sharing with them its triumphant energies; this is His redeeming work. Thereby, secondly, He takes them up into the fellowship of His blessedness, so freeing them from the unblest load of estrangement and guilt: this is His work of reconciliation.'[1]

It is also symptomatic of the philosophical trend of his thought that he appreciates the idea in the Epistle to the Hebrews of atonement by sympathy. Christ enters into men's lives 'as the most highly endowed of all the interpreters of Deity' and by sympathy with and for their miseries He makes them His own. In this act a union is created between the Saviour and the sinner. He takes men up into Himself as their recapitulation and representative. His conscience on sin makes reconciliation. It is often pointed out that the writer of the Fourth Gospel attempts to interpret the content of Christian faith by the help of the Logos philosophy of his day, and fails. Carried to its rigid conclusion the personality of the historic Jesus would vanish almost as completely as with some of the gnostic sects. By forsaking his philosophy when necessary, he remains true to the Christian faith.

Similarly, Schleiermacher introduces a philosophy of feeling that so eviscerates the term 'God' of all Christian content and reduces Him to a subjective immanence that he can only return to a full view of the work of Christ towards God and man by forsaking his philosophy. The best he can say is that Christ is the highest manifestation of the

[1] Mackintosh, *Types of Modern Theology*, p. 91.

Eternal, of Deity, of the Infinite, but he cannot bring himself to speak of Him as 'the everlasting Son of the Father', nor as the mediator of forgiveness to a guilty heart, but only as the Giver of the God consciousness to weak and erring men.

Finally, when we ask what has been Schleiermacher's contribution to the study of redemption, we find our best answer in Mackintosh's words:[1] 'It would be roughly true to say that he has put discovery in the place of revelation, the religious consciousness in the place of the word of God, and the mere "not yet" of imperfection in the place of sin.' Christ, the highest manifestation of Deity, is the mediator of sympathy, inner peace, and His own God-consciousness.

Maurice.

When we pass from the German Schleiermacher, to the English F. D. Maurice, we find much difference in thought, but at least one striking similarity. The great German had revolted against the arid scholasticism of the later reformers, and Maurice revolted against the 'philosophy of the conditioned' as expounded by Sir William Hamilton and applied to theology by Dean Mansel. The gist of Hamilton's view is in his brief thesis: 'To think is to condition.' God or the Absolute is not in Himself what is revealed in human experience. Further, the human mind can only be aware of an object in and by its relations, but the Absolute is unrelated and therefore unknowable. The only loophole left for religion is by the path of faith, because

[1] *Types of Modern Theology*, p. 100.

so far as reason was concerned philosophy had achieved an abstraction and called it 'God'.

But whereas Schleiermacher sought to establish a genuine knowledge of God, through introspection, in feeling, Maurice kept his eye on history and divine revelation, and reared or revived a new system on the basis of Christian theism.

Beginning as a Unitarian, he became dissatisfied with the interpretation of Christ and of man in the writers of that denomination. Only by a violent rationalizing could the distinctive wonder of Christ's life and work, death, and resurrection be dissipated. Only, too, by ignoring the tradition and doctrine of the Apostolic and Catholic Church could Christ be rendered so irrelevant. Maurice felt that as presented He was too inadequate to account for the religious and moral revolution that followed. Equally inadequate was the Unitarian analysis of human nature. Human responsibility, guilt, estrangement, spiritual impotence, were not treated with the seriousness that the facts demanded. These were elements of life or death.

For a brief interval, Maurice passed over into the Calvinism represented by one sect of the Baptists. This theology met his demand for a serious analysis of human nature, but when he proceeded to an examination of its doctrine of God he felt he had reached the crux of the whole matter. A secondary attribute in Deity had been turned into a primary essence. God was sovereign will. It was His divine prerogative as creator and ruler to use, control or appoint His creatures as He would. Power and impenetrable purpose were the outstanding and

227

essential elements in God. Such an interpretation provided an explanation of the fact that some human beings are penitent and some impenitent, some are 'vessels unto honour' and others are 'vessels unto wrath'. But it failed to satisfy the deeper moral demands in Maurice's nature concerning God, and to rise to the level of St. Paul's teaching concerning election when he concludes the great argument in Romans ix to xi: 'God hath shut up all unto disobedience that he might have mercy upon all' (xi. 32).

This led Maurice to a rigorous re-examination of the idea of God. There lay to his hand the invaluable tool of historical criticism. It helped him to see, not a static or mechanical revelation of God such as was offered in the theory of verbal inspiration by writers like Calvin and Flacius, but instead a progressive self-revelation adapted at every stage to the moral and religious capacity of man. Development in religious ideals was seen to be continuous, and consequently the good had to yield to the better and the better to the perfect. 'God, who at sundry times and in divers manners spake in times past unto our fathers through the prophets, hath in these last days spoken unto us in a Son' (Hebrews i. 1). Maurice felt that man's idea of God must be derived, not from the elementary gleams of dawn, but from the light that shined in men's hearts in the face of Jesus Christ. He is Lord of all.

This is the corner-stone of all his future work. The highest and fullest knowledge of God bestowed on man is in the filial consciousness of Jesus, and

the content of that filial relation is revealed on the
Cross. The spirit of the Cross is the spirit of the
Son of God, and God is best known, most truly
known, as the God and Father of our Lord Jesus
Christ. A careful examination of the New Testament Epistles will corroborate this view that the
clue to God's essential nature is in the sonship of
Christ. This, in turn, led Maurice over to a hearty
acceptance of the Catholic doctrine of Incarnation
and the Holy Trinity, but it also convinced him
that the work of Christ must be approached with
the idea of God, in mind, not simply as Creator,
King or Judge—these have their rightful but
subordinate places—but as the Eternal Father.
Men are sons, potential only in many cases, yet
sons who have erred from the home and must be
recovered. But if sons, then brothers under one
Father; hence the Fatherhood of God and the
brotherhood of men, which has become an over-
worked, and not always fully understood, slogan
in many quarters since.

It is difficult to understand the storm of opposition
and hostility that this emphasis on Fatherhood
provoked by the middle of the nineteenth century.[1]
But here our concern is to see how it compelled
even his opponents to rethink the meaning of
Christ's work in the light of divine Fatherhood, and
to present a more Christian and less Jewish or legal
presentation of the Atonement.

Maurice, like Anselm, begins with the question,
Why the Incarnation? At once he affirms man's
impotence and need of divine help. This point we

[1] See *Life*, vol. ii, pp. 188 ff. (2nd Edn.).

would emphasize. Maurice is so assured by, and amazed at, the love of the Father as seen in Christ Jesus that he sees God, regardless of Himself, His sovereignty, and honour, passing over in Christ to the rescue of His fallen children. The only satisfaction God requires is the glad obedience of the incarnate Son.

In a letter to Dr. Hort,[1] after speaking about Christ's victory over Satan and the assurance such a victory brings to the Christian, he continues: 'And if justice is done to the feeling which is implied in this language I believe the mind is freer to receive the full idea of that satisfaction which the Son made to the Father, that perfect reflex of His own love which He presented to Him, when He gave up His soul and body to death; when He showed forth the fullness of the divine love in human suffering. I cannot think there is any object so perfectly satisfying to Him who is absolutely and perfectly Love as this sacrifice. Though I see but a very little way into its meaning, I do feel that it is the atonement of God and man, and that to feed upon it must be the communion between God and man, the bond of fellowship between all creatures, the rest of each soul.' The atoning sacrifice is a life outpoured to the Father to accomplish His will in the recovery of sinners.

How, then, is this recovery achieved? By the emergence in humanity of a new kind of man 'a sinless root'. This new man will not only render to God the perfect sacrifice of an obedient, outpoured life, and unite God and man, and hallow

[1] *Life*, vol. ii, p. 72.

everything in human life, but He will also carry forward and perfect the work begun in Creation; for Maurice is not content to see the meaning of the Incarnation only in relation to the Fall. It is God's way of leading on to perfection the entire human race. Christ is the norm, in His union of divine and human, of all men. As He is, so should we be in the world. But as He is our elder Brother, so He acts on our behalf and provides what Dr. A. B. Bruce called 'Redemption by Sample'. In conclusion, a quotation from the *Theological Essays*[1] will best state Maurice's position: 'Supposing the Father's will to be a will to all good, the Son of God, being one with Him and Lord of man, to obey and fulfil in our flesh that will by entering into the lowest condition into which men had fallen by their sin; supposing this man to be for this reason an object of continual complacency to the Father and that complacency to be fully drawn out by the death of the cross is not this in the highest sense Atonement? Is not the true sinless root of humanity revealed? Is not God in Him reconciled to man. May not that reconciliation be proclaimed as a gospel to all men? Is not the Cross the meeting point between man and man, between man and God? Is not this meeting point what men in all times and places have been seeking for? Did any find it till God declared it?'

This self-originated atonement in God is shown in Romans iii. 24, he continues, because Paul introduces God 'as setting forth to us the one all-sufficient, all-satisfactory evidence that He has made

[1] p. 147.

231

peace with us'. Again, as to the unifying principle of divine love in God overflowing as grace on the Cross, Maurice writes:[1] 'All notions respecting a conflict in the Divine mind between the claims of justice and mercy; all notions of the Son winning from the Father that which did not proceed from His own free, gracious will; all notions which substitute the deliverance from punishment for the deliverance from sin, all notions which weaken the force of the words, or make them anything less than the classical words on this matter, "Lo, I come to do thy will, O God", are it seems to me, of this kind, subversive of the Divine Revelation, rationalistic in the worst sense of that word, not to be countenanced or tolerated.'

We may summarize the position taken by Maurice thus: Any true approach to the Atonement must be genuinely Christian. We have primarily to do with God revealed to us in Christ. Christ's sacrifice is spiritual, being His life outpoured in full obedience to the Father's will. This reached its utmost expression on the Cross in His death. In that sacrifice is found the atonement that reunites men to God. The Incarnation is a process of atonement. As men repent and unite themselves to the will and spirit of Christ they are accepted and forgiven. They also realize their sonship in Him.

In all this it will be seen that Maurice follows the Alexandrian school and, indeed, the Eastern Church generally rather than the Augustinian. He has nothing to say of the Law, or ethical demands in a perfect atonement. Rather, he conceives of the

[1] *Life*, vol. ii, p. 366.

hallowing of humanity in its various relations when the Word became flesh and dwelt among us.

Bushnell.

As will be seen from the introduction to his volume, *The Vicarious Sacrifice*, Bushnell begins from Anselm. He pays high tribute to Anselm's work as the great 'seed-view' of Christ's redemption, whose seedlings others transplanted and marred. Metaphors used with moral insight and skill by Anselm are turned into unimaginative prose by his feeble admirers and imitators; 'debt' comes to mean an unpaid bill which Christ will settle; 'justice' becomes a demand for penal suffering; 'payment' is simply suffering given to God as satisfaction to justice. Christ's obedience is a satisfaction because it is passive and carries within itself the necessary pains, and so on.

Having summarized the noble elements in Anselm, Bushnell casts around for the true and central idea in Christ's work. It is found in a careful analysis of the Christian word 'love' (*agape*). To understand love is to hold in your fingers the Ariadne's thread that guides you in all study of divine revelation and redemption. Its nature is self-communicating.

Wherever love is found, whether in a mother, a patriot or a friend, it overflows, because of its own essential nature, in vicarious sacrifice. It is the mainspring of all Christian ethics, superseding all legalism because it not only sees the duty to be discharged, but provides the motive power. While it may vary in degree, it can never vary in kind, for love is essentially the same in God, angels, and good men. It is the most fundamental principle in the universe; all other virtues in men, and attributes in God, are only manifestations of love. Its clearest expression is in the simple phrase, 'God is love'. But, according to Bushnell, the truth to be borne in mind is that love is always vicarious. To use a current metaphor, it is radio-active. It goes forth into the interests, problems, needs, miseries, and even enmities of those around and makes them its own. It seeks the well-being of foe as well as friend.

This vicarious element in the love of God in Christ is seen in such phrases as He 'was made a curse for us', 'bare our sins', 'hath laid on him the iniquity of us all', 'made to be sin for us . . .', 'tasted death for every man'. 'The whole gospel [he continues] is a texture, thus, of vicarious conceptions in which Christ is represented, in one way or another, as coming into our place, substituted in our stead, bearing our burdens, answering for us, and standing in a kind of suffering sponsorship for the race' (pp. 4, 5). The love of God that is in Christ Jesus our Lord revealed itself in Creation and in the Incarnation. It persisted to its highest point in death. It continues in the patient, unwearying activities of the Holy Spirit. It is shed abroad by Him in human hearts so that the Church which is the home or body of the Spirit of Christ shares in the vicarious sufferings of the Head. Love marches on from heart to heart, always missionary in its nature, always self-communicating, like leaven.

Next, Bushnell stresses the fact that the love in

vicarious sacrifice is never abstract and never acts impersonally. It is the vicarious overflow of a person to a person, it is not seeking merely to rescue abstract entities in God such as honour, justice or any moral principle, it is the expression in Christ of entire devotion to the Father's will as loving and good, but it is the spontaneous expression of Christ's love to all sinners which is also part of the eternal being of God.

Love has no frontier beyond which it finds no obligations towards the helpless. It has no maximum or saturation point that officially completes all its obligations, so that anything done beyond that point is an act of supererogation, and may really be placed in a separate reserve account, for the benefit, as occasion arises, of all who are in need. Or, in Bushnell's words, 'the fictions of superlative merit . . . which have infested for so many centuries the history of this great subject' must be ended. There is no nicely calculating less or more in love. He even goes so far as to say that God suffered pain through His love for sinners while He waited in the processes of His wisdom for the fullness of the times before His pent-up love could find release in Christ Jesus His Son. God's love was always the same, B.C. and A.D. alike, but the giving of the Son was a sacrifice of gladness, and the descent of the Spirit is a release of joy in seeing of the travail of His soul and being satisfied.

In a word, then, Christ atones, not by His office, but by the divine quality of His life, and in so far as each believer shares the same spirit of Christ and has the same love of God shed abroad in his heart he too becomes in his measure a partaker in the sufferings of Christ that continue to redeem the world. Nothing but vicarious sacrifice unites the members to the Head, genuinely Christianizes the ethics of society, or gives the work of the Church that eternal significance that inherently belongs to it. She is called on to fill up that which is lacking in the sufferings of Christ.[1] 'The supreme art of the devil [he writes] never invented a greater mischief to be done, or a theft more nearly amounting to the stealing of the cross itself, than the filching away thus, from the followers of Christ, the conviction that they are thoroughly to partake the sacrifice of their master.'[2] It is the spirit of the Cross in Him and in men that make both one and give us a reconciling power in the world still.

In Part III, Bushnell meets the criticisms of those who isolate the attributes of God, justice, holiness, &c., from God's divine personality, or, again, who set sovereignty over against fatherhood. There is no priority of one attribute to another in God; each is alike necessary to His divine perfection, 'justice and mercy are co-ordinate and co-operative'. If in the training of mankind, law and the sovereign aspects of God's character are more strongly or prominently expressed first, this is so because it was the part of man's spiritual culture that was needed first; and, secondly, it was the culture for which man's moral capacities were earliest prepared. What we regard as the severer qualities in God are as necessary to the true freedom of a perfect character as the milder.

[1] See pp. 71–7.   [2] p. 82.

Vicarious sacrifice never attains its ends by ignoring law or the divine precept. Christ's assertion of the Father's will, even unto the utmost possible degree in death, fulfils the law in a way that was never seen before. Perfect love is perfect fulfilment of law because it has the necessary motive power. 'Christ makes a contribution of honour to the law He obeys, that will do more to enthrone it in our reverence, than all the desecrations of sin have done to pluck it down—more too than all conceivable punishments, to make it felt and to keep it in respect.'[1] Christ fully reinstates the Law by its perfect incarnation in Himself and by His personal and perfect obedience to it, so that it is seen as 'God's own everlasting obedience'.[2]

Bushnell's exposition of Christ's relation to sin in man is not unfamiliar. To become man meant to enter the lot of a human being in which the curse of sin was working itself out in the individual and in society.

The divine anger against sin and the practice of sin have united to produce world-wide guilt and misery. No one can become man and avoid it. Whatever divine anger flames forth against must be destroyed. 'To this end was the Son of God manifested that he might destroy the works of the devil.'[3] Christ comes in His Incarnation into the condition in which sinners find themselves. He at once feels the full force of their sins and, because of His perfect holiness, even more intensely than any other. He clings to sinners and at the same time condemns their sins. His mediatorship lies in this

[1] p. 259.   [2] p. 265.   [3] 1 John iii. 8.

union with sinners in condemnation and salvation.

It is here, of course, that critics of the moral influence theory detect a weakness in Bushnell's position. Thus Dr. Scott Lidgett points out that, since Bushnell lays the major stress on the Incarnation as God's mode of redemption, he obscures the fact that the Incarnation is the entrance into humanity of the Son of God, with its result as the appearance of the *Man* Christ Jesus. 'The foundation of His life is in its God-ward relationship, His perfect Sonship, and in the spirit of self-surrender in which His sonship expresses itself. This God-ward relationship is not only real, but is primary, and the unfolding of it fills the gospels.'[1]   It would be difficult to turn the point of this criticism if we argue from Bushnell's writings; whether he would have deliberately and consciously repudiated this God-ward aspect of Christ's work is another matter.

On the question of a satisfaction being necessary to God, Bushnell argues negatively that if Christ can offer a satisfaction to God, then He is other than God. We find two gods: one who conciliates and one who is conciliated; or, if God provides the satisfaction within Himself, He must be a unique Ruler who secures justice by taking the punishments for violated laws out of Himself. 'There plainly could not be a weaker figure in the name of government.'[2]

The weakest part of Bushnell's argument is his attempt to distinguish between eternal law or right and law revealed in government. His words concerning these laws are: 'There was law before God's

---

[1] *The Spiritual Principle of the Atonement*, p. 198 (Epworth Press).
[2] *The Vicarious Sacrifice*, p. 317.

will and before His instituting act; viz. that necessary everlasting ideal, law of RIGHT, which, simply to think, is to be forever obliged by it. The perfections of God, being self-existent and eternal, were eternally squared by this self-existent law; for if they had any moral quality, it lay in their conformity to some moral law, apart from which no such perfection is conceivable.'[1]

Christ's work so far was twofold: first, to reinstitute in Himself this everlasting ideal law of right, and, secondly, to restore sinners to God and righteousness. Here, as in Dale over thirty years later, the weakness was the otherness of law as over against God, a kind of *alter deus* with which even the moral perfections of God must be squared, and which was regnant in unfallen man apart from the authority of God.

But we must end this brief summary as we began: Bushnell has left us his debtors by his analysis of love as at the centre a vicarious principle; and by showing with commanding clearness that in becoming a 'curse' for sinners Christ achieved atonement and bore away sin. What Christ's work meant towards God, if we judge by his writings, he never explored.

[1] *The Vicarious Sacrifice*, pp. 186–7.

Chapter 14

MORE RECENT TRENDS IN INTERPRETATION

ALTHOUGH the limits set out in this volume forbid anything more than a meagre survey, something should be said to indicate the trends of thought on the work of Christ during the past half-century or so. It seems better here, also, to indicate the lines of thought than to record a mere catalogue of names. We shall consider these tendencies under the following heads: Atonement and Fatherhood, The Revival of the Ransom Theory, The Objective and Subjective Views, Atonement and the Eucharist, and Neo-Calvinism.

I. ATONEMENT AND FATHERHOOD.

Following the example of Maurice and his school, most modern writers, however differently in other respects they may develop the theme, hold that belief about God must determine their interpretation of the work of Christ. If the supreme fact concerning God be His sovereignty, or His majesty, or His holiness, the interpretation of Christ's atonement will, as with the early reformers, be set forth in the light of these views. If, however, it be accepted that our profoundest knowledge of God is grounded in the self-consciousness of Jesus, and if the content of that self-consciousness be sonship derived from an immediate relationship with One whose nature is least inadequately expressed by the word 'Father', then Atonement will be expounded in the light of that truth.

Consequently Atonement in the light of this perfect revelation of Fatherhood has been the approach by the majority of thinkers inside the past half-century, particularly in Great Britain and the United States of America. Rashdall, Cave, Mozley, Moberly, and in some rare passages even Denney, have sought to understand Christ's work as the full and final manifestation of the eternal Father; they have related the death to the Incarnation, they have seen in the Incarnation the Eternal Son, who dwelt on the bosom of the Father, made visible, and they have set the work of Christ in eternity. It is the deed of God as Father coming forth in history to restore His fallen sons.

But no one has rendered finer service in this approach than Dr. Scott Lidgett. His style, like Butler's, is massive and, to a beginner, forbidding; but no student should be deterred by this from a careful study of his two masterly volumes, *The Spiritual Principle of the Atonement* and *The Fatherhood of God*, nor indeed should his *Sonship and Salvation* be omitted, since it is supplementary to the other two volumes and shows the inheritance of the believer in Christ Jesus.

Dr. Scott Lidgett subjects the concept of Fatherhood to a rigorous examination and shows, as Dr. Chalmers pointed out, that we are not to import 'the familiar waywardness of children on one side' and 'the unextinguishable fondness of a smiling and indulgent father' on the other side into a true conception of either sonship or fatherhood. 'This', says Dr. Scott Lidgett, 'may be the religion of poetry but it is not the religion of conscience.'[1] He shows that Fatherhood, as manifested in and regulated by perfect love, is the highest and truest expression of all the divine attributes. It is, as occasion requires, righteous, holy, judicial, severe; its aim is to bring many sons unto glory, not to indulge them in their misguided inclinations. All the divine activities in Christ Jesus are directed to the salvation and restored fellowship of sinful men. Rightly understood, no quality or excellence is lacking in divine Fatherhood. Other and subordinate qualities, such as holiness and righteousness, may have been revealed first to meet the immature conditions of ancient Israel, but in the fullness of time these were seen to be but the manifestation of a divine Being 'whose nature and whose name is Love'. They are subordinate in the sense that a stream is subordinate to its source. Once the source of the earlier manifestations is known, then the source becomes regnant. Fatherhood triumphs over creatorship, sovereignty and judicial power in the sense that it shows their true meaning. Similarly, the work of Christ takes on a new meaning when it is seen to be the expression of the Father's eternal purpose. Anselm's view must be lifted to a higher plane and his God be reconsidered in the light of the God and Father of our Lord Jesus Christ.

Dr. Scott Lidgett stresses another fact, much

[1] *The Spiritual Principle of the Atonement*, p. 231 (Epworth Press).

obscured in recent Barthian theology, viz. that while sin has entered and made havoc of man's moral nature, nevertheless the kinship between man and God abides. The message of the gospel is to lead men home in penitence and faith to accept their sonship. Further, by His Incarnation and death, the Son has sanctified all life and all human experiences. At the same time, since He is the perfect Son of Man, His death is a full, perfect, sufficient oblation and satisfaction to God because His sacrifice withheld nothing from God. All this is expounded with great fullness in Dr. Scott Lidgett's works. The permanent value of his labour lies in this, that his approach to atonement is genuinely Christian. It begins with Christ Jesus. It studies His sense of kinship and travail with that of the Old Testament prophets, such as Jeremiah, or the Prophet of the Exile, but it sees, as did the early Christian Church, that only in Jesus Christ was there a true fulfilment of the picture of the Suffering Servant. The testimony of Jesus is the spirit of prophecy, but it alone is its fulfilment. When this is recognized, it remains that any one who approaches the death of Christ by way of the Law (i.e. legal and ceremonial rites), or even the prophets, is inverting the true order, and much theology, now obsolete, would never have been written if men had begun with the noon-day sun and not with the twilight dawn.

Two other points call for attention: (1) Dr. Scott Lidgett's treatment of the Atonement has led the thoughts of many out into a broad place, where the work of Christ is seen *sub specie eternitatis*. The purpose of God is the source; Christ came to realize this purpose; He is the crown of the universe and of man; by His Cross every knee shall at last bow to Him, and then the reconciled universe He shall hand over to God as His final offering. (2) Meanwhile and secondly, through His death Christ has liberated a new power that turns all His commands into promises, and this new dynamic is the only condition of a new social order.

2. THE REVIVED RANSOM THEORY, OR THE CLASSIC IDEA.

The latter term belongs to Professor Aulén of Lund, a Swedish theologian whose Olaus Petri Lectures for 1930 have been translated into English under the title, *Christus Victor*.[1] The original title of the lectures was 'The Christian Idea of the Atonement'; the English title indicates only one aspect of Christ's work.

Although the author does not say so, we are convinced that this fresh approach by an old path is due to present world conditions. Half a century ago we were lulled to rest on the gentle precepts of a Christian humanism. By slow but sure increments, moral progress would land our children, if not ourselves, in the millennium. A world war seemed as unlikely as a collision with Mars. Racial misunderstandings and hatred would yield to reason and the march of science; and the angel of peace would brood over all. Liberal theology, nourished on Hegel and Harnack, seemed to provide all the stamina needed for earth's happy family.

But since 1914 we have left this mirage for the

[1] By A. G. Hebert of Kelham (S.P.C.K.).

days of Nero, Domitian, or Diocletian. We have
seen the depths into which the sons of men can sink.
We have seen materialism, insolence, violence, lies,
treachery, hatred, greed, with the accompanying
vultures of pestilence and famine. We have seen
bestial immorality and spiritual insensibility and,
finally, a denial of the existence of God and all
spiritual values. We ask, Is this man? From whence
come the volcanic forces of evil that surge in his
soul? Is he not the victim of mightier hostile powers,
whose enmity to God he expresses? These volcanic
forces were formerly explained in terms of biological
evolution. 'The ape and tiger' linger in the unsubdued soul of man, but in times of crisis break forth
with savage fury. Writers like Aulén go back to a
more Pauline interpretation. Men are under the
sway of 'principalities and powers and wicked
spirits in high places'. This is more naïve and will
repel some scientific thinkers. They will raise their
hands and cry, 'Animism!' But why should such
beings not exist?

The salvation of man, St. Paul and the Greek
Fathers and the new Swedish school contend, cannot
be achieved until these hostile principalities and
powers are destroyed. This is the clue to the central
meaning of Christ's work. By His Incarnation, He
came to make God known to men. The unseen
hosts of evil pursued Him and, finally, through the
hands of sinful men, nailed Him to the Cross. That
was the utmost that the Law, Sin, Death, and the
Devil could do. They seized His body, but they
actually liberated His spirit, and Christ arose victorious over all these foes. Through death He

245

destroyed him that had the power of death—that is, the Devil; and delivered them who through fear of death were in subjection to bondage.

After reviewing and finding unsatisfactory both the Anselmic and Abailardian views, Aulén returns to what he believes to be the true New Testament, Patristic, and Lutheran view. In this he finds conjoined both the objective and subjective elements in Christ's work. 'The Work of Atonement', he says, 'is accomplished by God Himself in Christ, yet, at the same time, the passive form is also used: God is reconciled with the world. The alternation is not accidental. He is reconciled only because He Himself reconciles the world with Himself and Himself with the world. The safeguard of the continuity of God's operation is the dualistic outlook, the Divine warfare against the Evil that holds mankind in bondage and the triumph of Christ.'[1] Later on, p. 170, he says: 'The atonement is set forth as the divine victory over the powers that hold men in bondage. Yet at the same time these very powers are in a measure executants of His own judgement on sin. This opposition reaches its climax in the tension between the Divine Love and the Divine Wrath. But here the solution is not found in any sort of rational settlement; it is rather that the Divine Love prevails over the Wrath, the blessing overcomes the curse, by way of Divine self-oblation and sacrifice. The redeeming work of Christ shows how much the Atonement "costs" God.' Later he adds: 'For my own part I am persuaded that no form of Christian teaching has any future

[1] *Christus Victor*, pp. 162–3.

before it except such as can keep steadily in view the reality of the evil in the world and go out to meet the evil with a battle-song of triumph. Therefore I believe that the classic idea of the Atonement and of Christianity is coming back—that is to say, the genuine, authentic, Christian faith' (p. 176).

It causes no surprise that, in days like these, this return to a conception of Christ's death as a triumph and conquest over the powers of evil should find a response in many hearts. Principal Hywel Hughes calls attention to the influence of Aulén on 'Bishop Headlam, Canon Kirk, Principal Cave, and Professor A. B. Macauley, to name only a few of the more recent writers'.[1]

Dr. Cave, in *The Doctrine of the Work of Christ*, seeks to develop Aulén's theory by making it a synthesis of the objective and subjective views. Christ does something unto God by asserting God's lawful dominion throughout the whole universe, and on behalf of men and within them in that He triumphs over all the powers of evil. Aulén is careful to purge away the offensive imagery and puerile questions that we have seen in certain patristic advocates of the ransom theory. He presents a view of Christ's work that fills men with confidence and hope, and whether he is justified in attaching the word 'classical' to his view or not, for it certainly does not cover the whole aspect of redemption, yet he presents an aspect that will speak to the condition of this baffled generation and of which we are sure to hear more in the near future.

[1] *Expository Times*, March, 1939.

3. THE OBJECTIVE AND SUBJECTIVE VIEWS.

Dale, Forsyth, and Denney, by exploring the possible significance of the Cross for God, reached a point where rationalizing almost over-reached itself. In his Congregational Union Lecture for 1875, *The Atonement*, Dale was so impressed with the need for a sound, individual, social, and international ethic that he searched for his moral foundations in the nature of God and His universe. Dale was a preacher of righteousness and an ardent social reformer, as well as an evangelist and theologian. Like Amos and Micah, his was a cry for righteousness and justice. Having satisfied himself of the great moral principles that belong to God-head and govern the universe, which he calls 'the eternal laws of righteousness', he proceeds to examine the atoning work of Christ in the light of these laws.

He says: 'Until we have considered the actual relations of the Lord Jesus Christ, both to the Eternal Law of Righteousness which the sins of men have violated, and to the human race—and until we have discovered what light these relations throw upon the Fact that His Death is the ground on which sin is forgiven—it appears to me that we are in no position to determine with any confidence to what extent the Death of the Lord Jesus Christ' is analogous to other propitiatory acts.

Dale then contends that Christ's death is a vindication of and satisfaction to the Eternal Law of Righteousness, and his Lecture is an examination of the teaching of our Lord and His Apostles on this point. He rejects the Abailardian view that Christ achieves our redemption by revealing God's love to us, and asserts that He reveals God's love to us by achieving our redemption. This is not a verbal quibble. A great deed had to be done at infinite cost towards the eternal principles on which the universe rests. 'God abideth faithful. He cannot deny Himself.' Christ died on account of men's sins. He made remission of sins a possibility. He was the propitiation for sin. He was a sacrifice to God on account of sin. Forgiveness of sins is grounded on what Christ did for men. All this is but the negative way of saying that by His sacrifice of Himself, Jesus met the claims to the uttermost of God's holy laws.

The Lecture is a noble contribution to one aspect of the Atonement; it reveals Dale's passion for righteousness and for an atonement that springs out of morality. It has had a powerful influence on thought—as witness the seven editions through which the volume ran in three years—and, in view of the assaults on the cardinal principles of morality among the nations to-day, it is likely to receive renewed attention. If Aulén is restoring interest in the conquering Redeemer, Dale is likely to be re-read as setting forth Christ as a Conqueror in righteousness.

Yet, as an interpretation of the work of Christ, it is over-simplified. It appealed so severely to the conscience and will that a reaction was sure to follow and an interpretation to be sought in closer relation to the needs of man's full personality. This has been attempted in a series of lectures instituted in memory of Dale himself by Principal Franks, of which we have seen something and can only say here that the author seeks to place the Abailardian view, not on an emotional or purely subjective, but on a rational basis.

But another point in Dale's theory has not escaped criticism. He makes the Eternal Law of Righteousness so central and refers the work of Christ so persistently to it that it has become a kind of *alter deus* that requires satisfaction in itself rather than a manifestation of God as the Eternal and Sovereign Father.

Dr. P. T. Forsyth accepted Dale's idea of Atonement as primarily made with reference to the divine righteousness, and develops it in two respects. Firstly, Christ's death is the perfect realization and meaning of all sacrifice as something done to God; and secondly, it carried with it the necessity of an experience of God-forsakenness. He writes of the dereliction on the Cross: 'It was death with a past of failure, a lonely present, and a dark future. It was a dreary hell, a dismal swamp, an icy grave. . . . If Christ sounded and tasted death to the uttermost, He conquered by principle a death like that.' It must be said that Forsyth's sense of the heinousness of sin, his feeling for expiation, his sense of the paradox of wrath and love, his moral earnestness, led him at times past the language of theology to that of poetry, and it is easier to enter into moral sympathy with his mood than to apprehend his meaning.

Professor Denney seems to have been the last distinguished member of this school, a thinker in whom ethics and discipline triumphed over tender emotion. He asserted not only the necessity for satisfaction of laws, but that broken laws will be followed by a penalty that will fall somewhere and on some one. The wrath of God is revealed from Heaven against all ungodliness and unrighteousness of men. It is not simply minatory; it follows sin as the night the day. Penitence is not enough, nor future obedience. The sin past must be met and the penalty imposed.

In the fact that Christ by His Incarnation came under the law and was integrated into the human race, Denney sees that Christ can act on man's behalf and suffer vicariously. The penalty due to the body can be borne in the Head. Denney has developed the legal and penal view so clearly and effectively that nearly all writers since his time have moved either towards the moral influence theory, or towards a synthesis of the objective and subjective theories in a higher and more ultimate view that will do justice to both.

The interpretation of Christ's work on the subjective side has rested so much on emotional appeal that it has come under fresh criticism. This corrective was needed. A great weakness in German Pietism and to some degree in the theology of Methodism, with which it is akin, was the undue appeal of the Cross to tender feeling. Bernard of Clairvaux and Zinzendorf, Bushnell, and some Roman Catholic theologians have made the appeal to feeling so strong that two evils followed: First, those who are of a more phlegmatic and severely rational temperament, and to whom this appeal carries small persuasion, begin to think that the work of the Cross is not for men of strong intelligence, and even to despise this presentation; and, secondly, since there is an inconstancy in all emotional states, the appeal of the Cross varies in the same person from time to time.

Canon Kirk has exposed this weakness in *Essays Catholic and Critical*, Part II, Essay vii, *n.*[1] He argues that since men vary in their imaginative and emotional endowments, it puts some at a disadvantage if the approach is subjective, and it fails to give due place to moral endeavour and the function of reason. Too often, also, the emotion stimulated was not that of awe or reverent love, but fear and distress, until in some pathological subjects the sufferings of Christ caused a sadistic reaction, or, again, in others a feeling of revenge towards those who executed our Lord. Some Jewish pogroms have been defended in Roman Catholic countries on this ground.

4. ATONEMENT AND THE EUCHARIST.

The idea of sacrifice has received fresh consideration in connexion with our Lord's death. Both anthropology and Old Testament studies have led to inquiry into the original meaning of sacrifice among Gentiles and Jews. The germinal idea was to establish fellowship with the god. The victim was slain, the blood poured out as a life offered, the meal was prepared. The smoking sacrifice was first placed before the god that he might receive its sweet savour; then the people drew near and ate and drank after, yet along with, the god. This

[1] S.P.C.K.

belief and usage are not wanting among the Semites or in the Old Testament. Atonement or reconciliation has one end in view—fellowship between the god and the people.

Gradually this conception became moralized, but it contained within itself the spiritual truth that must be our key, it is argued, to an understanding of Christ's death.

Writers like Bishop Hicks, in *The Fullness of Sacrifice*, call attention to the intimate way in which our Lord has related His death to the Supper in the Upper Room. By a method not made very explicit, this work of Christ on the Cross is related to the act in the Upper Room—the body and blood to the bread and wine. Bishop Hicks says: 'Up to the time of the Reformation . . . sacrificial language had been attached to the Eucharist at all times and in all parts of the Christian world. In the best and widest sense of the word "Catholic", the Eucharistic sacrifice, whatever it meant, was part of the Catholic tradition' (p. 331). Whereas the reformed Churches stressed the symbolism and the memorial aspects of the Lord's Supper, and made the mediation of the 'real presence' to the human heart to be conditioned by penitence and faith, those who follow the 'Catholic' tradition relate the saving efficacy of Christ's death to the bread and wine. The Eucharist becomes a perpetuated sacrifice and the work of Christ is applied afresh at the altar in seeking hearts. This is not the place to enter into a comparison of the reformed Evangelical view of the Lord's Supper over against that of Roman or Anglo-Catholic, but it may be said that for the Evangelical the term 'sacrifice' in the Eucharist is reserved for praise and thanksgiving, and the living sacrifice of our mortal bodies (Romans xii. 1), and not for a feast which, from its very simple character, can at best be only symbolical.

Nor, again, can the continuation of Christ's sacrifice for sinners in any localized or visible medium be reconciled with the idea of finality in redemption on the cross. The argument in Hebrews viii, ix, x, is completely against this view.

Principal Vincent Taylor, in the concluding chapter of *Jesus and His Sacrifice*, discusses the relation between our Lord's death and the Eucharist from another angle. As the ancient ritual sacrifice was not the work of one, but of all the people and of all in fellowship with their God, so it is in the Holy Communion. The death of Jesus is the point of reconciliation and fellowship between men and God and between men and men. The Eucharist, as the showing forth of our Lord's death till He come, is consequently the central act in Christian worship. Dr. Taylor says: 'The act of worship which bears most closely on man's corporate approach to God in Christ is the Sacrament of Holy Communion and it is from this standpoint that its importance is most clearly seen. Indeed, it will generally be found that neglect of the Sacrament accompanies an over-emphasis upon the individual and personal aspect of man's relationship to the work of Christ' (p. 321). It is this growing recognition that man apart from a society is nothing, and cannot have even a personality, that is tending to correct the exaggerated

individualism of the nineteenth century in both
religion and philosophy. Men only offer true
worship and realize their true selves as they take
their place in the *koinōnia* of the Church. Holy
Communion is a corporate act and its value does
not rest *wholly* or primarily on the personal faith-
union of individuals in Christ. The body of believers
is as a body more than the individuals who compose
it, just as the human body is not simply an aggregation of members. The body is one and the Crucified
and Risen Lord is its Head. It is in the fellowship of
the body that the individual receives most fully the
life and redemption of the Head.

The same truth holds good in regard to the individual and fallen humanity. '[The individual] is a
member of the community, wide as earth and
inclusive of heaven, for which Christ died. It is in
this consciousness that he approaches God, conscious not only of personal sins, but also of the sin of
the world, its blindness, cruelty and hardness of
heart. In this sin he is enmeshed, whatever his individual contribution to it may be, because he is a
child of man, a member of a sinful community. It
is not to be wondered at, that, in this conviction, he
sees a deeper significance in the self-offering of
Christ than can be gained in any other way.
Within him sound the words, "Behold the Lamb of
God that taketh away the sin of the world", and the
Amen of his spirit to Christ's offering of obedience,
submission and penitence attains its deepest in-
tensity' (p. 323). This truth of the corporate nature
of sin, redemption, fellowship, and unity in Christ,
all symbolized in the Sacrament of the Supper,

could scarcely find worthier expression. Only when Dr. Taylor says that 'neglect of the Sacrament' generally 'accompanies an over-emphasis upon the individual and personal aspect of man's relationship to the work of Christ' does one hesitate. This would hardly have been true when eighteenth-century Methodism was only a congeries of societies and often found access to the Lord's Table almost impossible. Then exaggerated individualism was skilfully corrected by Wesley by placing the individual in the corporate fellowship of the class- or band-meeting. This was a second best, since the relation of converts to the Catholic *ecclesia* was not by any means generally stressed; yet it is true that the sense of belonging to a great fellowship did characterize the Methodists of the eighteenth century under conditions in which the sacrament of the Lord's Supper was often entirely absent.

5. NEO-CALVINISM.

It is yet too soon to assess the permanent value of Barth's contribution to theology. One fact is already plain: he is the uncompromising enemy of all theories of redemption that spring from human effort or speculation, or that approach the question from the side of divine immanence. His doctrine of God governs his soteriology. There is no knowledge of God apart from revelation and no redemption apart from God's own act. He has not published any systematic work on the Atonement, but in *The Word of God and the Word of Man*, in his *Commentary on Romans*, and in his Gifford Lectures for 1938, entitled, *The Knowledge of God and the Service of Man*, it is easy to see the direction in which his thoughts tend on the Atonement.

God is, to him, the transcendent, the Wholly Other. The highest moral achievements in man can never pass over and become divine. Man's achievements are on one plane—God's achievement is on another. No 'wish-thinking' or speculative imaginings can ever carry man from the human to the divine level. Schleiermacher's idea of religion as a feeling of dependence on God is a deadly error to be resisted. Religions never rise above their own level—the human heart. Psychology is misleading when it offers an analysis of man's states of consciousness in relation to the unknown and calls that 'religion'.

'Religion forgets that she has a right to exist only when she continually does away with herself. Instead she takes joy in her existence and considers herself indispensable.'[1] There is therefore no road from man to God. God alone can bridge the gulf and cast up a highway. Unless He speaks—and God's word is a deed—man remains undone. But in Jesus Christ God strikes vertically into the naturalism of man and society, as the supernatural, 'and brings us the word of the Father of which we on the inside of historical appearances know nothing and can never know anything'.

If we accept Barth's exposition of the passage in the *Confessio Scotica* on Christ's death, passion, and burial as representing his own views, his interpretation of the Atonement is plain. And we must take the liberty of quoting a somewhat lengthy passage.

[1] *The Word of God and the Word of Man*, p. 67 (Hodder & Stoughton).

On p. 83 of the Gifford Lectures[1] he says: 'As man Jesus is *able* to offer Himself as a sacrifice, and as man He *does* so also. The death of Jesus Christ is the sum and consummation of the Incarnation of the Son of God, in so far as His death makes it clear that the Incarnation means the humiliation—the complete humiliation of God. The picture of Jesus Christ the Crucified reveals what the curse, the plight, and the despair of sinful man mean. Other pictures of human suffering exist as well, pictures too of comparatively innocent human suffering. But it cannot be said of any of the many others, who as men have suffered, are suffering and will suffer, that they have endured the wrath of God. It is the suffering of Jesus Christ utterly and alone which is "the revelation of the wrath of God revealed from heaven" (Romans i. 18).' Further, and in all this, it is God who is humiliated, who makes the sacrifice, who takes upon Himself 'everything which man's rebellion against Him has made inevitable—suffering and death, but also perdition and hell, punishment in time *and* in eternity in utter disregard of the fact that this is not worthy of Him as God. Where does God remain and what still remains His as God when God's Son has been slain on Calvary? It is certainly true that if ever there was a sacrifice, the death of Jesus Christ is the sacrifice of sacrifices' (pp. 83–4).

If we are right in thinking that this exposition is the expression of Barth's own doctrine of Atonement, it is obvious that he not only regards Christ's death as a sacrifice to God, but as a penal substitute

---

[1] *The Knowledge of God and the Service of God* (Hodder & Stoughton).

for man. Further, he so identifies the work of the
Son with that of the Father as to verge on a new
Patripassianism, and, finally, he makes redemption so entirely the act of God that no room seems
left for man's co-operation or response.

Emil Brunner is a distinguished member of the
Barthian school. In his great work, *The Mediator*, he
emphasizes the difference between evil and sin.
Evil may mean 'not yet', sin means 'no longer'. It
is a disrupted relation with God. Only when sin is
defined as guilt is evil comprehended in a personal
form. Guilt means that a man has done what he
cannot undo; human activity can only change
relations between men.

In *The Theology of Crisis* (p. 56) he reaffirms the
same fact: 'All human activity, even though it be
done in the name of God, with the exalted purpose
of building the Kingdom of God, must accept this
indictment.' If reconciliation or forgiveness is to
take place, a mediator must be provided by God.
'Forgiveness is not an idea or thought over which
man himself has power. A forgiveness which we
derive from an idea of God, when we say, "Men are
expected to forgive each other, therefore God also
must forgive, for forgiveness is a part also of divine
love"—such forgiveness is a presumption on divine
sovereignty. It pleased God to visit man who cannot
come to God. This approach of God to man, this
divine condescension, this entering into a world of
sin and sinners, burdened with their sense of contradiction to Him—just this constitutes the mystery
of divine revelation and reconciliation in the
incarnate and crucified Christ. That God removes

the contradiction by bearing it Himself, this is the cross—*Agnus Dei qui tollit peccata mundi*' (p. 60).

The incompleteness of this chapter, both in its scope and in its treatment of the individual writers, is only relieved by the hope that it may turn any beginners who read it to the volumes quoted. If they do so, they will find that thinkers on the work of Christ to-day are bringing things new and old out of their treasury—things that, though old, have a new voice.

Chapter 15

SUMMARY AND CONCLUSION

However partial and arbitrary the foregoing survey may have been, it may have served, at least, a twofold purpose: (1) It may have shown that, for close upon 2,000 years, men in every generation, in all lands, and on every level of culture have related the work of Christ to the forgiveness of sins and to fellowship with God. All are agreed that 'through this man is proclaimed into you remission of sins'. (2) It may have shown that the work of Christ is so many-sided in its relations to God and man and to all preparatory revelation, that no one single interpretation can cover all aspects of its meaning, or even, at any particular moment in Christian history, present an entirely consistent account of it. Like the roads to the famous Taj Mahal, each reveals its own wonder and inspiration.

The survey has suggested also that the roots of interpretation, tiny though they be, go back into the soil of pre-Christian thought, especially into the experiences of the godly Remnant in Israel, who are best represented by men like Jeremiah, and in such writings as we find in Isaiah xlii. 1–4, xlix. 1–6, l. 4–9, and liii. Some kinship of experience is discernible in ethnic literature, too, but here it must be passed by.

In the New Testament we have no clear rationale of the Cross. The first missionaries mostly addressed Jews, and as the Scriptures had come to hold such commanding authority among the Jews, especially concerning the Messiah, the Apostles naturally appealed to Old Testament prophecy when quotation lent strength to their appeal. Otherwise we have a variety of ways of proclaiming salvation through Christ, but they are the methods of the ardent evangelist and not the cool reflections of the systematic theologian. One throws the emphasis on Christ's sacrificial act of deliverance; another throws it on Christ's devotion to, and vindication of, the Father's righteous will; another represents Christ as acting on our behalf and on account of our sins, doing for men what they could not do for themselves; another represents it as victory over principalities and powers under whose awful spell men are in thrall every hour; another sees it as the cancelling of a bond, to which, under pain of death, we were bound; another as the opening of the doors of darkness and death and the leading forth of prisoners who had lived all their days in these gloomy concentration camps into 'the liberty of the glory of the children of God'; another as the mediation of forgiveness and the creation of fellowship: the list is not easily exhausted.

When we passed outside the Christian canon, the survey showed that almost every thinker and writer on the Cross regarded his views as based on New Testament teaching. Whether we discard these views or not, the writers believed themselves to be loyal exponents of apostolic teaching. This is important when we try to come to a conclusion for ourselves. So varied are the metaphors, analogies, myths, allegories, parallels used in the New Testament that each, torn from the rest and used, often apart from the passionate love of the apostolic writer, becomes a starting-point for a whole treatise, one-sided and exaggerated. This in itself is a warning against the pernicious mishandling of proof-texts. The unbalanced use of a solitary text has often led to most disastrous consequences; and a nemesis of revolt against the modicum of truth underlying the theory has followed. We shall presently find instances of this tragedy. It is not enough to find a single word or text upon which to build a doctrine of Atonement.

The survey of thought on the meaning of Christ's work since the second century has shown that it inevitably tended to move in one of three directions, viz. as it concerned the Devil, God, or man; this seemed to exhaust the possibilities.

1. When the Church was in its beginnings and exerting its main strength in Gentile territory and often among very primitive peoples, when science was as yet only the dream of a few Greek thinkers, when evil spirits and demons were as much a part of the mental furniture of St. Paul or Tertullian as they are of a primitive Bantu to-day, when demons were the true causes of all manner of temptations, calamities and miseries—physical and moral— Christ was inevitably conceived as the Redeemer from the Devil and his widespread agents and subordinates. How other and how better could one conceive of His saving work? If the Devil is the arch enemy, and if he has got control over men,

then we must conceive of salvation as somehow a deliverance from Satan. Both Martin Luther and John Wesley came too soon in history for nineteenth-century science. Witchcraft, demons, the 'evil eye', and a hundred other manifestations of Satan appear in their writings, all of which may be paralleled in animistic countries to-day. But, as recent hymn-books and handbooks on theology show, less use is made of the Devil to-day in interpreting the work of Christ.

To return, however, to the patristic efforts of interpretation along this road; the moment this theory fell into less delicate fingers it began to deteriorate until the Devil appears, almost on equal terms, demanding his ransom-money from God for the liberation of his captives, and God is compelled to resort to methods that hardly leave His moral rectitude unscathed. Yet, despite much coarseness in thought and not a little pernicious theology in these cruder patristic efforts, we must affirm that a moral truth underlies the so-called Ransom Theory. Let men conceive of the Devil and his angels as they will—and not even for Hegel must we sacrifice moral facts on the altar of a coercive intellectual consistency—or deny them outright, a thousand voices testify to deliverance in the name of Jesus from passions, lust, envy, jealousy, covetousness, pride, fear, and a legion of other powers which our noblest nature is compelled to regard as alien enemies.

Modern psychology may change the name; it may locate evil in the unconscious and not in Hell, or Devil, but at bottom man's moral ailment and moral remedy are the same in the first century and the twentieth. Call it 'demon' or call it 'animal instinct', it is man's undoing, and a Deliverer is needed. So true is this that one living writer has tried to rehabilitate this approach under the name of the 'classical theory'.

2. In Anselm we saw a thinker greatly and reasonably alarmed about the supreme sovereignty of God. Examining the ransom theories, he feared lest the foundations of the eternal throne should be shaken in thought by amateur theologians like Peter Lombard, or even by men of stronger calibre. Anselm is very jealous for the Lord God. His thought rises to indignation as he sees how the supremacy, majesty, and honour of God have been outraged by devils and men alike; and to suggest that God sacrificed His only begotten Son to buy off the Devil is too blasphemous to be contemplated. Anselm felt that we cannot be happy about a God who has to drop bribes to brigands and robbers. This phrase in his thought checks the march of the ransom theory. Why, then, did God become Man? Anselm says in order that God may vindicate His own character and office. A universe where God allowed His Person to be flouted, insulted or despised would soon become a moral hell. But all sin is such insult; it is robbery of God's honour, and all sinners are bankrupts, owing God what they cannot pay. Is it possible to restore God's honour, to pay Him what is due? Christ comes in His dual role—as Eternal Son, rendering a sacrifice of infinite merit, and as truly Man offering Himself on behalf of men. The sacrifice, though provided by God, is

offered by a Man on behalf of men. It is a penal satisfaction—the sin is expiated by the suffering Saviour. God, by the sacrifice on the Cross, is seen to be God over all, in righteousness and in majesty. The truth in the satisfaction theory is this: Every sin belittles God; it is contempt of His Kingdom, and God's sovereign control is a truth that needs expression in every age and in none more than the present. Christ presented a true *satisfactio activa* in perfect devotion to the Father's holy will.

3. Only one path remained. When the terrible defects in Anselm's interpretation became clear—its emphasis on a transaction between the First and Second Persons in the Trinity, the complete neglect of divine Fatherhood, the dangerously unethical appropriation of Christ's work, so far as some were concerned—men turned for relief to the remaining alternative. Could the meaning of Christ's work not be seen in its relation to man alone? It is not a sacrifice to devils; it is provided by God Himself. Can it have any meaning apart from its value for men? By pursuing this road, students grew hopeful that they could avoid all the antimonies between justice and mercy, between a just God and a loving Saviour, between a self-conscious Sovereign concerned for His divine prestige and the lowly Servant who poured out His Soul unto death, between One who must withhold forgiveness until a satisfaction is made and One who at great cost rendered the satisfaction and made forgiveness real.

If it is seen that man alone is the problem, it will

enable us to jettison much troublesome cargo and to travel faster. This sets our feet on the road to what has been called the 'moral influence theory', though Dr. Franks suggests as a more accurate title the 'experiential theory', since there is an objective gift in Christ and a subjective response by man, resulting in an experience of salvation. Almost all who accept this approach find the key in St. Paul's words (2 Corinthians v. 18, 19): 'All things are of God, who reconciled us to himself through Christ, and gave unto us the ministry of reconciliation; to wit, that God was in Christ, reconciling the world unto himself, not reckoning unto them their trespasses, and having committed unto us the word of reconciliation.' Here, clearly, Paul regards man as the problem, needing to be persuaded and turned from his sin to God; and God as the eternal source of our salvation, overflowing in redemption; and Christ as the Mediator by which man's reconciliation is achieved. All things are of God. Eternal love is free and discovers a way to reveal itself, not to the ignorant and indifferent only, but even to men who are hostile. God's love is infinite and the Cross most fully expresses what God is. It breaks hearts of stone and melts hearts of ice; it endures when man's hate has exhausted itself and it remains unconquered.

This love of God in Christ constitutes the Atonement and is seen in the Incarnation, Life, Passion, Death and Resurrection of Jesus. Here is nothing about 'eternal laws of righteousness' demanding satisfaction or 'something done unto God by Christ whether men respond to it or not', or 'satisfaction to divine honour', or 'justice'. Man is the rationale of the Cross and all notions of objective Atonement are ignored or denied or explained away. God as eternal love is eternally free to forgive on the simple condition of repentance and faith.

Thus far the summary: As we seek to reach a conclusion, some facts must be borne in mind.

1. To find a meaning in the work of Christ we must first ask what was His mission? Here we turn to the facts in the Synoptic teaching. Christ came to set up in human hearts the Kingdom or kingly rule of God. In Himself it found complete embodiment. 'If I by the finger of God cast out devils, then is the Kingdom of God come unto you.' But this fact carries others with it. There is a personal God whom He almost always describes as the 'holy Father' or 'Father'. There is a moral Kingdom where moral values are everything. There must be a moral constitution in man fit to receive this Kingdom or else the mission of Jesus is make-believe. These seem the postulates of redemption.

There is no key to the sacrifice of Jesus if God is only an immanent, or impersonal, or absolute force. Unless we can decide about God, our investigation will be fruitless. Christian theism, which is rooted in the New Testament, and pantheism or nomotheism, are entirely different postulates and can never yield the same conclusion. Neither can we make rhyme nor reason out of the Cross if we substitute the 'ethics of naturalism' for the moral demands of the Kingdom of God. Only confusion can come, we repeat, by failing to distinguish between a normative and a positive science, and no legerdemain can change the one into the other. Jesus made His choice between the moral demands of God upon Himself and the impulses of the flesh; and all inner controversy and conflict ceased after the fearful struggles in the wilderness. Jesus accepted the reign of God in Himself, and this fact guarantees that ethical quality in His work about which writers like Bushnell and Dale have written so largely. Just here, too, is the source of His Passion. He would fain have persuaded all men to accept this kingly reign of God. He urged them to it. He marvelled at their unwillingness to accept it. He used all His resources of entreaty, culminating in the so-called triumphal entry into Jerusalem; but whether men would spurn His offer and appeal or accept Him, He was adamant. The Holy Father and His Kingdom were eternal reality. Heaven and earth might pass away, but these would never pass away.

But in this condition we can see the genesis of a great and growing tragedy. Jesus has been calumniated as obstinate, as courting suicide, as intolerant; and the same charges have been made against some of His noblest followers in times of persecution since. But, given the reality of the Christian's God and His Kingdom, and 'intolerance' is nothing but heroic fidelity to truth. So John reports His answer to Pilate: 'To this end have I been born and to this end have I come into the world, that I should bear witness unto the truth' (xviii. 37). This is the primary meaning and purpose of the Incarnation, to establish the reign of the living God in the hearts of men, to bring them into the fellowship of obedience to Him, to establish His rule in men on earth as it is in Heaven.

2. Since Christ could be neither allured nor browbeaten from His mission, and since the men of His generation would have none of it, only one issue could result. He would not surrender. They would not be persuaded. But let us note carefully the new factor in His method. While His enemies used violence in its most brutal form, He relied entirely on spiritual weapons. His Kingdom was built on the principles of God and was indestructible, and He regarded His life as of small account if it could come into the lives of others. Christ was crucified, but by His death He asserted more strongly than he could have done by His life, the will of the Father and the principles of the Kingdom. Holiness, righteousness, mercy, truth, love, and whatever else there be in God are purchased to us for ever and established for ever by the blood of Christ. Or, to repeat Bushnell's words once again: 'In such a way of obedience, Christ makes a contribution of honour to the law He obeys, that will do more to enthrone it in our reverence than all the desecrations of sin have done to pluck it down—more, too, than all conceivable punishments to make it felt and keep it in respect.'

This satisfaction of the holy purpose of the Father and His moral claims John finds completed even before Jesus reaches the Cross. In the Upper Room, Jesus says in the High Priestly prayer, 'I have glorified thee on the earth, having accomplished the work which thou hast given me to do' (xvii. 14). No point, then, is served by turning this personal, kingly character of God, to which Jesus bore witness and on account of which He died, into an abstract system of eternal laws of righteousness, and finding the meaning of Christ's death in a general homage to them. All that is holy and good in God found its first perfect expression in Christ Himself in concrete obedience and filial service.

3. This brings us to St. Paul. Much controversy has raged and still rages in some remote quarters, about the way Paul has befogged 'the simple gospel' with an artificial and obsolete theological jargon. The cry 'Back to Christ!' makes an appeal to beginners even yet who delight in the charm of the Synoptic teaching, but grow weary with St. Paul's involved arguments. But, worse still, theologians of the left wing assert that St. Paul perverted the gospel of Jesus and taught another gospel that misrepresented the character of God. In these concluding pages it would be impossible to cover this ground again—it has been done by abler pens elsewhere[1]—but two or three points should be borne in mind. Is, or is not, St. Paul true to the principles of Christ in his Epistles? Again let the contrast between the quality of our Lord's mind and that of St. Paul be kept in mind. Jesus was always concrete and pictorial in His teaching. His terse epigram, His vivid parable, His quick, rhetorical question kept His teaching in contact with the minds of plain people.

Again, how far Jesus' thought may have travelled

---

[1] e.g. C. A. Scott, *Living Issues in the New Testament* (chaps. i, ii), also *Christianity According to St. Paul*, p. 59, and Howard, 'The First Interpreter of Jesus', *London Quarterly and Holborn Review*, January, 1939.

forward into the consequences of His teaching and work we can only surmise. He seemed sure they would result for Himself in a violent death and He had faith in His 'little flock' to perpetuate His work, but in His Ministry He knew Himself, as we say, to be making history and achieving a work that others must interpret and proclaim. He took the meaning of the Kingdom of God and made it visible in the simple acts of daily life. Righteousness was dear to St. Paul's thought, but it was the righteousness made visible in Christ's treatment of the ostracized and oppressed, of publicans and sinners; gentleness was exalted, but it was the gentleness towards these 'little ones' expressed so often in Jesus; humility was a badge of the true disciple, but it was the humility of Him who laid aside His garment, girded Himself with a towel, and washed His disciples' feet. 'The word had breath, and wrought with human hands the creed of creeds.'

Paul stood in every respect in a different position. He was challenged by accomplished facts. He was compelled to explore the meaning in recently written history. By personal contact with the Risen Christ, he knew himself to be a transformed man. He knew there were the things Jesus *did* as well as said. But Paul was a Pharisee, and his contact with Jesus did not divest him of all his early thought-forms and training. Paul had an alert mind and knew what was thought in the Gentile world. So when this man, Paul, became the bond-slave of Christ and went forth as the ardent missionary, any word, or metaphor, or myth, or simile that would convey the good news to his hearers' hearts he instantly used. Some words were imported from Eastern mystery cults, some from grosser pagan religions, some were tags from a Greek poet, some were from Moses or the prophets; but anything was grist to St. Paul's mill, if, by any means, he might save some. Sometimes his experience of Christ outran his language and his amanuensis had to put a dash and leave the sentence unfinished.

No doubt the Apostle would have been pained or amused often since, could he have seen pedestrian literalists, who, perchance, lacked his passion, dissecting and analysing words like 'propitiation' and 'justification' to fit them into a new plan of salvation. Paul was saved from pedantry because he was interested in men and their salvation primarily; and in system-making only secondarily.[1] The contrast between Our Lord and St. Paul seems to be principally in this: Christ was the good news of God, revealed in His Incarnation, Death, and Resurrection. Paul was a subject of the 'good news', and in its presence he was compelled, first, to re-think his earlier beliefs about God and righteousness, and, secondly, to proclaim his gospel, in whatever form was most effective, to Jew and Gentile. But any one who will seek out the underlying principles in Paul's gospel will find in them the spirit of the Cross, or, in his own words, 'the love of God which is in Christ Jesus our Lord' (Romans viii. 39).

[1] It is interesting that Paul's most theological treatise, Romans, seems to be an enlargement of his most urgent and practical Epistle to Galatians. His theology grew out of his experience.

4. At this stage we must bear in mind another point. Men's hearts were not clean, virgin soil, waiting for the good seed of the Kingdom. Here and there Christ could detect wheat in the field, sown by some long-forgotten prophet or psalmist, but the harvest was small and easily gathered. Let Him assert God's claims on men, let Him preach repentance, and soon He discovered an ancient growth of prejudice, jealousy, resentment, self-interest, malice, and deadly hatred, as we saw in Chapter III. Some theories about the origin of this growth were considered in Chapter II. Moral estrangement from God is a fact of human experience; it needs no demonstration in this century. Decency is not only not enough; men are discovering themselves to be incapable of the decencies. Country after country that at least rendered formal homage to God makes no effort to test its conduct by the principles of the Kingdom. Whatever democracies may do now, Jesus challenged such men. He did not compromise with them. He came on a mission of destruction as well as mercy. No metaphor is more frequently on his lips than fire. 'I came to cast fire on the earth' (Luke xii. 49). 'Gather up first the tares and bind them in bundles to burn them' (Matthew xiii. 30). 'He that is near me is near the fire' (Unwritten Saying No. 79).

On the human side, there was need for moral response. How could the reconciliation be achieved, the estrangement removed? Only by a call to repentance and the response of repentance. The ushering in of the kingly rule of God must be preceded by a great expulsion of individual and national idolatry. There are pagan ideologies and Christian ideologies and they can never become friends, even if they are gathered in one room around a common table. If the Cross proclaims a personal God, it also demands a return to His will, and volition is the greater part of repentance.

5. How, then, did Christ achieve the reconciliation of sinners? He did not always succeed, but His method was, and is, twofold. (1) He comes right into their lot. This is where the sacrifice begins. If men are to be helped and delivered it is by One who enters into their basest and worst condition. It involves spiritual strain, disappointment, unrequited love; yet there is no other way to redemption. The cold shoulder or contempt, a refusal to accept responsibility or trouble lack the cardinal elements of redemption. Any one who would atone must suffer. This fact is developed in the Epistle to the Hebrews: 'For verily not of angels doth he take hold but he taketh hold of the seed of Abraham' (ii. 16). By sympathy born of self-identification, Christ enters into man's deepest woe and makes it all His own. It involves surrender to the consequences of sin and folly and shame. It involves loneliness and, at last, a consciousness of human foulness and crime more real than the presence of God Himself.

There is a tradition that when the fortunes of the Federal States were at their lowest in the American Civil War and Lincoln was the target for all manner of calumny, rancour, and abuse, a friend said to him: 'Why not resign and let them sink or swim?' To which Lincoln slowly and sadly replied: 'If I resign they perish.' Only love can redeem the loveless, and all redeeming love is and must be suffering love. God in Christ refuses to shut His heart against man's sins and miseries—He bears them. He straightens out the tangles; He encourages; He empowers; He befriends; nothing is too foul, too guilty, too complex, too hopeless for His irresistible love. (2) This same truth concerning self-identification, St. Paul expressed in the enigmatic sentence: 'Christ redeemed us from the curse of the law, having become a curse for us' (Galatians iii. 13). 'This deliverance he achieved for us when we were under the curse of the Law by becoming in the fullest sense one with us, even to the extent of sharing our curse.'[1] A little reflection will find modern parallels, however weak and inadequate. The measure of our self-identification with the needs of others is the measure of our love. Only divine and infinite love can bear the sins of enemies and effect their reconciliation.

6. Given this sin-bearing love and sacrifice, will these inevitably restore sinners? In this life optimism must be tempered with facts. The appeal of Christ hardens some. Its demands are too exacting. Its claims are too personal. Its action is too revolutionary. It provokes hostility. This fact challenged the thought of many, if not all, New Testament writers. The frankest statement is in the Fourth Gospel. Why is it that, of two men who hear the same call, one responds to and the other rejects the appeal? John falls back on an original defect in the moral nature of some; the light lighting every man is insufficient in these: 'Ye believe me not because

[1] Duncan, *Galatians*, p. 97 (Hodder & Stoughton).

ye are not of my sheep' (x. 26). 'No man can come to me except the Father which hath sent me draw him' (vi. 44). John regards some who do not respond as spiritually colour-blind, lacking a power to discern the meaning and grace of Jesus. St. Paul finds a similar reason for the rejection of Christ by Israel—'blindness in part hath fallen' to them. The brutal Crucifixion of Jesus by the Gentile rulers he attributes to ignorance of Him (1 Corinthians ii. 8).

We cannot deny that some are less interested and less responsive, at least outwardly, to the message of the Cross than others; that environment, early education, and public opinion make some insensitive to its appeal; that to-day these ideals of the Cross have to fight for their lives in presence of the demand in all nations for military and economic rearmament. Yet these admissions do not make a reason for man's lack of response. So long as any human being can be regarded as a moral agent, even in however elementary a degree, there is a latent power of discernment and appropriation— it may be as a grain of mustard seed. There in that sensitive place God enters into judgement with us by displaying Christ; there responsibility must be accepted; there the eternal problem of divine action and human freedom meet; and there the evasive attitude of unbelief can neutralize the work of Christ in and for that soul. By resting our eye only on the resources of divine love, we may preach optimistically about the victory remaining with love, but when we watch slow, sure deterioration of character here and now through neglect of Christ and denial of His claims, we cannot say the victory remains always with love. Beyond this we cannot go. Sin has appalling powers of disintegration and we are less sure of inevitable moral progress than were writers in the seventh decade of the last century.

7. So far we have been considering the work of Christ almost entirely as a divine movement towards men, overcoming their hostility and winning them to God in penitent response. Is there nothing to be said as to the effect of the work of Christ on God? We have seen that in Christ's perfect devotion to the Father's Will there is the guarantee that the reconciliation shall be in holiness and righteousness. It is pre-eminently an ethical Atonement. It is not a transaction between persons in the Trinity remote from the life and character of men. New Testament scholarship has shed light on some of the technical terms of a bygone soteriology; it is worth while to add a word on these. The word 'propitiation' needs care. As Dr. Maltby says with characteristic felicity: 'The word "propitiation" has made a long journey from its native country. . . . The truth is that this word, like many others, once baptized into Christ, has become a new creature; old things are passed away, they are become new.'[1]

No pagan deity was ever conceived as coming to the help of his suppliant devotee and providing the means by which he could return to fellowship and joy. No pagan could say, 'All things are of God'. Propitiation meant placation, appeasement; and the means lay with men or they lay nowhere. But, in

[1] *Christ and His Cross* p. 123 (Epworth Press).

the Christian gospel, this is gone and if Paul uses this old word (and its meaning is dubious)[1] he conceived of Christ as God's means of re-creating fellowship between sinners and Himself. The effect of Christian baptism on this word is that God is always the subject and never the object of the verb 'to propitiate'. If Charles Wesley meant to imply by the line 'My God is reconciled'[2] that there was a time when God was not reconciled and was unwilling to receive sinners, then the familiar line goes beyond the New Testament. We hasten to add that Wesley's words do not necessarily carry this meaning, but they have often been quoted in this sense and the previous verse lends colour to this view.

Similarly, the word 'satisfaction' needs such careful handling and depolarizing, if used at all concerning God, that a less ambiguous word might with benefit be used.[3] It is not a scriptural word. In the Authorized Version it is used twice (Numbers xxxv. 31, 32), but in the Revised Version the word is changed to 'ransom' in both cases. It was introduced into Christian theology by Tertullian, a lawyer by training and profession, at the end of the second century. In Roman Law, no doubt, it did excellent service when indicating 'reparation for an injury or offence, pecuniary or otherwise, of a debt or obligation', but when used to interpret Christ's work it had to make assumptions about the character of God and His relation to sinners that are untrue. It assumed that God was unwilling to approach

---

[1] See Sanday and Headlam, *Romans*, pp. 87–94; Dodd, *Romans*, p. 54.
[2] See *Methodist Hymn Book*, 368, verses 4–5.
[3] It has been omitted from 'The Order of Service for Holy Communion' in the *Methodist Book of Offices*.

sinners until His principle of anger was satisfied by the penal sufferings of some one, and here New Testament teaching is forsaken for a revived paganism.

If it were possible to use the word 'satisfaction' to indicate God's delight in the unfaltering devotion and loving obedience of the Son in whom He was well pleased, it might still be rescued from oblivion and put to noble uses; but old associations make the conversion of words difficult.

Similarly, the word 'substitution' has thrust itself into Christian thought, carrying a load of alien ideas with it. Grotius, like Tertullian, strove to interpret Christ's work in terms of law. He understood Dutch Law better than he understood the spiritual principles of the gospel. By reconstructing the drama of the law courts, he put God as King and judge, the Law behind all requiring justice, sinners as transgressors of law who must be punished; and then he introduces the novel idea that the punishment can be borne by proxy. All the guilt of mankind can concentrate on the innocent person of Christ and He, as man's substitute, can bear the punishment that must be visited on some one by a just God. This is at once the most immoral and perilous theory that has found its way into popular theology. Common British Law repudiates it. No innocent person can ever stand in a true or intelligible sense in the place of the guilty. No theory so easily lends itself to a superficial interpretation of Christ's death.

That God should punish Christ for our sins is immoral as it is unscriptural. St. Paul often speaks of Christ giving Himself for us, but the preposition he uses is always *huper* ('on our behalf' or 'in our interest') but never *anti* ('instead of' us). Even the favourite illustration of those who find Leviticus full of archetypes and symbols, viz. the account of the scapegoat, fails. The passage (xvi. 21, 22) must be quoted: 'And Aaron shall lay both his hands on the head of the live goat, and confess over him all the iniquities of the children of Israel, and all their transgressions, even all their sins, and he shall put them up on the head of the goat, and shall send him away by the hand of a man that is in readiness, and the goat shall bear upon him all their iniquities into a solitary land and he shall let go the goat in the wilderness.' Here there is a very moving symbol of the bearing away of sin which found its fullest meaning in Christ, but there is no hint about penal suffering, and the creature sent away is not even put to death. Christ suffered on our behalf. He bore our sins and He carried our sorrows, but He never stood as our substitute to bear the strokes of divine anger. Such a notion can only appeal to those who are more concerned to be saved from suffering than from sin; to be made secure than to be made good. It is an un-Christian notion that should be expunged from every form of worship.

One other term requires attention. Phrases such as 'the blood of Jesus his Son cleanseth us from all sin' (1 John i. 7) and 'loosed us from our sins by his blood' (Revelation i. 5—R.V.) are difficult in modern ears. Some who ponder the meaning of words are repelled by them, and others who lightly adopt such phrases come to regard them as having a vague, magical, and even literal significance. The legends in Roman Catholic hagiology about the drops of blood, and appalling representations of Christ in which crimson blood-stains are so realistically present, find their parallels in crude Protestant evangelism. Two or three truths should be borne in mind: (1) The New Testament writers were nearly all Jews by birth and early training. Every Jew regarded the blood as the life and the life as in the blood; the reason for this is obvious. We should not go amiss if in reading allusions to 'the blood of Christ' we substituted the word 'life' for 'blood'. (2) As is obvious from the first of these examples (1 John i. 7), this is the true meaning, because the verb used is in the continuous present. Christ, by His outpoured life in the believer, continues to keep us clean from all sin. (3) There is a figure of speech in the English language called 'synecdoche', which means that we indicate the whole by a part. This not infrequently happens in the New Testament. Christ's blood indicates His entire sacrifice of Himself on our behalf.[1] The word is symbolic of an outpoured life. Isaac Watts writes surely in the inspiration of genius when he lifts our thoughts from everything physical in Christ's sacrifice and says:

> See from His head, His hands, His feet,
> Sorrow and love flow mingled down.[2]

Though Cowper[3] admittedly took his imagery from

---

[1] See, e.g., Romans iii. 25, v. 9; Ephesians i. 7; Colossians i. 20.
[2] *Methodist Hymn Book*, 182, verse 3.
[3] ibid., 201, verse 1.

Zechariah (xiii. 1) in a stronger figure than Western thought now relishes, yet if many critics had equated the 'fountain filled with blood' with a 'fountain of life', their criticism of Cowper's lines would have been less severe.

* * *

The word of the Cross stands in jeopardy. It represents a distinctive way of life, a peculiar attitude of mind to God and man. It proclaims self-surrender, self-effacement, self-denial, crucifixion for the sake of others. It is utter foolishness, it evokes derision and persecution, yet it has its own ideology, its own way of life, and this way was established in Jesus. Through Him we come to know it as the way of God. It is the perfect revelation of God. The Cross is the sign in Heaven of eternal, suffering love.

But it is in organic relation to men, and every man is called to share in it, for Jesus offers every follower his own cross; and as the spirit of the Cross enters each believer, so in this new community or Body, the Church, Christ in every generation can be crucified afresh.

Each student must approach the mystery of the Cross in his own way, but, while we speak of rationale, or ideology, or theory, let it be made plain that no man can plumb the depths of Christ's sacrifice by the intellect alone. The Cross as a principle of life must be embraced and set in one's own heart. So embraced, it is found to be the power of God and the wisdom of God; it reconciles, it heals, it gives life, it creates fellowship. It becomes the only wisdom. But it is in jeopardy. It is opposed by every primal instinct in man. It is assailed by all preachers of self-sufficiency and by all who deny moral values. It is being trampled on with raging contempt by all who believe in self-assertion, violence, and every other usage of the jungle. It has been so, somewhere, in every generation, yet Christian history bears witness that where men are strong in faith the Crucifixion is always followed by the Resurrection.

EPILOGUE

PERSONAL AFFIRMATIONS

1. I believe that God made man in His own image and designed him for fellowship with Himself.

2. I believe that sin has alienated man in his thought and affections from God.

3. I believe that God was in Christ seeking to recover man to Himself and to perfect his nature.

4. I believe this reconciliation could only be effected by One who was Himself sinless, and who was prepared to lay down His life in His redemptive mission.

5. I believe reconciliation could not have been achieved unless, and until, every attribute in God's holy nature had found perfect expression and satisfaction.

6. I believe, therefore, that there is a God-ward and a man-ward significance in the life and death of Jesus.

7. I believe that Christ tasted death for every man.

8. I believe that all who trust in Christ share in the death and resurrection of Christ.

9. I believe that the Church of Christ (i.e. all who believe in Him) is called upon to express His work to the world in suffering love.

10. I believe the Risen Lord continues His work of redemption in Heaven.

INDEX

Abailard, 47, 214–20
Adeney, W. F., 129
Adonis, 69
Ahriman, 36
Anselm, 15, 180, 205–13, 214, 215, 229, 233, 265
Arius, 190
Arnold, Matthew, 177
Athanasius, 169, 189–92
Attis, 69
Augustine, St., 15, 37, 182, 200–5
Aulén, G., 176, 244, 246, 247, 249

Babbitt, Irving, 22
Bacon, B. W., 150
Badcock, F. J., 134
Barnardo, Dr., 48
Barth, Karl, 256, 257, 258
Bartlet, J. Vernon, 103, 124, 129
Baur, F. C., 130
Bennett, W. H., 130, 161
Berdyaev, Nicolas A., 26
Bergson, H., 15
Bernard of Clairvaux, 217, 251
Bicknell, E. J., 35
Bradlaugh, Charles, 25
Branscomb, B. H., 53, 58, 62, 114, 122
Brightman, E. S., 15
Brooke, Stopford, 123
Bruce, A. B., 145, 231
Brunner, Emil, 259
Bultmann, R., 159
Burkitt, F. C., 57
Bushnell, H., 220, 233–9, 251, 270
Butler, Bishop, 29, 30, 241

Calvin, John, 15, 179, 228
Campbell, McLeod, 123
Carlyle, Thomas, 190
Cathari, 38
Cave, S., 91, 241, 247
Chalmers, T., 241
Chapman, J. A., 221
Chase, F. H., 129
Comte, Auguste, 20
Cowper, W., 282
Cyprian, St., 180

Dale, R. W., 123, 208, 216, 239, 248, 249, 250

Darwin, Charles, 31
De Quincey, 52
Denney, James, 39, 125, 127, 162, 165, 248, 250, 251
Dibelius, M., 106
Diocletian, 245
Dodd, C. H., 99, 279
Domitian, 245
Driver, S. R., 39, 163
Duncan, G. S., 276

Eusebius, 130

Fairweather, W., 184
Findlay, G. G., 163
Flacius, 228
Foakes-Jackson, F. J., 125
Forsyth, P. T., 248, 250
Franks, R. S., 219, 250, 267
Freud, Sigmund, 17, 34

Galloway, G., 40
Garvie, A. E., 88, 148
Gibbon, E., 177
Glover, T. R., 177, 186
Goethe, 222
Gotama, 35
Gregory Nazianzus, 169, 199
Gregory of Nyssa, 169, 192
Grensted, L. W., 69
Grotius, 280

Hamilton, Sir W., 226
Harnack, Adolph von, 70, 166, 182, 185, 189, 190, 244
Harris, Rendel, 17
Harrison, Frederic, 20
Hauer, 16
Headlam, A. C., 17, 247, 279
Hebert, A. G., 244
Hegel, 18, 19, 41, 244
Henson, H. H., 37
Hermes, 74
Hicks, F. C. N., 253
Holyoake, J. G., 25
Hort, F. J. A., 230
Hoskins, Sir Edwyn, 165
Howard, W. F., 115, 155, 159, 271
Hughes, Hywel, 247
Huxley, Julian, 22, 23, 24, 25

287

INDEX

INGE, W. R., 41, 160
Irenaeus, 169–76, 179, 180, 187

JOSEPHUS, FLAVIUS, 50
Jung, C. G., 33, 34

KANT, IMMANUEL, 30, 220
Kirk, K. E., 247, 252
Kittel, Gerhard, 152
Klausner, J., 119
Knox, John, 179

LIDGETT, J. SCOTT, 19, 127, 141, 187, 238, 241, 242, 243
Lightfoot, R. H., 121
Lincoln, Abraham, 275
Lippmann, Walter, 22
Loisy, A., 70, 122
Lombard, Peter, 265
Luther, Martin, 58, 179, 264

MACAULEY, A. B., 247
Macgregor, G. H. C., 152, 157
Mackenzie, J. S., 32
Mackintosh, H. R., 45, 223, 225
Maltby, W. R., 278
Mani, 37
Mansell, Dean, 226
Manson, T. W., 44, 58
Marcion, 167, 177, 179, 183
Maurice, F. D., 139, 220, 226–33
Mauthner, Fritz, 16
Mazda, 36
Milton, John, 39
Moberly, R. C., 241
Moffatt, James, 53, 77, 129, 130, 136
Montefiore, C. G., 119
Morison, F., 75
Mozley, J. K., 241
Murry, Middleton, 57

NARBOROUGH, F. D., 136
Nero, 103, 245
Nietzsche, F., 21

OMAN, J., 222, 223
Origen, 134, 169, 171, 182–9
Ormuzd, 35, 36
Orr, J., 70
Osiris, 69

PAPIAS, 76
Peake, A. S., 95, 136
Pelagius, 218
Philo, 51
Plotinus, 182

QUICK, O. C., 17

RAMSAY, SIR W., 129
Rashdall, H., 114, 116, 143, 178, 184, 186, 198, 211, 219, 241
Reitzenstein, R., 159
Renan, E., 70, 124
Reventlow, 16
Robinson, H. Wheeler, 28, 49
Robinson, T. H., 135
Ruskin, John, 32

SANDAY, W., 279
Schiller, 222
Schleiermacher, F., 220–6, 257
Schopenhauer, A., 15, 221
Scott, Sir W., 207, 222
Scott, C. Anderson, 84, 271
Scott, E. F., 44, 97, 110, 136
Shaw, Lord, 67
Sikes, J. G., 47
Simeon Stylites, 160
Smith, David, 174, 207
Socrates, 24, 150
Spencer, Herbert, 20, 31
Strachan, R. H., 91
Strauss, D. F., 70, 74
Streeter, B. H., 76, 101

TANSLEY, A. G., 62
Taylor, Vincent, 101, 115, 156, 254, 256
Tertullian, 169, 177–81, 187, 280
Turner, C. H., 112

VALENTINUS, 38
Valentinians, 182

WALDENSIANS, 38
Watts, Isaac, 282
Webb, C. C. J., 25
Wesley, Charles, 279
Wesley, John, 15, 58, 220, 256, 264
Westcott, B. F., 139, 154, 157, 162
Whitman, Walt, 31, 32
Wilson, W. E., 163
Wordsworth, William, 222

XENOPHON, 150

ZAHN, T. H., 129
Zeus, 74
Ziehen, T., 16
Zinzendorf, N. L. G. von, 251
Zoroaster, 35, 36

Printed *by* The Camelot Press Ltd., London *and* Southampton